FAMILY AND COUPLE PSYCHOANALYSIS

The Library of Couple and Family Psychoanalysis

Series Editors: Susanna Abse, Christopher Clulow, Brett Kahr, and David E. Scharff

Other titles in the series:

FAMILY AND COUPLE PSYCHOANALYSIS
A Global Perspective

Edited by

David E. Scharff and Elizabeth Palacios

From the Committee on Family and Couple Psychoanalysis of
the International Psychoanalytical Association

KARNAC

First published in 2017 by
Karnac Books Ltd
118 Finchley Road
London NW3 5HT

British Library Cataloguing in Publication Data

A C.I.P. for this book is available from the British Library

ISBN-13: 978-1-78220-508-1

Typeset by V Publishing Solutions Pvt Ltd., Chennai, India

www.karnacbooks.com

CONTENTS

ACKNOWLEDGEMENTS

Isidoro Berenstein's chapter "Interference" is edited by David E. Scharff from an interview with Carlos Slepoy. *Página/12* (newspaper), Sunday, 21 March 2010. By permission of his heirs.

Barbara Bianchini's case "Giuseppe and Noemi" was previously published as "Reflections on the container-contained model in couple psychoanalytic psychotherapy" by B. Bianchini and L. Dallanegra, in *Couple and Family Psychoanalysis*, Volume 1, Number 1, edited by Molly Ludlam (published by Karnac Books, 2011), and is reprinted here by kind permission of Karnac Books.

Bion's Grid (used by Timothy Keogh in his discussion of David E. Scharff's clinical material) was originally published in *Learning from Experience* by Wilfred R. Bion (Tavistock, 1962, republished by Karnac Books in 1984), and is reprinted with kind permission of Karnac Books.

Elizabeth Palacios and Alicia Monserrat's "The Link and the Argentinian approach to families" was previously published as (2015) "Contributions to the link perspective in interventions with families: Theoretical and technical aspects, and clinical application" by A. Monserrat and E. Palacios in *Couple and Family Psychoanalysis* (Chapter 5, pp. 76–88). It appears here by permission.

David E. Scharff's clinical material was published in a different form in *Object Relations Couple Therapy* (D. E. Scharff & J. S. Scharff, Jason Aronson, 1991). By permission of the publisher.

John Zinner's case of a family was previously published in another version as "A journey from blame to empathy in a family assessment of a mother and her sons" in 1997 in the journal *Psychiatry: Interpersonal and Biological Processes, 60*:104–110). This version is reprinted by permission of The Washington School of Psychiatry (www.wspdc.org).

Cover illustration

This drawing was completed by a family of four during assessment, each drawing their self in a shared family activity of ice skating. The girl holding her parents' hands was the index patient, while her sister is off to the side with a "penguin", a device to hold on to while learning to skate.

ABOUT THE EDITORS AND CONTRIBUTORS

Editors

Elizabeth Palacios, MD, is a psychiatrist, and adult and child psycho-analyst; trained in Argentina and Spain in Madrid's Psychoanalytical Association, IPA member and member, IPA's Committee on Family and Couple Psychoanalysis. She is a member of the child and adolescent department in APM (The Psychoanalytic Association of Madrid). She is founder, president, professor, and supervising analyst in Aragon's Society for the Research of Child and Adolescent Psychic Life, and member of the Spanish Federation of Associations of Psychotherapists. Private practice in Zaragoza, Spain. She has published several books and papers on child and adolescent psychoanalysis.

David E. Scharff, MD, is Chair, the International Psychoanalytical Association's Committee on Family and Couple Psychoanalysis; Chair of the board, founder, and former director, the International Psycho-therapy Institute, Washington, DC; clinical professor of psychiatry at Georgetown University and the Uniformed Services University of the Health Sciences; former vice-president, International Association for Couple and Family Psychoanalysis; founding editor-in-chief of the journal *Psychoanalysis and Psychotherapy in China*; author and editor of numerous books and articles, including *The Sexual Relationship*, and with Jill Savege Scharff: *Object Relations Family Therapy, Object Relations Couple Therapy, The Interpersonal Unconscious* and *Psychoanalytic Couple Therapy*.

Contributors

Isidoro Berenstein, MD (1932–2011) was an internationally recognised figure in psychoanalysis. He was founding chair of the IPA's committee on family and couple psychoanalysis. Winner of the Sigourney Award for Contributions to Psychoanalysis. He trained as a psychoanalyst in the Argentine Psychoanalytic Association (APA). Founder of Buenos Aires Psychoanalytical Association (APdeBA) in 1977 where he was a full member and training analyst. He published *The Oedipal Complex. Structure and Significance* (1976); *Family and Mental Disease* (1976); *Psychoanalysis and Dream Semiotics* (1978); *Psychoanalysis of the Family Structure: From Destiny to Significance* (1981); *Psychoanalyzing a Family* (1997). With Janine Puget he published *Psychoanalysis of the Marital Couple* (1988). Together with Janine Puget he produced new conceptualisations published in *Lo vincular: Clínica y Técnica Psicoanalítica* (*The Linking: Clinical and Technical Approaches in Psychoanalysis*) (1997). He was a founder of the department for family and couple in APdeBA (1985), and director of the master's in family and couple in the University Institute of Mental Health (IUSAM) in APdeBA.

Barbara Bianchini is a psychotherapist, full member of the alumni association of Tavistock Relations (London), member of IACFP; full member of APG (Milano). She teaches and supervises couple and family therapy at COIRAG Postgraduate School of Psychotherapy (Milano).

Delia G. de la Cerda Aldape is a doctor of psychology (UIA, Mexico), a training and academic analyst, and coordinator of the Community Attention Commission at Institute of the Mexican Psychoanalytic Association. She trained in couple therapy at the Family Institute, A.C. (Mexico). She is a member of the International Psychoanalytical Association, and former co-ordinator of the master's programme in child and adolescent psychotherapy.

Lia Rachel Colussi Cypel is a full member and training analyst, the Brazilian Society of Psychoanalysis of São Paulo, and International Psychoanalytical Association; former coordinator of the families and couples committee of the Latin American Psychoanalytic Federation—FEPAL. Coordinator of psychoanalysis, family and couple links study group. Member of the Committee on Family and Couple psychoanalysis, IPA.

Timothy Keogh, PhD, is training analyst and full member, Australian Psychoanalytical Society; member (for Oceania), IPA Committee for Family and Couple Psychoanalysis; member, International Association of Couple and Family Psychoanalysis; member, International Advisory Board for Couple and Family Psychoanalysis; IPA research fellow; honorary senior lecturer, medical school, University of Sydney. Author, *The Internal World of the Juvenile Sex Offender*.

Lin Tao, MD, is a graduate psychoanalyst of the IPA's Beijing programme and direct member, IPA, member of the IPA's China Committee and the board of the China Psychoanalytic Association; member, IPA Committee for Family and Couple Psychoanalysis; a couple psychoanalytic psychotherapist qualified by Tavistock Relationships, London; visiting psychotherapist at Tavistock Relationships; member, British Psychoanalytic Council.

Roberto Losso, MD, is a psychiatrist, full member and training analyst, the Argentine Psychoanalytical Association and member of the IPA. Professor of psychiatry and mental health at the School of Medicine, Buenos Aires University. Professor of family and couple clinics, John F. Kennedy University. Co-chair family and couple committee, FEPAL. Founder and member of the board of the International Association of Couple and Family Psychoanalysis; invited professor of the Università degli Studi di Bologna and Università degli Studi di Firenze. Author of the book *Psicoanálisis de la Familia*.

Daniela Lucarelli is a psychologist, psychoanalyst of the IPA and the Società Psicoanalitica Italiana; expert in psychoanalysis with children and adolescents. She teaches and supervises in the post-specialisation course in clinical research in couple and family psychoanalytic psychotherapy in Rome. Editor of the review *Interazioni: Clinical Psychoanalytic and Research on Individual, Couple and Family*.

Hanni Mann-Shalvi, PhD, a graduate of the Hebrew University of Jerusalem; director of the Psychoanalytic Couple and Family Center in Israel and the International Institute for Psychoanalytic Couple and Family Training, which is affiliated with the International Psychotherapy Institute (IPI) of Washington, DC; adjunct faculty to the couple, child and family programme of IPI. She is vice president of the International Association of Couple and Family Psychoanalysis (IACFP); and is on the international advisory board of the *Couple and Family Psychoanalysis Journal*, and the Italian journal *Interazioni*. She is in private practice in Tel-Aviv in individual and couple psychoanalysis, psychotherapy, and supervision. Author of *From Ultrasound to Army: The Unconscious Trajectories of Masculinity in Israel* (Karnac).

Alicia Monserrat, PhD, is a doctor in psychology from the Complutense University; psychoanalyst, member and coordinator of the child and adolescent department of Madrid Psychoanalytical Association. Full member, IPA; professor of postgraduate courses; mental health supervisor in several hospitals. She has published several books on child psychoanalysis.

Julio Moreno, MD, PhD, is a full member of the IPA from APdeBA, Argentina; co-director, family and couple master's programme at IUSAM; full professor, Buenos Aires University and the Italian Hospital University. He is author of the books *Ser Humano* (Letra Viva) translated as *How We Became Human* (2014, Rowman & Littlefield), *Tiempo y Trauma* (2010, Lugar Editorial), *La Infancia y sus Bordes* (2014, Paidós Editorial), and *El psicoanálisis en clave vincular* (2016, Lugar Editorial).

Mary Morgan is a psychoanalyst and couple psychoanalytic psychotherapist, Fellow of the British Psychoanalytical Society. Reader in couple psychoanalysis at the Tavistock Relationships; Member, IPA Committee for Family and Couple Psychoanalysis; board member of the International Association for Couple and Family Psychoanalysis (IACFP); editorial board member of the journals *Couple & Family Psychoanalysis* and *Interazioni*. She has developed and led couple psychotherapy trainings in several countries and lectures internationally.

Susana Muszkat is a full member and faculty, Brazilian Society of Psychoanalysis of São Paulo; IPA member and adjunct member, IPA Committee for Family and Couple Psychoanalysis; co-chair for Latin America of the IPA Mental Health Committee; private analytic practice with families, couples, and individuals.

Eliana Riberti Nazareth is a full member of the Brazilian Psychoanalytic Society of São Paulo; consultant in IPA law and psychoanalysis committee; master in clinical psychology, psychology, and law.

Anna Maria Nicolò, MD, is a training analyst (SPI-IPA); IPA recognised in child and adolescent psychoanalysis. She has been regional representative (from Europe) to the board of representatives of the International Psychoanalytical Association (IPA) and member of the forum for adolescence of the European Psychoanalytical Federation (FEP); founder member of the Society for Psychoanalytic Psychotherapy for Children and Adolescents (SIPsIA); editor-in-chief of *Interazioni;* president of the Italian Society of Psychoanalysis of Couples and Families. She lives and practices in Rome, Italy.

Diana Norsa, PhD, is a psychoanalyst member of SPI and IPA, child analyst. Member, IPA Committee for Family and Couple Psychoanalysis. Teacher and supervisor for Istituto Winnicott (*iW*) Rome, ASNEA Milan, and PCF (Psicoanalisi della Coppia e della Famiglia), Italy. Editorial board member, *Richard & Piggle Review* on infant and adolescent psychoanalysis, and *L'annata Psicoanalitica Italiana*, the *International Journal of Psychoanalysis'* yearbook in Italy.

Karen Proner is an adult and child psychoanalyst who originally trained in England at the Tavistock Clinic. She resides in New York and is a faculty member of the Contemporary Freudian Society and IPTAR; member of the American Psychoanalytic Association; Member, IPA Committee for Family and Couple Psychoanalysis. She is a training supervisor for Contemporary Freudian Society's child analysis training and the International Psychotherapy Institute's child analysis training. She has written and published on primitive defences, borderline states, and infant observation.

Janine Puget, MD, psychoanalyst, full member of IPA, APdeBA, and AAPPdeG. Winner of the Sigourney Award. Books: *Subjetivación* *discontinua y psicoanálisis. Incertidumbre y certezas* (2015). *Lo vincular: Teoría y Clínica Psicoanalítica* (1997), *Violence d'Etat et Psychanalyse* (1989), *Psicoanálisis de la pareja matrimonial* (1988), *El Grupo y sus configuraciones: Terapia Psicoanalítica* (1982).

Jill Savege Scharff, MD, is an adult and child analyst working with individuals, couples, and families in Chevy Chase, MD; founder and supervising analyst, International Institute for Psychoanalytic Training at the International Psychotherapy Institute; adjunct member, IPA Committee for Family and Couple Psychoanalysis; clinical professor of psychiatry, Georgetown University; author and editor of books on object relations theory and practice. Her most recent books are *Psychoanalysis Online 1*, *Psychoanalysis Online 2*, and *The Interpersonal Unconscious*.

Caroline M. Sehon, MD, is a psychoanalyst and child psychiatrist; clinical associate professor of psychiatry at Georgetown University in Washington, DC; chair of the DC Program, International Psychotherapy Institute, and board member of the International Association of Couple and Family Psychoanalysis. She maintains a private practice in Bethesda, Maryland.

Gabriela Tavazza is a psychologist and psychoanalyst IPA/SPI (Società Psicoanalitica Italiana); head of the task force for the prevention of mental disorders and education to mental health at the mental health department ASL RMD in Rome, Italy; editor-in-chief of the review *Interazioni: Psychoanalytic Clinic and Research on Individual, Couple and Family*.

Yolanda de Varela, PhD, is a member of the International Psychoanalytical Association and a training analyst of the IPA's Panamanian Psychoanalytic Study Group. Founding faculty of the International Psychotherapy Institute, and founder of IPI Panama. She has published numerous articles, and has a private practice in adult psychoanalysis and couple therapy.

Félix Velasco Alva, MD, is a psychiatrist and is former president, training psychoanalyst and coordinator of the couple and family committee, Mexican Psychoanalytic Association. Master's in family psychotherapy at the Instituto de la Familia, A.C. (Mexico). Doctorate in psychotherapy (SEP, Mexico). Member, IPA Committee for Family and Couple

Psychoanalysis; Member, International Association of Couple and Family Psychoanalysis. He has written: *Manual de Técnica Psicoanalítica, Conflictos de Pareja, Parejas en Conflicto, Psicoterapias Psicodinámicas; Los Amorosos y sus Descontentos*.

Monica Vorchheimer is a training and supervising analyst from the Buenos Aires Psychoanalytical Association (APdeBA) in Argentina; full member of the International Psychoanalytical Association; member, IPA Committee for Family and Couple Psychoanalysis; member of the Latin American Psychoanalytic Federation (FEPAL), European Federation of Psychotherapy (FEAP) and honorary member of AAPPIPNA (Spain); member, University Institute of Mental Health in Buenos Aires, Argentina, where she is in private practice.

Janine Wanlass, PhD, is director, The International Psychotherapy Institute and faculty, International Institute for Psychoanalytic Training; professor of psychology and counseling, Westminster College, Salt Lake City, Utah. Articles on family and couple analytic therapy, individual child and adult therapy, and distance psychoanalysis. Private practice of child, adult and family therapy and psychoanalysis in Salt Lake City, Utah.

John Zinner, MD, is vice-chair of the contemporary psychoanalytic couple and family therapy training programme of the Washington (DC) Center for Psychoanalysis; clinical professor, George Washington University department of psychiatry and behavioural science; adjunct member, IPA Committee for Family and Couple Psychoanalysis. Dr. Zinner maintains a private practice of psychoanalysis, individual, family, and couple psychotherapy and is a supervisor of mental health professionals.

SERIES EDITOR'S FOREWORD

We humans are story-telling creatures. We like to tell ourselves and others stories about our relationship to the world around us. By doing so we forge connections with others and feel connected within ourselves. In their telling, our stories change. We edit the details as memories, and motivations reorder the prominence given to aspects of our narratives and in response to the reactions we receive from those who listen to us. Our stories connect us with some and alienate us from others. Stories define who we are as social beings. They draw on remembered history to account for how we come to be where we are, they provide a filter for understanding what we are experiencing now and they guide our behaviour in the future. Stories identify us to others and to ourselves.

Psychoanalytic theories are stories. They define our stance in understanding the human predicament and guide our actions in trying to make the world a better place. History is important in these stories since we cannot fully understand the world and ourselves in it without knowing where we have come from (the word history itself derives from the Greek for "'knowing"). Our stories of development allow us to distinguish between and account for adaptive and non-adaptive ways of being in the world in those we try to help. They help us to know ourselves and those who consult us. We, like they, are drawn to the stories that resonate with experience and are familiar. We often delight in the retelling of familiar stories and know where we are with them, sometimes finding it difficult to understand and accommodate new stories. Conversely, we may become dissatisfied with the stories that are familiar to us, and enlivened by new stories that enlarge our understanding and have practical value in guiding our endeavours. The psychoanalytic method—the 'talking cure"—relies, in part, upon the telling and revising of stories that no longer sustain people in their lives.

The Library of Couple and Family Psychoanalysis, whose first volume appeared in 2009, is a library of stories. It was set up to stimulate exchange about ideas and practices that increase understanding of unconscious forces in couple and family relationships and inform psychotherapeutic practice with this constituency of patients. This volume is the fifth in the series, which has placed a premium on valuing the diversity of ideas and approaches in the psychoanalytic community, attending to knowledge generated by research in the field and supporting initiatives that not only benefit psychotherapists in their consulting rooms but also influence public policy relevant to the mental health of communities. Its title, *Family and Couple Psychoanalysis: A Global Perspective*, reverses the ordering of couples and families contained in the title of the series and expands the international breadth of contributions that has been a feature of the previous volumes. This volume includes contributions from four of the six continents in our globe; only Africa and Antarctica are missing. Africa and Antarctica have been represented as the alpha and omega of the human story, but their omission should not be taken as a snub to history or a disregard for the significance of interactions between people and their environment for how that story will unfold in the future.

This volume is the outcome of several meetings of a working group of distinguished couple and family psychoanalysts set up to foster the exchange and testing of psychoanalytic stories applied to family relationships. It is structured in two parts. The first provides a concise and authoritative summary of key theories that currently inform contemporary couple and family psychoanalysis. The second, the main part of the book, examines details of clinical practice, subjecting them to the scrutiny of colleagues. This dialectical approach has similarities with the therapeutic process: a conversation in which experiences are recounted, accounted for, and reappraised in the context of a respectful working relationship. The frame and method encourage the cross-pollination of thinking about clinical practice and provide a seedbed that has real potential for germinating new ideas.

The stories recounted in this process have two main conceptual threads. The first, and longer established, is object relations theory, a thread originating in Europe as Freud's theory of mind increasingly took a relational turn. Its focus is on the internal world of relationships, pithily summarised by John Milton in *Paradise Lost* as he described the mind as "its own place, and in itself can make a heaven of hell, a hell of heaven …" This thread sees psychopathology and relationship distress originating from the attempt to deal with the disjunction between internal and external realities through colonising one or the other, and attempting to by-pass the relationship between the two. The intra-psychic and the interpersonal then become fused in unconscious fantasy and belief as if they are one and the same. Here, the influence of the intra-psychic is the primary focus of therapeutic interest as it becomes manifest in and accessed through the interpersonal.

The second and more recent thread, originating in South America, is link theory. Link theory shares with object relations theory a concern with the influence of intra-psychic and interpersonal subjectivities in defining the psychic space within and between people. But the "otherness" of others is understood not only in terms of narcissistic projective processes but also as distinct realities that "interfere" with the presuppositions of the unconscious mind. Moreover, the intra- and interpersonal realities exist within and are influenced by superordinate realities dictated by social, political, economic, and cultural forces. As families provide (or fail to provide) group membership for individuals, so too do communities and the societies of which they are a part provide (or fail to provide) group membership for families. Link theory connects with the work of Bion in directing our attention to the significance of groups. In the moment-by-moment experiences in the consulting room we encounter not only the ghosts of our ancestral families but also the sunlight and shadows cast by those larger than family groups that define our identities as social beings. In the detail of our work in the consulting room we are then truly challenged, as William Blake would have it, "to see a world in a grain of sand".

These two conceptual threads interweave with each other in the clinical details recounted by the contributors, and in the responses they evoke. The presentations in this book provide us with a detailed and engaging experience of the therapeutic process that allows the reader to form his or her own responses to the stories told and to compare them with those that appear in print. They push us to widen our horizons, develop our reflexive muscle, check our omnipotence, and increase our capacity to bear uncertainty, even—and especially—when this threatens to tread uncomfortably on the dream-like stories that we might be tempted to weave to cope with the unbearable realities that are often part and parcel of the work we do. Here is a book that links us to ourselves as well as to global perspectives on couple and family psychoanalysis, one that exposes us to the new and unfamiliar as much as to what we think we know. It is a book that unites us in a shared appreciation of what it means to be human, and in the value of striving to promote the best of humanity.

Christopher Clulow
Series Editor
London

PREFACE

This book can rightfully be considered a "foundational contribution" to the study of family and couple psychoanalysis. Having explored and appreciated its structure, contents, and general style, I can say that in my view it represents now the most advanced progress in this specific area, thanks to some uncommon features that characterise it.

First, this is a scientific production that follows general criteria based on what I call an "IPA mentality": while it focuses rigorously, precisely, and coherently on a specific object of interest, it collects contributions from different geographical areas and theoretical schools across the international psychoanalytical community. This feature gives the book a wider vision, allowing the reader really to get in contact with the current advancement of psychoanalytic studies on families and couples all over the world.

I want to underline that this is not at all obvious: it is very difficult to conceive and to realise this kind of work without having actively co-participated in a wide institutional scientific group. So, I am inclined to highlight how the "IPA Family and Couple Committee" is today the natural basis and frame that provides a number of researchers with regular international and inter-regional contacts and exchanges that generate an extremely enriching and updated "cross-fertilisation" that would be impossible to achieve not only individually, but also within a single scientific group or local society.

Of course, the regional organisations of Europe (EPF), North America (NAPSAC-APsaA), and Latin America (FEPAL) also have their own well-structured working areas and fruitful scientific events dedicated to this topic. However, it is the task of the IPA to connect all of them in an inter-regional scientific network, offering the widest and most complete opportunity for interchange.

A second important aspect is that of having unequivocally and officially overcome an old mistrust (and underlying, crawling devaluation), connected with a hyper-conservative, "purist" psychoanalytic attitude by some traditionalists, which for decades had labelled as "applied psychoanalysis" the many areas where psychoanalytic reflection is extended to situations other than the classic two-persons-only session. Such a restrictive attitude may have been appropriate to the early stage of growth of psychoanalysis, which had to consolidate itself for a long time before daring to expand into further settings and scenarios, while maintaining a feeling of belonging, continuity, specificity, and peer dignity.

However, today the situation has changed considerably. Like a tree with many branches, contemporary psychoanalysis does not limit its own image to its trunk: on the contrary, psychoanalysis today enjoys an unexpected flourishing development of its "branches", precisely thanks to these openings to more specific and well-differentiated research areas, without losing its foundational theoretical and clinical premises which we cannot renounce.

The International Psychoanalytical Association has the role of recognising this progress, and of organising and officially supporting these studies through the creation of institutional committees, which is an acknowledgment at the highest level of their scientific meaning, mandate, and function.

This issue is much more substantial than mere bureaucracy, since in fact it allows a number of colleagues to go ahead and work more in depth with their specific clinical and theoretical reflections on the topic; it encourages young researchers and professionals to involve themselves in further specialisation; and finally it provides all interested analysts and therapists with new knowledge and tools, allowing them to better help their patients by improving their recognition and treatment of family and couple issues.

A third important aspect to be mentioned regarding this extremely stimulating text is its potential function as a proactive generator of new ideas (I would say: "happy boomerang-ideas"!) feeding back into the classical psychoanalytic theory it comes from.

This would not be surprising, for many of us: historically, several psychoanalytical areas initially seen only as "further and collateral", have generated important developments, integrations, achievements, and changes in the original root they came from: that is, let's think of child and adolescent analysis; groups (from Bion, on); serious pathologies and the field of mental health; and the list could go on, after the many fertilisations that have occurred in specific areas and have come back to influence and enrich the classic setting of all analysts at work.

Last but not least, I want to emphasise the relevance of the clinical part of the book, which—once again—shows analysts from different regions and schools at work, allowing the reader to experience a clinical full immersion and to engage with different styles, as well as different cases.

Finally, my sincere congratulations to the editors: David E. Scharff, the chair of the IPA family and couples committee, and Elizabeth Palacios, a respected member of the same committee. They are well known and esteemed all over the world for their experience and competence in this field, and have been able to carefully select and to harmoniously combine wonderful scripts from some of the most prestigious contributors today in this area. A great scientific achievement for the psychoanalytic movement, and a great help for practitioners and patients.

Stefano Bolognini
President of the International Psychoanalytical Association

PART I

INTRODUCTION: THEORETICAL AND CLINICAL APPROACHES TO FAMILY AND COUPLE PSYCHOANALYSIS AROUND THE WORLD

CHAPTER ONE

Theoretical diversity in family and couple psychoanalysis around the world

David E. Scharff and Elizabeth Palacios

F amily and couple therapy were born into the cradle of psychoanalysis from diverse sources. In the United States in the 1950s, Nathan Ackerman realised that his psychoanalyst colleagues had overlooked the influence of the most important relationships of their patients, and began to see whole families therapeutically. In the United Kingdom, Enid Balint formed the Family Discussion Bureau at the Tavistock Institute in the late 1940s, where the focus on couple and marital relationships characterised an institution that has continued its pioneering work under several names, currently as Tavistock Relationships. At the Tavistock Clinic, John Bowlby, through his studies of human attachment understood the family to be of overweening influence. His remark to this effect inspired John Elderkin Bell to begin seeing whole families in the United States. However, before any of them and already in the early 1940s, perhaps as early as the 1930s in Argentina, Enrique Pichon Rivière began seeing whole families with the theoretical support of what he described as the concept of *"vínculo"*, or the link, which connected persons to the family in which they grew as well as to previous generations and to the wider social world.

Psychoanalytic couple and family therapy has grown from these roots. However, in the United States and Europe, family therapy became largely cut off from psychoanalysis because of the systems family therapy movement that turned its back radically on psychoanalytic ways of thinking despite the fact that many of its founders were originally trained as, or heavily influenced by, the psychoanalysis of America or from the research centre in California around Bateson.

In part, this may have been deserved on the part of the analytic community, because the majority of psychoanalysts focused exclusively on individual patients almost as though each person developed *sui generis* without a family and as though his life revolved around analytic treatments with little attention to the fundamental relationships to life partners, children, families, colleagues, and friends. There was, however, significant loss to the family therapy community. Any understanding of unconscious processes and of the way the inner life of the individual shapes the family was lost in the process. Family and couple treatments became increasingly surface and behaviourally oriented, employing psycho-education and behavioral manipulation more than insight or understanding.

Another significant development was the birth of significant understanding of sexuality in relationships, notably through the work of Masters and Johnson in the 1960s and 1970s, as translated into psychoanalytic terms by Helen Singer Kaplan in the 1970s and 1980s. This made new understanding of the actualities of sexual response and sexual relating available to therapists for the first time, transforming what had only been Freud's psychosexual developmental theory into more of a reality concerning adult sexual interaction.

With the advent of object relations, group analytic, and later intersubjective and relational approaches to psychoanalysis, bridges to family and couple psychoanalytic perspectives became easier. Because all these theoretical approaches relied on the idea of unconscious communication and unconscious fantasy, they offered language that could be applied to the understanding of couples and families in richer ways.

Ironically, the burst of enthusiasm that marked the family therapy movement in the latter part of the twentieth century has faded in many regions of the world. It is now much more difficult to find training programmes in systemic family therapy, although interest in couple therapy remains high. It is now usual only in child training programmes that families are regularly discussed, but even here the divide between psychoanalytic ways of understanding individuals and systemic ways of understanding families and couples remains.

In many European and South American countries, however, psychoanalytic interest in families and couples remains strong. In these regions, there is a tradition of psychoanalytic family and couple therapy that has never been eclipsed by the non-analytic family therapies. In part this is due to the abiding influence of Pichon Rivière's theory of the link, which will be described in the next of these introductory sections by Roberto Losso, who was a student of Pichon Rivière. Pichon's students and those influenced by him have contributed to the global spread of forms of psychoanalytic family and couple therapy (and group therapy too!) that continue to flourish.

This book is the result of the researches of the working group on family and couple psychoanalysis of the International Psychoanalytical Association. The group was founded in 2009 by Argentine family therapy pioneer Isidoro Berenstein, who along with Janine Puget, wrote some of the foundational texts in Spanish on analytic family therapy. Since his death in 2011, the group has continued to study varieties of couple and family therapy around the world. Members of the group along with other colleagues meet regularly to present case material and discuss similarities and differences in theoretical understanding and clinical technique.

In this volume, the first of several that are planned, we begin with theoretical introductions from a variety of perspectives. While we cannot of course include all ways that family psychoanalysts view couples and families, this gives an introduction to our similarities and differences. We then follow with detailed case studies that have been presented in the group's meetings over the last years during meetings in Mexico City, Prague, and Washington, DC. By presenting discussions of these cases from differing theoretical vantage points, we hope to illuminate strengths and weaknesses in our ways of seeing families and couples, and, most of all, to explore both our differences and our agreements. Through this method of examination, we hope readers will be able to compare their own assumptions and ways of working with those of the presenters and discussants represented in this volume, in order to stimulate dialogue about how we can best understand and help couples and families in need. And, finally, we hope these discussions will also add to our understanding of psychoanalytic therapy for all modalities, whether it be individual, couple, family, or group analytic therapy.

We begin in Part I with several summary statements of our theoretical approaches, each written by a representative from a different geographical and/or theoretical area. Then, Part II, the main part of the book, is constructed by case presentations discussed by colleagues from their own points of view. In the conferences and meetings of our group, these presentations and discussions have led to spirited discussion of the tenets and practice of our psychoanalytic work with couples and families. It is our hope in producing this book, that readers will use it as a vehicle to inspire examination and discussion of their own approaches to family and couple therapy, and that this will spur further development of our field around the world.

CHAPTER TWO

Brief introductions to theoretical and clinical approaches around the world

An Argentine approach to family therapy

Elizabeth Palacios (Zaragoza, Spain)

The origin of family and couple psychoanalysis in Argentina goes back to the 1960s. Until this time, most clinical approaches employed Freudian and Kleinian theoretical concepts, along with communication theory from American authors and conceptualisations from group psychotherapy.

From about 1960 on, the family started to be thought about as a group. Enrique Pichon Rivière had much to do with the origin of thinking about the family as an internal group and of family dynamics as group dynamics. Carlos Sluzki brought in ideas from communication theory, opening the possibility of thinking of the family as a communicational system. Later, Isidoro Berenstein and Janine Puget considered the link between members of a family from a structural perspective, making connections between the conceptualisations of Freud, Klein, and Lévi-Strauss.

Pichon Rivière stands out as a leading figure in this field. Using Freudian and Kleinian notions, he reformulated the Oedipus complex, taking into account the internal representations of family members each person produces in his mind. From a group and social perspective he took ideas from K. Lewin and G. H. Mead, thereby bringing new concepts into psychoanalysis, such as that of "spokesperson" (*portavoz* in Spanish), someone who acts as "an informer" of what is going on in the group's dynamics and who often is the one who is outwardly the most mentally disturbed. He saw the Oedipus complex as a configuration external to the subject, not solely as an internal pattern as in Freudian theory. The parental couple's configuration leads to the concept of *roles* rather than fixed positions. Pichon Rivière left a legacy to all psychoanalysts, pioneering the way in which the family plays a defining role in individual psychic constitution. How a family is structured is important in diagnosis, prognosis, treatment, and prophylaxis, offering the possibility of enhanced understanding of individual psychic constitution and the individual's social network. His ideas are as important to the social sciences as they are to psychoanalysis. For him the family also has the function of interweaving each of its members with the wider social network. This fact is central in the socialisation of the family's children.

From this starting point, Argentine psychoanalysis has made many important contributions, such as those by Isidoro Berenstein beginning in the 1970s, who developed the concept of "unconscious family structure", using not only Freudian and Kleinian notions but also incorporating the conceptualisations of French anthropologist Claude Lévi-Strauss. Berenstein blends concepts from individual psychoanalysis, such as identification and object choice, with those derived from interpersonal linkages in family organisations. He viewed the Oedipus complex as an unconscious determination within the parents' psychic life that determines both the couple's link and the kinship of family bonds. The Oedipus complex unfolds as a structure that deals with interpersonal linking. Later, Berenstein developed a fourth term or dimension in the Oedipus structure of a more distant member of the mother's family, the uncles, aunts, cousins and other relatives (*avunculate*). From his perspective, the prohibition of incest governed by castration anxiety extends to the cultural dimension, where rules of exchange with prohibitions, prescriptions, and alliances are fundamental in kinship structure, as they regulate endogamy and exogamy, and define pathology in family structure.

García Badaracco, another influential Argentine psychoanalyst, used Pichon Rivière's ideas to formulate a different conceptualisation of the Oedipus complex based on links, especially in the configuration of a psychotic member within the family bond, providing an interesting theoretical contribution from an intergenerational perspective. He describes how the non-resolution of the Oedipus complex in one generation is inevitably repeated in the next. Psychosis in children is deeply rooted in development prior to resolution of the Oedipus complex. If the mother has been unable to achieve a proper resolution of the Oedipus complex, she will tend to establish a narcissistic pathological relationship with her child, who will then be trapped in a symbiotic link that excludes the father, with pathological consequences for the child. The ill member is thus an *emergent* of pathological family dynamics.

From the point of view of Argentine psychoanalysis, the reformulation of these concepts was necessary in order to understand couple and family organisations. Different models intertwine, but in all of them the internal representation of family members in psychic life parallels the family dynamic of the family as a group, forming what Pichon called an "internal group".

Today we can say that there is an Argentine perspective, which is usually referred to as the "link" perspective in psychoanalysis (*el vínculo*). Janine Puget, working with couples, and Isidoro Berenstein, working with families, together with the contribution of other Argentine psychoanalytic thinkers, have given birth to an original theoretical view. Although this view developed originally to understand and treat the link in pathological organisations, it has also enabled others to develop and redefine numerous concepts, such as those of difference, presentation, representation, uncertainty, event, and interference. As these ideas have grown in acceptance as new formulations within psychoanalysis, they have led to a metapsychology of the link. Berenstein and Puget held that individual psychoanalysis alone was insufficient treatment for couples and families. They suggested three psychic spaces across each subjectivity: an intrasubjective space that has to do with drives and phantasy: intersubjective space where two or more subjects meet; and a trans-subjective one where subjects participate in a specific culture and are part of a society that gives a sense of belonging. The logic of the internal world is totally different to that of the link. The importance of novelty versus repetition defines the new view, where transference in the link is not only seen as pure repetition compulsion, but as a field in which the radical novelty of fate and unpredictable new events break repetition and introduce uncertainty.

Uncertainty in this sense is considered to be a new principle that regulates all link organisations.

These new contributions provide an epistemological break with traditional psychoanalytic understanding of clinical material for individuals, and especially for the psychoanalytical treatment of families and couples. Isidoro Berenstein (1932–2011) and Janine Puget have published widely in elaboration of these ideas, including their co-authored books in Spanish, *Psychoanalysis of the Marital Couple* (1981) and *Linking* (*Lo Vincular*) in 1997. They were twice granted the Sigourney Award for outstanding contributions to psychoanalysis (1993 and 2011).

Other Argentine authors are now well known in family and couple psychoanalysis for their contributions to the link theory, all offering alternative perspectives on the link. These include Silvia Gomel, Miguel Spivakow, Rodolfo Moguillansky, Guillermo Seiguer, Roberto Losso, Juan Carlos Nocetti, among many others.

A Brazilian approach: clinical foundations of couple and family link psychoanalysis

Lia Rachel Colussi Cypel (São Paulo, Brazil)

Psychoanalytic listening and new demands

Our current clinical practice, with its multifaceted demands and interfaces, poses challenges to the psychoanalytic approach. A world that is rapidly changing raises questions about new forms of subjectivity, links, and prevailing pathologies. We are led to reflect and to update our theory and practice in order to address the different dimensions of emerging demands. The search for the expansion of psychoanalytic research is thus manifested in the re-contextualisation of its concepts and practices.

Today we are being urged to discuss both current challenges to the family and those faced by psychoanalysis as it seeks to study this institution. The link perspective on family psychoanalysis does not deal merely with relationships among family members. It seeks to develop psychoanalysis further by establishing connections between internal and external realities in their most diverse expressions. The emergence of "the new" will be possible if we are able to tolerate a relative lack of knowledge and the lack of clear answers, letting ourselves open to the unknown.

The family is the primary human group. It is the matrix responsible for maintaining the species and a processing agent for changes intrinsic to human evolution at both the individual and the collective levels. It is in charge of individuals' development, enabling their individuation and autonomy, forming creative beings capable of building a society where justice, freedom, and respect for differences prevail. It is the point of contact between nature and culture, between the biological and the psychic, and is engaged in a dialectical relationship with its context whereby it shapes and is shaped by the historical moment of the society it inhabits. Every family is an expression of its time.

Thinking and working with families and couples from a psycho-analytic perspective entails a willingness to approach a broad, complex area. This endeavour generates challenges and resistances of different kinds owing to: 1) the nature of the object of study and the subject of the treatment, which constitutes a stronghold of powerful emotional forces; 2) difficulties in facing the continuous demand to develop suitable psychoanalytic tools to treat families and couples and in using them.

Such a demand arises from new inquiries and findings derived from clinical practice that expand theoretical questions and reveal unex-plored areas. It is also difficult to conceive human beings as part of a link that constitutes us and thereby also threateningly puts us off-centre from the sense of individuality. Putting us off-centre breaks the illu-sion of identity and the lack of limits. Psychoanalysis is undergoing a process of research and development, and the path that is proving most enriching is approaching it as an expansion of psychoanalysis. Analysts and patients create an analytic dialogue that promotes specific inter-pretations as well as the ability to change. It thus penetrates the field of the living unconscious and modifies it to achieve fuller self-knowledge.

Foundations of link psychoanalysis

Psychoanalytic work with families involves a methodology that has as reference customary psychoanalytic parameters, which articulate the characterisation of the analyst's role. These are the rule of abstinence, free association, unconscious phenomenon, and psychoanalytic listen-ing and interpreting. The aim is to transform unconscious phenomena involved in the link by means of transference, countertransference, and the analysis of the ongoing emotional experience. Nonetheless, it is assumed that this basic reference will suffer variations in clinical practice according to analysts' conceptual framework, in terms of both their definition of psychoanalysis and the theoretical model that guides their understanding of family and couple links.

Two main theoretical approaches have influenced couple and family psychonalysis in Brazil in the last thirty years. One is centred on the notion of object relations (the English School including the Tavistock Institute, and the French School with Ruffiot, Racamier, Eiger, and Kaës, among others), and sees family dynamics as a web of crossed projective identifications determined by individual object relations. The individual (and infantile) intrapsychic world of those involved defines the relationship, and "the other" operates as an intrasubjective object or a representation of subjects' unilateral desire and fantasy.

The other reference point is the Argentine School (with Pichon Rivière, Berenstein, Puget, Moguillansky, and Spivacow). These thinkers aim to distinguish object relations from the intersubjective relation or the link (*el vínculo*). This is redefined as a relationship between two egos that have a quality of extra-territoriality. Because he or she is different and distinct, and cannot be reduced to the subject's desire and fantasy, the other can generate a new circumstance, an origin (which goes beyond individual, infantile desire) for each participant, who is transformed by this relationship of presence into a new subject, known as "the subject of the link". These authors highlight the idea of the foreign aspects of the other, which lack unconscious inscription and hence cannot be repressed. Mechanisms of imposition (this is not introjection), pertaining to power relations, thus become part of the link.

Subjectivity is then determined not only by the drives, through the network of identifications and ensuing object relations, but also by each meaningful link. This is why while childhood events constitute a starting point, they are not the only beginning point.

In our clinical experience we have found that it is possible to make connections between these two contributions. They can be articulated by incorporating Bion's ideas, which already contain an intersubjective vertex. Discrepancies can be seen among these approaches, which are neither radically different nor mutually exclusive. They reflect the complexity and the dynamics of the psychic elements, which interconnect in the several dimensions of subjective experience in family relations. Bion's ideas can thus be used to look at object relations and links not just as opposed notions but also as the two ends of a spectrum of development of the capacity to think. The physical presence of the other does not ensure his being recognised as a different subject in the individual's mental representation of him. This spectrum contains the psychoanalytic notion of a gradient of narcissism and orientation towards the object.

Theoretical–clinical correlation

Here I'm trying to put together a few theoretical–clinical ideas that, in my view, constitute basic guidelines for the analyst's job in order to pursue their consistent interrelation. The theory becomes the expression of our clinical observations and when we use it in our practice to guide our method and technique, it may bring benefits and a true and lasting psychodynamic reorganisation in families or couples undergoing treatment.

Bion's theory can be used as a path to integrate these diverse contributions according to which the family is both responsible for instating the psyche and forms a matrix for the ability to think. The purpose of working with the family would be to offer it a space to think about its emotional states, and thus develop the ability to control and deal with its members' frustration and psychic pain.

Another key concept that supports our practice is that we conceive of the psyche as an open system that is in continuity/discontinuity with the other(s). For this reason, every psychic event is two-dimensional. In other words, the intrasubjective and intersubjective dimensions constitute two sides of a single mode of functioning, with no clear boundaries between them.

As to the link, it is constituted by reciprocal investitures between two or more subjects that generate modes of functioning, mutual unconscious influences, and determinations. It is hence pivotal to the genesis and maintenance of the psychic apparatus, to the constitution of the unconscious, and generates the ongoing subjectivation process that unfolds over the course of individual lives. Individuals are subjected to demands both from childhood history, which determines them, and from chance, indeterminacy—from new, unknown events that are part of the emotional experience of the link. These events are unpredictable and unique for each individual with that particular other. Reciprocal influence redefines and modifies those aspects that are specific to each participating subject. Unconscious creation and transformation phenomena unfold in all subjects involved thanks to mental processes taking place between them.

From a psychodynamic point of view, linking should be envisaged as happening in dialectical movements between subject and others. Dialectical linking is expressed in the in-between of alternation:

intrasubjective	$\rightleftarrows$	intersubjective
internal world	$\rightleftarrows$	external world
narcissistic links	$\rightleftarrows$	object links
repetition	$\rightleftarrows$	innovation

and of determination

by childhood	$\rightleftarrows$	indeterminacy
object relation	$\rightleftarrows$	link
absence	$\rightleftarrows$	presence

The dimension that predominates at a certain moment most characterises the psychodynamic of the link.

These ideas lead to a therapeutic process that favours transformation. A family (couple) that has a sterile mental life and is imprisoned in a fusional, rigid, and repetitive functioning (a "combined family figure"), where members use massive projective identification and where roles and functions are undifferentiated (denying gender and generational differences), may, through therapy, turn their psychic field into a fertile one that expands to promote containment, the working-through of mental suffering, and the development of its members, thus being able to individuate and enjoy freedom and autonomy. The goal is for them to leave behind a primitive, fragmentary, and narcissistic functioning, especially regarding concrete thinking and absolute beliefs.

These achievements entail participating in integration and symbolisation processes that facilitate members' acknowledgement of and concern for the other as well as tolerance of difference in a link, being able to look at things flexibly in perspective.

It becomes relevant to observe the natural alternation between these different levels of mental functioning. At the same time, it is essential to analyse the psychic resources of couple members. These will determine the constructive or destructive quality (fragmentation $\rightleftarrows$ integration) of their linking ability and linking states during the session. We must also examine family life cycles in order to understand the anxieties triggered in each phase of the therapeutic process or by external reality.

As Freud stated, individual and group functioning are inextricably linked. Two significant issues that may be clarified through psychoanalytic work with families are: 1) how individuals' mental functioning or defense mechanisms find expression within the family group; and 2) how unconscious processes can be revealed by treating the family as a psychic unit (the family as a patient), individual symptoms finding meaning in the combination of family members' linking dynamics.

The analyst's function will also focus on the analysis of the linking states, which are supported by a negative capability (tolerance of the unknown) that leads to the tolerance of alterity. Such tolerance transforms the intrapsychic subject–object relation into an intersubjective subject–subject relation and makes it possible for a new order (of meaning) to be established when a couple is formed (Moguillansky, 1999).

As a key circumstance the constitution of a couple or a nuclear family requires a symbolic operation that will define a symbolic rupture with (consciously and unconsciously) learned relationship patterns stemming from the families of origin. These patterns represent narcissistic feelings and a matrix of omnipotence, wholeness, and immortality. To establish a new family, it is essential that couples create and recreate this new space built in the void left by the symbolic rupture with the foundations laid by their families of origin (unconscious conceptions, projects, and ideals about marital and family life). A new vertex of rationality (multi-subjectivity) can emerge, with a new meaning for each member that is compatible with the times he or she lives in. An inter-generational process takes place versus a trans-generational process.

Binocular vision will support the analyst in these multiple perceptions, favouring the instatement of the "pairing function" in the family (Meltzer, 1978). This tendency to form units larger than the individual enables our development as human beings, something we could never achieve on our own.

The clinical link situation: the analytic function and the analyst's mind

The construction of the clinical situation, starts in the analyst's mind (internal setting), where the link context is placed. Analysts know that the latent meanings of manifest events can be apprehended by means of transference and countertransference dynamics (the repressed unconscious), but also through other modes of expression that transcend the transference and speak of preconceptions contained in unconscious emotional experience of the link.

Articulating these ideas, there should be space in the session for the analysis and interpretations of the two dimensions. We must address the intrasubjective or individual aspects of the subjectivity constituted around unconscious childhood conflicts. We must be alert to the repetition of the first marks left by original objects—the "mark of the *absence*" of the other projected into the present. Yet we cannot overlook the dimension of unconscious link events that occur in the "here-and-now" of the session with the *"present* other" (giving access to the multisubjectivity of each member of the family in the intersubjective context). These events must therefore refer to the other, to unknown unconscious dimensions originating in that unique and specific link and in the new psychic event. From this perspective, the historical past does not explain the present. Rather, our understanding of the present re-signifies the past. So, analyst and patients will achieve a worked-through reintegration of the nuclear family with the families of origin in order to grant continuity to their lineage, to phylogenetic connections, and to achieve an inner reconciliation with the transmission of tradition.

When we address intrasubjective aspects, we must always go right back to the link perspective and identify the role of this "individual psychic something" in the link. We should be able to determine what purpose it serves within this specific link configuration (i.e., unconscious alliances and collusions in the mode of interaction).

Active interpretation of the family's (or couple's) use of projective identification or of the unconscious alliances prevailing in the link field promotes link members' awareness of how they experience each other and their analyst, and of how the analyst experiences them. Thus the right conditions for insight on the dynamics of family (or couple) relations are created. Interpretation makes it possible for participants in the link to take greater responsibility in relation to the treatment and to their lives in general.

The fluctuation of analysts' attention between these diverse conditions by means of a "zoom-like" gaze offers them a more particular and panoramic view that could lead to the emergence of an interpretation as a "selected fact".

Our clinical approach seeks to pull analysts away from the omnipotent position of absolute knowledge, from intellectualisation towards favouring an emotional experience. The apprehension and tolerance represented by a multiplicity of dimensions and the ongoing movement among them have to do with the nature of the psyche. In clinical practice this attitude represents a basic analytic position in which constant inquiry about our observations, thoughts, and feelings is necessary. The mind can thus be conceived as a complex, multidimensional, and multi-factorial system with an endless ability to transform in response to internal and external reality.

Analysts who agree with this view search for meaning rather than causes. They aim for psychic expansion rather than the narrowing of thinking and feeling. They advance hypotheses and tackle doubts. This leads them to question themselves and their hitherto unshakeable truths. They develop a reflective attitude and ponder their participation in the resulting conflicting link.

This analytic attitude reveals a tolerance for "not knowing", and should be directed first to analysts' own theoretical framework and clinical experience so that there will be a fluid back-and-forth between theory and practice that will facilitate their constant revitalisation and recreation.

Contributions from British object relations

David E. Scharff (Washington, DC, USA)

The group of ideas developed in Great Britain beginning about 1940 that can be loosely grouped together as "British object relations" stem from the work of Fairbairn, Klein, Winnicott, Bion and Bowlby. They were first elaborated as an approach to couples by Henry Dicks in his ground-breaking book *Marital Tensions* (1967), in which he synthesised the work of Fairbairn and Klein. Much of the work of the family discussion bureau, founded by Enid Balint at the Tavistock Institute in 1948, later continued as the Tavistock Marital Studies Institute, Tavistock Centre for Couple Relationships, and currently as Tavistock Relationships (TR), now with its own buildings separate from the main Tavistock complex, also stems from Klein, Bion, and Bowlby, with added influence of such others as Donald Meltzer and Ron Britton. Mary Morgan's separate introduction to the approach by Tavistock Relationships (see later in this chapter) will present that line of development. Therefore, in this contribution, I will introduce the work that Jill Savege Scharff and I elaborated beginning in the 1980s, variations of which have been developed by colleagues at the International Psychotherapy Institute and elsewhere. We have spelled out our basic integration in *Object Relations Family Therapy* (1987) and *Object Relations Couple Therapy* (1991), and elaborated on sexuality (D. Scharff, 1982), trauma (Scharff & Scharff, 1994), integrated treatment (Scharff & Scharff, 1998), and recent developments provided by such modern theories as chaos theory, attachment theory, the social unconscious, and link theory (Scharff & Scharff, 2011). Meanwhile, colleagues at IPI and many others have elaborated on this core, taken up certain aspects other than our core concepts, and have thereby enlarged the reach of this set of ideas (Bagnini, 2012; Caruso, 2005; Poulton, 2013). For instance, the ground-breaking research done by a group headed by Roger Shapiro and John Zinner at the family studies branch of the National Institute of Mental Health in the 1960s and 1970s was later gathered as a volume that shows this group's fundamental contribution, which also drew heavily on British object relations (J. Scharff, 1989).

The core theoretical ideas of our approach can be summed up as:

1. Unconscious communication exists from the beginning of life, transmitted through the mechanisms of emotional communication and of projective identification.

   The baby is born into relationships and with a need to relate. The earliest communications are highly affective, and are the crucible in which each person develops. Interaction and unconscious affective transmission through the mechanism of projective identification establishes bonds with parents and early caregivers. Each person takes in central aspects of these formative relationships through continuous cycles of projective and introjective identification with caregivers and in other important relationships. Emotional communication, which is largely unconscious, is central to this process.

2. Families and couples need to be understood as special group organisations, with interactional and emotional links between members.

   Each couple and family is organised both by the individual psychic structure of each person, and by the family's function as a group. Therefore principles of group interactive dynamics are fundamental to understanding their shared functioning. This includes the idea of unconscious shared organisation, shared assumptions, and intra-group conflict.

3. Members of a couple or family share links in the space between the individuals. The link is defined as the organisation—both conscious and unconscious—created by all the interacting individuals.

   We have learned from the tradition begun in Argentina by Pichon Rivière that links are both conscious and unconscious, and are expressed in action, words, and the body. In turn, they contribute to the organisation of each of the individuals who operate together to construct the ever-evolving shared link. Such links are unique to each pair or family group. While each individual contributes, no two groups or couples have identical patterns of linkage. Therefore the individuals are influenced differently depending on which group or sub-group they are relating to at a given moment. Links are also installed internally (through introjective identification) in the individual as psychic structure where internal links between self and internal objects continually influence external behaviour.

4. The couple forms a link that is at the cross-hairs between the inherited legacies of previous generations, and between the current nuclear family and the couple's extended families, their social groups, and society.

   The couple is cradle to the family, carrying the legacy of previous generations. In their care of the children, the couple extends what we can call a vertical axis of the link to future generations. So the vertical axis is the connection to past and future. In the horizontal axis of the link, the couple connects to extended family, neighbouring families, and groups, and the wider society and culture—that is, to concentric circles of the current world.

5. Sexuality is a crucial couple link. The object relations of the couple's sexual and romantic interaction influences and is influenced by the organisation of the larger family.

   The sexual life of couples is often overlooked clinically. Because it combines the possibility of heightened pleasure, procreation and its failures, and both emotion and body, it has a special role in the expression and development of object relations and links within the family.

6. Families and couples provide psychological holding, containment, intimacy, and the facilitation of individual development of their members.

   Couples and families are work groups. Their tasks are, first, to provide for the emotional and practical safety of the members. This psychological holding is analogous to the mother's arms-around provision for her infant. The second major task of the family group is to provide for the development of each individual member of the couple or family at whatever level is appropriate to their age, stage of development, and personal capacities. A major part of this in the emotional realm is the provision of containment. Bion described how the parent unconsciously takes the infant's primitive anxieties into her mind through projective identification, metabolises them, and feeds them back to the infant in more mature, less anxious, and emotionally more comprehensible form. It is not just the individual mother, but the family or couple as a group that has this task. If it is neglected or badly done, all individuals in the family suffer. The family group provides for each individual's need for love and intimacy.

Some central therapeutic principles of our clinical approach are:

1. We work to create space so each member of the family can tell us of his or her experience, and create an atmosphere that facilitates increased individual understanding, understanding of each other, and of the family or couple as a group.
2. We use a variety of "languages" depending on what is most appropriate and effective: words that describe family experience or important events outside the immediate family. We also work with children's play, dreams, fantasy, and descriptions of bodily experiences.
3. We track affect, looking for *core affective moments* within sessions that provide inroads to the object relations organisation of the individuals and the family group.
4. In this way, we begin to see how the couple or family's object relations history influences both difficulties in the family and central moments in treatment.
5. We think of symptomatic family members as *spokespersons* for overall family difficulty, but we also look to other family members to speak for particular issues.
6. We are interested in a couple's sexual and romantic life.
7. We examine the *developmental stages* of the overall family and how that relates to the developmental needs of individual family members.

8. We work to understand various levels of *group organisation* of the family.
9. We follow *couple and family transference*, using our countertransference as a central guide.

While this list is not exhaustive, it serves to describe varying levels of engagement and of the understanding we seek. No list can create a sense of exactly how we would like to work, and it is with this shortcoming in mind that we present many clinical examples later in this book.

To summarise, the object relations approach assumes that the therapeutic relationship is the chief engine of change. We work to produce change by continually enlarging our understanding of the couple or family's difficulties in relating, autonomous functioning, and support of family needs. We do so by engaging with the family, and allowing the family's emotional climate to enter the consulting room where it is emotionally absorbed by the therapist, who through conscious and unconscious processes, joins in the family's emotional experience. Because understanding is a chief medium of exchange, we value verbal interpretation of what we learn. We employ all levels of interpretive feedback, to include simple things such as clarification, linking, pointing out contradictions, and highlighting the object relations of basic misunderstandings and anger within the family. However, we understand that unconscious communication occurs at all times and is equally important for engagement with the family, for communication of care, concern and understanding, and for interrupting existing family organisation in so far as it is dysfunctional and shortchanges family needs. Ultimately, it is the quality of care and of underlying hope that the therapist brings to therapeutic encounters that is central to the process of couple and family growth and change.

Tavistock Relationships' object relations approach to couple relationships: past, present, and future

Mary Morgan (London, England)

The psychoanalytic understanding of couple relationships I describe has evolved within Tavistock Relationships (TR) over the last sixty-eight years, beginning with pioneering family caseworkers working in collaboration with psychoanalysts and others. The early work of Enid Balint (1993), Henry Dicks (1967/1993), and Lily Pincus (1960) was later influenced by broadly based analytic thinking, particularly from the 1990s by post-Kleinian ideas.

Object relations theories about the couples all concern the complex relational interplay between two people's internal object relations, unconscious phantasies, conflicts, anxieties, and defences in interaction. Several strands of thinking have had prominence in the history of TR, all informing current thought. These are influences of the past on relationships, their developmental dynamic nature in the present, and their potential in the future.

The influence of the past

The unconscious determinants bringing couples together based on past experience shape new relationships, and perhaps set up to repeat, to manage, or work through unresolved early anxieties. Lily Pincus wrote: "Although there is often a wish to start afresh in marriage and to escape the frustrations or disappointments of unsatisfactory early relationships, the strong unconscious ties to the first love-objects may help determine the choice of partner with whom the earlier situation can be compulsively re-enacted" (1962, p. 14). We analyse the meaning of unconscious choice of partner, unconscious contracts, and projective systems in which each partner splits off, projects into, and carries aspects of the other. In more defensive relationships there are wishes to keep these aspects firmly located in the other, but in developmental relationships with more flexibility, these aspects have potential for reintegration. Early clinical publications detailed meanings of object choice, couple fit, and complex unconscious arrangements as couples seek equilibrium.

Freud noted that defensive versions of couples' transference relationships repeat early unresolved relationships carried internally. In *Beyond the Pleasure Principle* (1920), he gave examples of individuals whose relationships all had similar outcomes: similar objects are repeatedly chosen but nothing is worked through, no new relationship develops. For example, he speaks of "the lover each of whose love affairs with a woman passes through the same phases and reaches the same conclusion … . If we take into account observations such as these, based upon behaviour in the transference and upon the life-histories of men and women, we shall find courage to assume that there really does exist in the mind a compulsion to repeat which over-rides the pleasure principle" (p. 22). Each new relationship becomes a version of the old.

These early clinicians observed wishes to repeat alongside wishes to create something new. Enid Balint stated: "One of the most striking, and perhaps encouraging, things that psychoanalysts have discovered, is that people never give up trying to put things right for themselves and for the people they love. Even when they may appear to be doing just the reverse, we often discover that what appears to be the most desperate and useless behavior can be understood as an attempt to get back to something that was good in the past, or to put right something that was unsatisfactory ... . We could say then, that in marriage we unconsciously hope to find a solution to our intimate and primitive problems" (1993, p. 41).

Thus relationships provide potential opportunity for working through and development. If projective systems are flexible enough, parts of self are held by the other, improved within the safety of the relationship, and over time can be reintrojected. Optimally each partner continues to individuate and develop within the relationship's container (Colman, 1993).

Cleavely wrote: "The marriage relationship provides a containment in which each feels the other to be part of themselves—a kind of joint personality. What at first attracts and is later complained of in the other is often a projection of the disowned and frightening aspects of the self. It might be imagined that the best thing to do with unwanted aspects of the self is to project them onto someone or something and get as far removed as possible. That would, however, be placing a part of oneself in danger of being lost forever, and of losing one's potential for becoming a more complete person" (1993).

All these writers speak to the tension between developmental and defensive needs of relationships. The optimistic view of couple relationships as potentially therapeutic relies on capacities to repair the past and enable individuals to work through earlier conflict.

Another important thread is the way couples share experience of the world through unconscious phantasy, unconsciously believing, for example, that love or hate are dangerous (Bannister & Pincus, 1965). Couples set up shared defences to manage their shared unconscious phantasies, leading to relationships in which, for example, the avoidance of strong feelings attacks intimacy and sexuality. Recently fixed unconscious phantasies have been thought about as unconscious beliefs about being a couple (Britton, 1998; Morgan, 2010). Such thinking prevalent in TR in the 1960s through to the 1980s is illustrated in *Psychotherapy with Couples* edited by Stanley Ruszczynski (1993).

The present

Two areas of thought relate to the nature of the relationship in the developmental and in the dynamic present.

The couple's psychic development in becoming a couple

Becoming a couple is part of psychic development from birth on, but development can become stuck because development towards being a couple is not secure. In this process of couple psychic development, the relationship to the primary object, working through the oedipal situation and adolescence are all crucial (Morgan, 2005).

Sometimes as couple therapists we ask what kind of couple exists in the present. Do partners feel part of a couple and what kind of couple? The relationship may be set to repeat an idealised version of mother/baby. Or there may be problems in becoming a couple because of difficulties relinquishing earlier stages of psychic development, for example, adolescent autonomy. Couples frequently seek to create perfect, idealised unity. Equally we see individuals terrified about commitment, as if they will lose themselves.

The present relationship dynamically

How do couples manage being in relationships with an "other" who is separate but intimate? This ordinary difficulty is also often a narcissistic problem. Being in a relationship (unless the relationship is fused) faces individuals on a daily basis with another person's view that cannot easily be engaged with or understood. The emphasis here is about the impact on each partner of being with a differentiated "other". For some, the fact of a separate other is intolerable, and so the couple resorts to primitive defences. One common solution is the attempt to force the other to accept one's own view, resulting in endless conflict, or sado-masochistic dominance and submission. I have described "projective gridlock" in which couples collapse into each other, using projective identification to create a sense of living inside the object, or the object living inside the self, as a way to deny others' separateness and difference that threatens the self. This can lead to comfortable fusion (for a while), or to controlling, rigid couples who are trapped in gridlock that they created (Morgan, 1995).

Ideas about narcissistic couple relating that developed in TR from 1990 onwards were presented in *Intrusiveness and Intimacy in the Couple* (Ruszczynski & Fisher, 1995) and in Fisher's *The Uninvited Guest* (1999).

Fisher described ongoing tensions between narcissism and psychological states of marriage: "The capacity to pursue the truth of one's own experience and also to tolerate the truth of another's experience, acknowledging and taking the meaning of the others experience without losing the meaning of one's own, especially when these experiences not only differ but conflict, is a major developmental achievement. The achievement of this capacity is not a fixed state and in intimate relationships they are always under pressure of our own infantile wishes, fears and anxieties to redraw the boundaries between self and other" (1999, p. 56). This shift in thinking suggests that intimacy is not just about being close while remaining separate, but that each partner is changed through encountering the other. Because the way the self is changed cannot be known and is unconscious, contemplating a relationship may be experienced as a frightening step into the unknown.

Another theme involves developing triangular psychic space by working through the oedipal situation (Britton, 2000; Morgan, 2000). For example, Ruszczynski (1998) wrote about 'the marital triangle', and Balfour (2016) highlighted the triangular situation's potential in couple therapy for creating psychic space. I have described the "couple state of mind" (2001) as often missing in couples, and how this is provided by the therapist and internalised through treatment. The couple state of mind, a third position represented by the relationship, helps couples be themselves, and in relationship. This is important for containing inevitable turmoil in intimate relationships where both otherness and the impact on the self has to be managed.

Scharff and Scharff (2011) have pointed out in their important exposition that there are similarities but also differences between link theory and object relations theory. Even considering couple relationships as constructed through object seeking, unanticipated aspects of the "other" are discovered and inevitably challenged in the relationship: not all of the other can be assimilated or known. We commonly see couples expending enormous psychic energy trying to deny this fact.

Berenstein (2012) from the perspective of the "link" (*el vínculo*) describes the notion of how the "presence" of the other impacts the self through "interference". He says interference "is what is produced in the space *in between* as a result of there being two or more subjects whose presence generates something new and unknown. The unknown forces these subjects to do something with it, to inscribe it, and to attempt to produce a *becoming* based on difference while dealing with the uncertainty about what they may be able to achieve."

The future

My third area concerns the future, containing the couple relationship's potential for development, for creating something new. What gets created in the coming together of two people is unique to each configuration. Here I bring together ideas developed in the object relations tradition—"the creative couple" and the notion of *vínculo* as an *exchange* between two or more people. Berenstein wrote:

> [The link's] product is an expanded, modified, renewed subjectivity that makes it possible to negate the ego's (narcissistic) confinement in its identity and to establish this subjectivity as novelty. The couple has its own life as an aggregate, which is different from the sum of its parts. Its member's carry in them the psychic developments of their own history and childhood as well as those produced within this aggregate, which is ceaselessly being constituted in each of the numerous "nows" they experience together. The present time gives rise to a past, a history, and a future in the form of a project that may not necessarily be realized but is a determining factor nonetheless. (Berenstein, 2012 p. 573)

The point of a relationship is that there is an "other" in continuous exchange. In creative couples, two people, separate and different, come together, are changed by each other and produce a "third", symbolised by the "baby", or let us say "thirds", as the couples who function creatively produce many "thirds".

In therapy we are interested in whether couples can discover their relationship as a resource for containment, but can also use difference and otherness to create new thoughts, resolutions, and ways forward. The internalisation of the therapist's "couple state of mind" helps couples find capacity for self-observation in relationship. This helps them manage conflict through achieving perspective on their relational dynamics and on what each partner brings, including past experience. But in order for couples to be creative, "the foreign aspect of the other" has to be engaged. "Interference is not about working through, as is the transference, but about making room for the other as a different subject. It is about the couple's members' ability to produce something new and different, instead of *reproducing* what each carries from childhood and what he or she has brought to the couple" (Berenstein, 2012 p. 576). In this way, the individual's psychic development continues because of working through the past, and through a new creative couple relationship with another person.

To recap, the ways in which I have conceptualised and summarised this object relations approach to understanding the couple relationship are: first, what couples bring of their past and how this is responded to defensively and developmentally; second, how couples do at "being a couple"—how they manage the dynamics of there being an "other"; and third, how they might continue developing in a relationship which can be creative for them together and individually.

The Italian approach to family and couple therapy

Anna Maria Nicolò and Diana Norsa (Rome, Italy)

Starting in the 1970s, a group of Italian child and adolescent psychoanalysts with grounding in the systemic family model, began to study parent and family dynamics. They founded the journal *Interazioni* in 1992, edited by Anna Nicolò. Psychoanalytic research focused on married couples, parents, and families, resulting in a publication by Anna Nicolò and Gemma Trapanese (2005). Later, publications drew from the object relations theory of Kleinian and Winnicottian ideas (Norsa & Zavattini, 1997; Nicolò, Benghozi, & Lucarelli, 2014). As a result, it is now possible to acknowledge ways in which psychoanalysis can be practiced beneficially in various developmental stages and with severe patients.

The psychoanalytical setting with couples and families allows consideration of shared psychopathological areas of relationship that often defy individual therapy. Knowledge of couple relational dynamics shows that often the person who seeks therapy, while suffering more, is also better able to use therapy. The partner, often sicker, shies away from the challenge. In collusive situations, the partner who enters therapy often meets analytical impasse due to the partner's resistance to change. Couple and family psychoanalysis opens new paths for psychic understanding, while also facing us with new obstacles.

Focus on intrapsychic and interpersonal dimensions; the multi-dimensionality of families and couples

In clinical practice, we focus on the intersection and exchange between intrapsychic and interpersonal dimensions of life. Individuals have inner worlds, of which they are only partly aware, and, at the same time, are part of interpersonal worlds they help build, most significantly the family into which we are born and which we then build.

The family's multi-dimensional organisation consists of layers of psychic functioning. The interaction between individuals and members of their family, both internal and external, involves continuous elaboration. Coexistence of levels of function affords flexibility to the family, and allows for changing operations depending on members' needs in the cycle of life or in particular crises. A family is therefore a network of more or less differentiated, more or less primitive or undifferentiated, interrelations where distinction between mental and somatic, external and internal, individual and group may vanish periodically. Psychoanalysis has taught us to consider psychic functioning in a continuous processing of sense, between the inside and outside and between the primitive and current (Sapisochin, 2013, p. 967). Through co-construction of shared unconscious meaning, individuals establish lasting links between spouses and between generations of parents and children (Nicolò, Norsa, & Carratelli, 2003, p. 285).

Family myths are complex group constructions whose tasks include transmitting the memory of past events and characteristics inherent in its history and in family identity. There are other levels that Reiss (1989) called interactive co-ordinated practices, now called procedural memories. Recent neuro-scientific discoveries have proven that there are several ways to store memories related to these myths and memories. Daily interactions, remembered as unprocessed facts and interactive habits, hide fundamental systems of psychic life and transmit unelaborated traumatic memories, and repetition of relational rules unconsciously learned from previous generations and renegotiated in the new family. To understand psychotic functioning, narrations, myths, and dreams will no longer be enough. Observations of these unfolding concrete operations are needed, in addition to observation of interactive co-ordinated practices, because families do things without thought. A child is born into networks of actions and behaviours that express and deny lived memories, fantasies, and emotions.

Couple sexuality and care of newborns represent relational use of the body for communication that "updates" primitive levels of somato-psychological functioning, taps past relations, and sensory and pro-cedural memories sometimes precluded at more organised levels of personality. Clinical study of marital couples and families with small children or families coping with the nascent sexuality of a teenager has been a rich field for studying psychopathology and the dynamic nature of family ties (Norsa, 1993).

The link

A psychoanalyst of families, couples, or institutions sees not only recip-rocal and crossed projective identifications and collusion, but also a third element defined as the "link" (Kaës, 2015; Puget & Berenstein, 1989). Once constructed, it takes on a life of its own, independent from the subjects, able to influence them, and constituting a third element, a new entity affecting the functioning of family and couple, acting on the context and on the members who produced it. At pre-symbolic lev-els, links are established between partners in a couple and with each of their children. Split-off elements and unconscious agreements suitable to protect against non-elaborated experiences or traumas are elaborated in links. The subject of the relationship is not only the object of projec-tion, but also "the end of a process of psychic exchange and, therefore, is like the other subject, another subject who does insist and does resist in so much as he is the other" (Kaës, 1994, p. 190).

These links constitute a background web that characterises inter-actions, like a stage on which the actors play their parts. These links involve more than a member and a child who grows in their midst learns them (Nicolò, 1997, 2000a, 2000b, 2003, 2005). The organisation of common defences, such as malignant merger, intrusion, and coloni-sation of others' minds, or identity grown from birth, reveal links that unite members, Because of links' reciprocal nature, they defy causal explanations of symptoms, and show the needs of everyone involved in the network. Meltzer (1978) assumes that the mental pain's "location can be shifted rather than its existence denied" (p. 81), shifted to objects of the outside world and transferred to other persons.

The concepts of "depository" (Bleger, 1967), "spokesperson" (Pichon Rivière, 1965), and "porte-parole" or "speech bearer" (Kaës, 2015) are examples in which the symptomatic person simultaneously expresses personal suffering and collective unease. Family and couple therapy demonstrates the possibility of "healing oneself in the other" or "becoming ill in his place" (Nicolò, 1990).

Therapeutic tools

The basic tools of the family psychoanalyst are the same as in the dual setting. Sticking to timetables, fees, and regulated interruptions are intrinsic elements. Couple and family therapies are normally scheduled once a week, at a given time and for a fixed duration (e.g., one hour and fifteen minutes), with breaks for scheduled holidays. The therapeutic contract does not provide time limits, but ensures the availability of psychoanalysts for as long as is necessary. Transference and countertransference dynamics need to be considered. One psychoanalyst is enough for family treatment. For couples, we have experimented with Dicks's (1967) model—two psychoanalysts representing a fantasy parental couple with capacity for containment. We also consider the "internal setting" (as understood by Grinberg), characterised by the analyst's mental attitude. With teenagers, psychotic patients, or in other situations with families and couples, a more flexible setting may be required.

The two types of settings proposed by Bleger are useful: one is maintained by the psychoanalyst and consciously accepted by the patient, while the other is projected by the patient."The setting 'is' the most primitive part of personality, the ego-body-world fusion", building from primitive and psychotic parts of personality (Bleger, 1967, p. 235).

The therapeutic relationship

Unlike individual therapy, during a family or couple session, the real presence of several members entails that the therapeutic setting presents real relations between the members in the "here-and now", representations of past relations, and fantasy relational aspects. The partner constitutes not only internalised relations, but also a real other. Frequently, couples stop speaking about their children only after a few sessions, and instead bring their more personal issues to the surface. Then, if parents and children have their own therapies, children can use psychotherapy more freely, often with full transference to the analyst.

In treatment, families re-enact the processes characterising their relational functioning, acting on their analyst, luring him into their defensive system, or pushing him to action rather than understanding. A psychoanalyst with little training risks acting to rid herself of emotional pressure. Instead, analysts must be containers of unsorted and non-integrated aspects of the self (Winnicott, 1956). Rigorous training, including personal analysis and supervision, is needed to use countertransference well. A psychoanalyst who can articulate her inner experience adds meaning, so that experiences, previously lived as frightening or intolerable, can now be accepted and integrated.

In family analysis, each family member develops his own personal transference, not being directed only toward the psychoanalyst, but also to other family members. For instance, a parent may project her relationship with her parents onto her child. Interpretation of such lateral transferences is important because it increases individuals' degrees of freedom, allowing better definition of expectations, mutual functions, reciprocal representations, and role attributions.

We think that the setting with the family and couple is a multi-corporal, multi-personal field. In it, "the characters of the respective internal groups" (Pichon Rivière, 1971) undergo a process of diffraction (Kaës, 2007) in the members of the family, couple, and the psychoanalysts, and "interact with those belonging to the internal groups of psychoanalysts" (Losso, 2000, p. 188). This encounter creates new relationships. The interpretation of transference in this regard will concern differences between repetition of the past and the possibility of building something new. We also consider transference to the therapeutic context (contextual transference) (Scharff & Scharff, 1991), directed toward the holding function of the setting.

Understanding and interpreting histories

Members of couples or families communicate with the psychoanalyst in the presence of the other, perhaps strengthening resistance due to fear of retaliation, or to shame about communicating facts or private experiences to the partner. Psychoanalysts must maintain a safe space for specific privacy of each spouse, delimiting occasions for safe communication. Then, associating freely in the presence of the other becomes a powerful therapeutic factor.

With the analyst's guidance, confronting projections of each patient not with respect to reality but with respect to past experiences of other members, leads to shared understanding. Then, narrative of the individual histories creates a shared history, allowing for new knowledge of the other and constituting new family identity. Narrative offered in the family setting is never individual, but is the collective product of many stories, a "co-narrative" built by all the members interacting with one another and the psychoanalyst. The observation of their intersection is important in the construction or reconstruction of a "sufficiently true", plausible family history. The history of the family is different from the story each member has. Subjectively, there is a different family for each member and different parents for each child.

History always crosses generations. Multiple generations are present in the culture of the current family group, transmitted through identification, and coalescing in family myths (Nicolò, 1993).

Interpretation concerns the content communicated by individual members, as well as the link between the members, which, being a third element, draws from complementary versions of individual members. Interpretation highlights relational configurations that have immobilised family members, especially interpretation of transpersonal defences that members have built over time together to cope with shared anxieties that are re-enacted in the here-and-now of sessions. Interpretations are generally provided by the psychoanalyst, but sometimes members of the family communicate them. Sometimes a member's dream will embody an interpretation, triggering new insight for all.

Dreams, play, and metaphor

Our group has developed techniques for intervention that maintain consistent levels of psychotherapeutic care. We pay special attention to unconscious language that conveys affective meaning, even in situations dense with conflicting, incoherent, and contradictory elements, as is often the case in verbal material of family and couple sessions. Unconscious language consists of childhood games, dreams, and metaphors (Nicolò, Norsa, & Carratelli, 2003, p. 294). The psychoanalyst fosters emergence of co-constructed fantasies in order to stimulate each person to reveal and elaborate on emotions, sensations, and fears toward the others.

Having children in family sessions is valuable because while adults often find difficulty describing their past in words, children play, providing opportunities for easy interpretation capable of reaching all family members. Play is like free association, as Klein posited. Winnicott added that play can communicate intense and contradictory emotions directly, and organise them into stories that build psychic meaning. By recognising the language of play, one can also detect when adult language is used in a way that discards or denies the other, and can see opportunities for coming together. Play sessions, therefore, should involve all family members. Similarly, telling of dreams enables psychoanalysts to get an overall idea of their patients as individuals, couples, or families, and to build integrated affective images of their unconscious organisation. The resulting metaphors form valuable therapeutic instruments, often taking the place of interpretations too complex or verbose for digestion.

Other dimensions of work with families include elaboration of rites and myths built over multiple generations that contribute to family and personal identity, and narration of the collective history of the family that may reveal unconscious aspects that are still present. Through continuing psychoanalytic work, these elaborations of experience, which may have been traumatic, may be transformed into new versions and new narratives.

Couple and family psychoanalysis in Oceania: history, influences and development

Timothy Keogh (Sydney, Australia)

Identity is the history that has gone into bone and blood and reshaped the flesh. Identity is not what we were but what we have become and what we are at this moment.

—Joaquin, 2004, p. 64

The emergence of psychoanalysis in Australasia

A particular set of social and cultural factors has fostered both resistance and limited receptivity to psychoanalytic ideas and development in Australia. As Boots notes:

> Our national history is one of diaspora, migration forced and chosen, destructive conflicts between an old indigenous culture and recent non-indigenous arrivals … . [T]he first European settlement … was conceived in a very strange climate of fear, dread, separation—and opportunity. These psychic elements, I believe, have continued to haunt a national identity that has only recently undergone a revisionist historical analysis. (2010, p. 1)

The profession of psychoanalysis in Australia can be thought to have begun in 1910 with an invitation to Freud to attend the Ninth Session Australasian Medical Congress held in Sydney 18–23 September 1911 (Thomson-Salo, 2011). Freud could not attend but sent a paper for the congress "Outlining the central tenets of psychoanalysis" (Damousi, 2005). Clinical psychoanalysis began when the British-trained analyst, Dr. Roy Winn commenced practice in Sydney in 1931. Dr Claro Lazard-Geroe from Budapest established the Melbourne Institute in 1940, and in 1949 Dr. Andrew Peto of the British Society founded the Sydney Institute. The Australian Society of Psychoanalysis (APAS) was formed in 1952 and made a provisional society at the 1971 IPA Vienna Congress. Currently there are three Australian IPA psychoanalytic institutes in Adelaide, Melbourne, and Sydney. As psychoanalysis developed in Australia, so too did institutes of psychoanalytic psychotherapy. Its umbrella organisation, the Psychoanalytic Psychotherapy Association of Australia (PPAA), has several hundred members, most based in Sydney and Melbourne.

New Zealand, with no IPA component society, has a number of psychoanalytic psychotherapist members of the PPAA, and a small group of Jungian analysts of the Australian and New Zealand Society of Jungian Analysts (ANZSJA).

Two waves of development in couple and family psychoanalysis

The development of couple and family psychoanalysis (and psychoanalytic psychotherapy) in Australasia arose in response to social and cultural factors at first related to the social and emotional complexities resulting from World War II. In New Zealand, psychoanalysis and psychoanalytic psychotherapy were pioneered by Eva Fishman, a German-Jewish refugee. Arriving in 1939 after her own psychoanalytic training had sadly been disrupted, she began a small practice and reading group. She had a special interest in child and family work, and after World War II she inspired renowned pediatrician Alice Bush to join her in setting up the Family Guidance Clinic, with the purpose of offering psychoanalytically informed child and family therapy. Later the clinic found a welcome benefactor in the Paykel family, who endowed it with a large house that became the first Auckland Family Counselling Service (Blumenfeld-Hoadley, 2015).

At the same time, based on the British model, marriage guidance councils were established in Melbourne and Sydney in 1948. It was, however, in the Citizen's Welfare Service (later renamed as the Drummond Street Centre, in 1990) that psychodynamically oriented couple work found its real home. The Drummond Street Centre remained a government funded clinic until 2007.

A second wave of couple and family development occurred in another era of social change in Australia and around the world, culminating in the formation of associations, institutes, and societies dedicated to advancing the knowledge and understanding of theory and practice. This social change brought about a re-examination of social norms concerning gender roles, sexuality, marriage, and family, particularly in the 1960s and 1970s, and occurred in an increasingly materialistic and narcissistic culture. With this development, Australia saw the practice of couple and family psychoanalysis and psychotherapy emerge as a sub-specialty at roughly the same time this took place in Europe and North America.

In Melbourne during this period, couple and family work was significantly influenced by Peter Fullerton, a Jungian analyst trained in London in the early 1980s and later staff of the then Tavistock Institute of Marital Studies (TIMS). In 1989 Fullerton brought his training and experience to Melbourne and established a clinical study group known as the "Vivaldi Group". The group includes Melbourne-based analyst Roslyn Glickfeld and continues to be influential in promoting couple and family psychoanalysis and psychotherapy and through offering supervision.

Meanwhile, a Sydney-based group developed in a more formal way, ultimately establishing the New South Wales Institute for Family Psychotherapy in 1990 (Berg, Jools, & Keogh, 2011), renamed in 2012 as the Couples and Family Psychoanalytic Psychotherapy Association of Australasia (CAFPAA). Whilst there are not organised groupings of couples and family psychoanalysis or psychotherapy in other major Australian cities, there has been growing interest. The psychoanalytically oriented interest group (POPIG) of the Australian Psychological Society, with branches in Brisbane, Perth, and Adelaide, has also promoted psychodynamically oriented couple and family work.

Links with Europe

Charles Enfield, a psychiatrist and psychotherapist who immigrated to Australia from London, established and was the inaugural president of the New South Wales Institute for Family Psychotherapy (NSWIFP). Like Fullerton, Enfield had trained in couple and family therapy at the Tavistock Clinic with John Bowlby, Henry Dicks, and Pierre Turquet. In planting the seeds of British influence in Australia, he originally established in 1977 the practice of couple and family psychotherapy at the Royal Alexandra's Children's hospital, where he was director of psychiatry. The child and family psychiatry department at the hospital had a culture supporting psychoanalytic practice. Like Fullerton in Melbourne, Enfield trained a number of psychiatrists, social workers and psychologists within the department, and the staff went on to play significant roles in in couple and family therapy in the hospital and community.

In New Zealand, from the 1990s until 2006, it was the Auckland Family Counselling and Psychotherapy Centre which provided a base for the provision of dedicated and psychoanalytically orientated individual, couple, child, and family therapy. It also offered subsidised services to families in need and offered a two-year psychoanalytic psychotherapy course for health professionals in Auckland. The course developed by the director, Ms Annette Asher, and visiting psychoanalyst, Arnold de Jong, ultimately became a diploma in psychoanalytic psychotherapy. Later Judi Blumenfeld-Hoadley piloted a well-received psychoanalytically orientated couple work course, later developed into a master's course for Auckland University of Technology.

Recent developments

Through his connections with Jill Savege Scharff, Charles Enfield encouraged the development of a link with the Washington-based

International Psychotherapy Institute (IPI) in 2008. Subsequently, connections were made by Sydney-based therapists with other couple psychoanalysts and psychotherapists at the Tavistock Centre for Couples Relationships (TCCR) and with the Scottish Institute of Human Relations (SIHR). Further networking also led to an NSWIFP-sponsored invitation to IPI couple psychoanalysts (including David and Jill Scharff) to visit Sydney. In Melbourne, the Australian Association of Relationship Counsellors had also sponsored a number of prominent overseas couples and family psychoanalysts and psychoanalytic psychotherapists to conferences and workshops, included Mary Morgan, and Jill and David E. Scharff.

A link was also made between Australia and China when a group of Australian therapists and analysts presented a paper at the Freud in Asia Conference in 2010, the historic first IPA-sponsored psychoanalytic conference in China (Berg, Jools, & Keogh, 2010). Later, as a psychoanalyst from the Australian Society, Timothy Keogh, was invited to join the IPA working group (now an IPA committee) on couple and family psychoanalysis as its representative for Oceania. This enabled further linkages between China and Australia, especially through the group's China representative, Dr. Lin Tao. It offered formal representation of Australian couple and family psychoanalysis within the IPA, and resulted in Oceania being represented at several significant IPA events, including pre-congress and congress workshops at IPA congresses in Chicago (2010), Prague (2012), Boston (2015), as well as the historic IPA-FEPAL first-ever couple and family psychoanalysis conference held in Buenos Aires in 2015 (Keogh, Vorchheimer, & Gregory-Roberts, 2015).

An emerging theoretical framework

The original theoretical model applied to couple dyads and the family constellations in Australasia was the Kleinian object relations model, with its attendant modes of psychic experience (paranoid-schizoid and depressive) and psychic (especially projective and introjective) mechanisms of unconscious communication. The approach was strongly influenced in Australia by the work of Henry Dicks (in particular as articulated in his classic 1967 text *Marital Tensions*), John Bing-Hall, and later by Sally Box and others who had helped to forge the specialty of couple and family work at the Tavistock Clinic (Enfield, 2015). Charles Enfield (Sydney) and Peter Fullerton (Melbourne) were influenced in their Tavistock Clinic training by Bowlby's notion of "internal working models" and how insecure attachment results in proto-typical defensive reactions in relationships.

Later, as a result of David and Jill Scharff's writings and visits to Australia, the conceptual model was expanded to incorporate Fairbairn's view of object relations theory, and in particular his endopsychic model (Scharff & Scharff, 1991). Recent contemporary British therapists, including Mary Morgan and her elucidation of concepts such as "the couple state of mind" and "projective gridlock" in couples, have been particularly influential (Morgan, 1995; Morgan, 2001). A renewed focus on Bowlby's seminal findings concerning attachment theory and their relevance to couples articulated by Clulow (2001) also encouraged integration into contemporary practice (Byrne, Berg, and Jools, 2007; Keogh, Kourt, Enfield, and Enfield 2007). The work of Ruszczynski and Fisher (1995), especially on the understanding of narcissism in couples, also had a significant impact on couples work in Australia.

Thomas Ogden's ideas also led to a recognition of the importance of primitive mental anxieties associated with early un-integrated states of mind (that is, autistic-contiguous anxieties) and their relevance to couple and family work, allowing understanding of deeper anxieties to be incorporated into conceptual frameworks about couples and families (Berg, Jools, & Keogh, 2010; Berg, 2012; Keogh & Enfield, 2013).

In New Zealand couple and family psychoanalytic psychotherapy was also strongly influenced by the Tavistock object relations approach, including the work of Henry Dicks and Robin Skynner. This framework remains an abiding influence, although in Auckland in recent years there has been a more post-Kleinian influence in contrast to Fairbairn's influence in Australia.

Antipodean couple and family psychoanalysis has continued to flourish with the benefit of global nourishment, home grown inventiveness, and cautious optimism, so that we are now "feet sandaled with dreams treading paths of vision (hopefully) leading to wisdom's sharp peaks" (Aberjhani, 2010, p. 67).

Acknowledgements

Timothy Keogh wishes to gratefully acknowledge the assistance of Charles Enfield, Peter Fullerton, Judi Blumenfeld-Hoadley, and Roslyn Glickfeld for their generous contribution to this chapter. I thank

Elizabeth Orr (psychoanalyst, Melbourne) and my couple and family peer group (Charles Enfield, Cynthia Gregory-Roberts, Sylvia Enfield, and Maria Kourt) for valuable input.

Couple and family psychoanalysis in China and Taiwan

David E. Scharff (Washington, DC, USA)

In China, couple and family psychoanalytic therapy training is at an early stage, only beginning in Beijing in 2010. At first, training was for couple psychoanalysis alone, but subsequently family and child therapy were added. Conducted by faculty of the International Psychotherapy Institute (IPI) of Washington, DC, recently augmented by members of the IPA's committee on family and couple psychoanalysis, it is directed by David E. Scharff and organised by Fang Xin of Peking University's Department of Psychology. Training is offered to therapists with previous individual dynamic psychotherapy training who come from across China and Taiwan. The training is offered to seventy to 100 students in two-year cycles of four five-day institutes, and was initially co-sponsored by Peking University's Department of Psychology and the Beijing Association for Mental Health. It is now independently offered with sponsorship by IPI. The international object relations theoretical orientation includes daily small affective groups for processing the learning, a model IPI uses in the United States (Scharff & Scharff, 2000; 2016, in press for the *International Journal of Psychoanalysis*). To this end, IPI faculty have been training Chinese group leaders in order to grow a Chinese-run programme.

Lin Tao, MD, who undertook IPA analytic training in Beijing as well as psychoanalytic couple psychotherapy training at the Tavistock Centre for Couple Relationships in London, and who is now a member of both the IPA's China Committee and the IPA Committee on Family and Couple Psychoanalysis, now commutes from London to teach regular programmes in his hometown, Jinan City, capital of Shandong Province, on "the emerging analytic mind" and on the Kleinian school. He has not as yet offered specific training in analytic couple therapy in China.

There are also a few senior therapists in Taiwan who have trained in the object relations tradition and who plan to institute training in analytic couple therapy. In support of these efforts, five of David and Jill Scharff's books have been translated into Chinese, including

The Sexual Relationship, Object Relations Couple Therapy and *Object Relations Family Therapy.*

References

Aberjhani. (2010). "Poets of the Angels." In: *In the River of Winged Dreams* (p. 62). Savannah, GA: Black Skylark Publications.

Bagnini, C. (2012). *Keeping Couples in Treatment*. Lanham, MD: Jason Aronson.

Balfour, A. (2016). Transference and enactment in the "Oedipal setting" of couple psychotherapy. In: A. Novakovic (Ed.), *Couple Dynamics: Psychoanalytic Perspectives in Work with the Individual, the Couple, and the Group*. London: Karnac.

Balint, E. (1993). Unconscious communication between husbands and wives. In: S. Ruszczynski (Ed.), *Psychotherapy with Couples* (pp. 30–43). London: Karnac.

Bannister, K., & Pincus, L. (1965). *Shared Phantasy in Marital Problems: Therapy in a Four-person Relationship*. London: Institute of Marital Studies.

Berenstein, I. (2012). *Vínculo* as a relationship between others. *Psychoanalytic Quarterly, 81*: 565–577.

Berg, J. (2012). "A bad moment with the light." No-sex couples: The role of autistic-contiguous anxieties. *Couple and Family Psychoanalysis, 2*: 33–48.

Berg, J., Jools, P., & Keogh, T. (2010). "The family within." A paper presented at the International Psychoanalytical Association's Freud in Asia Conference, Beijing.

Berg, J., Jools, P., & Keogh, T. (2011). Antipodean object relations: The development of object relations couple and family therapy in Sydney, Australia. *Couple and Family Psychoanalysis, 1*: 136–138.

Bleger J. (1967). *Symbiosis and Ambiguity: A Psychoanalytic Study*. Sussex: Routledge.

Blumenfeld-Hoadley, J. (2015). Personal communication.

Boots, J. (2010). What to do with Australia. *Psychoanalysis Down Under, the Online Journal of the Australian Psychoanalytical Society, 10*: January, 2010.

Britton, R. (1998). *Belief and Imagination. Explorations in Psychoanalysis.* London: Routledge.

Britton, R. (2000). On sharing psychic space. *Bulletin of the Society of Psychoanalytic Marital Psychotherapists, 7*: May.

Byrne, N., Berg, J., & Jools, P. (2007). Love in a warm climate: a partnership between object relations theory and attachment theory. In: M. Ludlam & V. Nyberg (Eds.), *Couple Attachments: Theoretical and Clinical Studies* (pp. 105–118). London: Karnac.

Caruso, N. (2005). A troubled marriage in sex therapy. In: J. Scharff & D. Scharff (Eds.), *New Paradigms for Treating Relationships* (pp. 385–396). Lanham, MD: Jason Aronson.

Cleavely, E. (1993). Relationships: interaction, defences, and transformation. In: S. Ruszczynski (Ed.), *Psychotherapy with Couples: Theory and Practice at the Tavistock Institute* (pp. 55–69). London: Karnac.

Clulow, C. (2001). *Adult Attachment and Couple Psychotherapy: The "Secure Base" in Practice and Research.* London: Brunner Routledge.

Colman, W. (1993). Marriage as a psychological container. In: S. Ruszczynski (Ed.), *Psychotherapy with Couples: Theory and Practice at the Tavistock Institute* (pp. 70–96). London: Karnac.

Damousi, J. (2005). *Freud and the Antipodes: A Cultural History of Psychoanalysis in Australia.* UNSW Press: Sydney, Australia.

Dicks, H. V. (1967/1993). *Marital Tensions: Clinical Studies Towards a Psychological Theory of Interaction.* London: Karnac.

Fisher, J. (1999). *The Uninvited Guest: Emerging from Narcissism towards Marriage.* London: Karnac.

Freud, S. (1920). *Beyond the Pleasure Principle. S. E., 18:* 1–64. London: Hogarth.

Joaquin, N. (2004). *Culture and History.* Manila, Philippines: Anvil Publishing.

Kaës, R. (1994). À propos du groupe interne, du groupe, du sujet, du lien et du porte-voix chez Pichon-Rivière. *Revue de Psychothérapie Psychanalytique de Groupe, 23.* Also in: *Psychanalyse et psychologie sociale: Hommage à Enrique Pichon-Rivière* (pp. 181–200). London: Karnac.

Kaës, R. (2007). *Linking, Alliances and Shared Space.* London: The International Psychoanalytic Association.

Kaës, R. (2015). *L'extension de la psychanalyse.* Paris: Dunod.

Keogh, T., & Enfield, S. (2013). From regression to recovery: Tracking developmental anxieties in couple therapy. *Couple and Family Psychoanalysis, 3:* 28–46.

Keogh, T., Kourt, M., Enfield, C., & Enfield, S. (2007). Psychopathology and therapeutic style: Integrating object relations and attachment theory in working with borderline families. In: M. Ludlam & V. Nyberg (Eds.), *Couple Attachments: Theoretical and Clinical Studies* (pp. 239–252). London: Karnac.

Keogh, T., Vorchheimer, M., & Gregory-Roberts, C. (2015). It takes three to tango? International perspectives on couple and family psychoanalysis. First IPA/FEPAL Congress on Couples and Family Psychoanalysis, Buenos Aires, 9–11 April 2015. *Couple and Family Psychoanalysis, 5:* 234–237.

Losso, R. (2000). *Psicoanalisi della famiglia.* Milano: FrancoAngeli.

Meltzer, D. (1978). *The Kleinian Development.* London: Karnac, 1998.

Moguillansky, R. (1999). *Vínculo y relación de objeto*. Buenos Aires: Polemos.

Morgan, M. (1995). The projective gridlock: A form of projective identification in couples relationships. In: S. Ruszczynski & J. Fisher (Eds.), *Intrusiveness and Intimacy in the Couple* (pp. 33–48). London: Karnac.

Morgan, M. (2000). Response to Ron Britton's paper "On sharing psychic space". *Bulletin of the Society of Psychoanalytic Marital Psychotherapists, 7*, May, 2000.

Morgan, M. (2001). First contacts: The therapist's "couple state of mind" as factor in the containment of couples seen for consultations. In: F. Grier (Ed.), *Brief Encounters with Couples: Some Analytical Perspectives* (pp. 17–32). London: Karnac.

Morgan, M. (2005). On being able to be a couple: the importance of a "creative couple" in psychic life. In: F. Grier (Ed.), *Oedipus and the Couple*. London: Karnac.

Morgan, M. (2010). Unconscious beliefs about being a couple. *Fort Da, XV1*, No 1.

Nicolò, A. M. (1993). Il transgenerazionale tra mito e segreto. *Interazioni, 1*, 1996: 138–152.

Nicolò, A. M. (1997). L'importanza diagnostica delle interazioni nella valutazione della famiglia e delle sue difese transpersonali. *Interazioni, 10*: 53–66.

Nicolò, A. M. (2000a). Il sogno nella psicoanalisi con la coppia e la famiglia. In: A. M. Nicolò & G. Trapanese (Eds.), *Quale psicoanalisi per la coppia?* Milano: FrancoAngeli, 2005.

Nicolò, A. M. (2000b). La memoria nella trasmissione generazionale della famiglia. *Psiche, 2*: 111–122.

Nicolò, A. M. (2005). La folie à deux: hypothèse dans la pathologie trans-personnelle. *Le divan familial, 15*: 13–29.

Nicolò, A. M., & Trapanese, G. (2005). *Quale psicoanalisi per la coppia?* Milano: FrancoAngeli.

Nicolò, A. M., Benghozi, P., & Lucarelli, D. (2014). *Families in Transformation*. London: Karnac.

Nicolò, A. M., Norsa, D., & Carratelli, T. J. (2003). Playing with dreams: The introduction of a third party into the transference dynamic of the couple. *Journal of Applied Psychoanalytic Studies, 5*: 283–296.

Norsa, D. (1993). Modelli di Identificazione Genitoriale. *Interazioni, 1*: 9–29.

Norsa, D., & Zavattini, G. C. (1997). *Intimità e collusione*. Milano: Raffaello Cortina.

Pichon Rivière, E. (1971). *Del Psicoanálisis a la Psicología Social* (2 vols.) Buenos Aires: Galerna.

Pincus, L. (1960). Relationships and the growth of personality. In: *Marriage: Studies in Emotional Conflict and Growth* (Part I) (pp. 11–34). London: Tavistock Institute of Marital Studies.

Pincus, L. (1962). The nature of marital interaction. In: *The Marital Relationship as a Focus for Casework*. Institute of Marital Studies.

Poulton, J. (2013). *Object Relations and Relationality in Couple Therapy*. Lanham, MD: Jason Aronson.

Puget, J., & Berenstein, I. (1989). *Psycoanalisis de la pareja matrimonial*. Buenos Aires: Paidós.

Reiss, D. (1989). La famiglia rappresentata e la famiglia reale, concezioni contrastanti della continuità familiare. In: A. J. Sameroff & R. N. Emde (Eds.), *I disturbi delle relazioni nella prima infanzia* (Relationship Disturbances in Early Childhood: A Developmental Approach). Torino: Bollati Boringhieri, 1991.

Ruszczynski, S. (1998). The "marital triangle": Towards "triangular space" in the intimate couple relationship. *Journal of the British Association of Psychotherapists, 34*: 33–47.

Ruszczynski, S. (Ed.) (1993). *Psychotherapy with Couples*. London: Karnac.

Ruszczynski, S., & Fisher, J. (Eds.) (1995). *Intrusiveness and Intimacy in the Couple*. London: Karnac.

Sapisochin, G. (2013). Second thoughts on Agieren: Listening to the enacted. *International Journal of Psychoanalysis, 94*: 967–991.

Scharff, D. E. (1982). *The Sexual Relationship*. London: Routledge & Kegan Paul.

Scharff, D. E., & Scharff, J. S. (1987). *Object Relations Family Therapy*. Northvale, NJ: Jason Aronson.

Scharff, D. E., & Scharff, J. S. (1991). *Object Relations Couple Therapy*. Northvale, NJ: Jason Aronson.

Scharff, D. E., & Scharff, J. S. (1998). *Object Relations Individual Therapy*. Northvale, NJ: Jason Aronson.

Scharff, D. E., & Scharff, J. S. (2011). *The Interpersonal Unconscious*. Lanham, MD: Jason Aronson.

Scharff, J. S. (Ed.) (1989). *Foundations of Object Relations Family Therapy*. Northvale, NJ: Jason Aronson.

Scharff, J. S., & Scharff, D. E. (1994). *Object Relations Therapy of Physical and Sexual Trauma*. Northvale, NJ: Jason Aronson.

Thomson-Salo, F. (2011). The Australian Psychoanalytical Society: the evolving relationship with the IPA. In: P. Loewenberg & N. Thompson (Eds.), *100 Years of the IPA: The Centenary History of the International Psychoanalytical Association 1910–2010: Evolution and Change* (pp. 345–355). London: The International Psychoanalytical Association.

Winnicott, D. W. (1956). *Through Paediatrics to Psychoanalysis*. London: Hogarth.

CHAPTER THREE

Pichon Rivière and the theory of the link

Roberto Losso (Buenos Aires, Argentina)

From Freud's epistemological jump in his *Group Psychology and the Analysis of the Ego*, where he affirms: "In the individual's mental life someone else is invariably involved as a model, as an object, as a helper, as an opponent; and so from the very first individual psychology (…) is at the same time social psychology as well", Pichon Rivière developed this line of thought in the 1950s introducing the concept of the link (*vínculo*) in psychoanalysis. He repeated in his teaching that "psychic life does not exist outside the link with the others". He also highlighted the importance of interviewing patients inside their own environment, their family, and social contexts. He moved forward trends that have centred on intersubjectivity recently. Taking into account that Bion also stated that individual analysis is in fact the analysis of a couple (patient-analyst), both American and European authors have emphasised the importance of intersubjectivity in the frame of the analytic session for the last twenty years.

Pichon Rivière defined a link as "a complex structure which includes the subject, the object and their mutual interaction through communication and learning processes", where the third (or thirds) function as the "noise" of the communication theory. For Pichon, the individual is built inside a triadic link structure, which he defined as bicorporal and tri-personal. He considered that although the relationship between mother and baby could seem dyadic at the beginning, the third element functioned from the very beginning through its place in the mother's or the caretaker's mind. In this sense, the situation is triangular from scratch.

For Pichon, the motivational fundamentals of the link are the psychobiological needs for love, contact, protection, heat, nutrition, and so on, all related to the initial helplessness of human beings who are not viable outside of their links with others. The individual is born with these needs, which pave the way for experience from the start that will be both frustrating and gratifying. In this way, all subjects are born from links and live in links throughout their lives. All of us are "chained" to links (In a parallel and contemporary development in London, S. H. Foulkes described the weave of human links as a net or *plexus*, whose knots represent the subjects. Therefore, if the net is undone, the knots—in other words the subjects—disappear as well).

Pichon Rivière also considered transgenerational links. The subject is tied to a double chain: that of the generations and that of the contemporaries. He expressed this idea through his metaphor of the cross. The individual lives at the intersection of a cross: the vertical axis corresponds to links with previous generations (the transgenerational chain) and the horizontal axis corresponds to the links with his contemporaries, firstly with its family group, but ultimately to current culture and society (the social chain).

Link and internal group

In every link structure, subject and object interact in a dialectic relationship. Along this interaction, the link structure is internalised, thereby acquiring an intrasubjective dimension through which what was interpsychic becomes intrapsychic. Intrasubjective relations, or internalised link structures, articulated in an internal world are to integrate what Pichon Rivière has called the "internal group" (as a modification of the Kleinian concept of internal world), which represents the inside "stage" where a reconstruction of the external reality is staged and then modified by the individual's needs in a process that goes from intrasubjectivity to intersubjectivity and back again to intrasubjectivity. In this process, links of intersubjectivity turn into unconscious intrasubjective links, transforming from sociodynamics to psychosocial. The internal group is constituted from the internalisation of the external links (at the beginning, basically the family links), which are however constantly distorted by the individual's needs. The life of all subjects takes place in this continuous dialectic between external and internal links. Pichon makes use of the metaphor of the internal field to refer to his idea of the internal group as something dynamic. The continuous interaction and movement inside this "internal field" is always in tension with the interactions with the "external field". He also developed the concept of ecologic internalization together with the notion of the hometown you belong to (*querencia* or *pago*), as the internalisation of the environment in which the life of the subject takes place, highlighting the importance of the social environment in the constitution and support of individual identity. Intrasubjective relations or internalised link structures articulated in the internal group will influence the learning of reality, and will be facilitated or hindered depending on the degree to which confrontation between the intersubjective and the intrasubjective is a dialectic or a dilemma.

Instinct (or drive) theory

Pichon worked during the peak of Kleinian influence in Argentina. He valued not only Klein's work, but also Fairbairn's pioneering ideas. In this way, he started from instinct theory in the Kleinian sense of life and death instincts, but gave his ideas an intersubjective dimension. Modifying Fairbairn's ideas of "good and bad objects", he proposed not to speak about instincts alone, but about two models of links: a good link, coming from gratifying experiences, and a bad link, coming from frustrating experiences. Gratifying experiences are the ones that give the subject the life sense. We cannot help evoking certain of Winnicott's ideas here, like the idea that the mother must seduce her child into life. Therefore, when Pichon defined life instinct as a gratifying link and death instinct as a frustrating link, he gives drive theory an intersubjective sense in which drives originate in intersubjectivity.

Pichon then proposed a psychiatry of the links, where the pathology did not have to be studied as pathology of isolated individuals but as that of the links. In this line of thought, the spokesperson is the one considered "ill", but who is in fact the one who is strong enough in some ways to express suffering and group insecurity. Thus, family group psychotherapy is an indispensable tool for our work.

From Fairbairn's ideas, Pichon Rivière came to understand pathological patterns as the result of a certain distribution of links in three interrelated phenomenological areas of expression of behaviour that he took from Lagache: the mind, the body, and the external world. The individual can express himself/herself in these areas, either through psychological illness, body symptoms, or ways of behaving in society. These three areas coexist, co-operate, and interact. There is always a surface predominance of one of them, but the other two are always expressed as well.

Since subjects are first and foremost subjects of necessity, they are always subjects of desire. Pichon does not separate the individual from social life because he is born in a certain environment and society, and at the same time with his body's demands. In this way, Pichon restates the importance and complexity of the mixture of the demands of necessity and reality in the development of social relations. I finish by quoting one of Pichon's phrases: "The human individual is a being of necessities which are only socially satisfied in relations which determine his or her identity. The subject is not only a related subject, but also a produced subject. Everything is the result of the interaction between individuals, groups and classes."

CHAPTER FOUR

The link and its interferences

*Isidoro Berenstein**

Presentation of interferences

The use of new terms is not only an academic or technical problem. It derives from and has clinical implications. Like legal categories such as robbery and larceny, it has to do with the theft of a belonging or a value, the first one accompanied of violence and the second without it. The sentence is different. Between homicide and aggravated homicide, there is premeditation. In this same way it is of most importance to differentiate words that define different psychoanalytical concepts. This will be so with *interference* and *transference* or with *presence* and *presentation* in relationship to *absence* or to *representation*. The relationship between the therapist or the psychoanalyst and the patient implies a level of complexity due to the non-uniqueness of each of them. The patient offers herself to talk about herself (whether aware of it or not) and at the same time she is a listener to her own affairs: ideas, fantasies, events, experiences, dreams. The analyst offers a way of listening

---

*Edited by David E. Scharff from an interview with Carlos Slepoy. *Página/12* (newspaper), Sunday, 21 March 2010. By permission.

and poses a specific way of talking that defines him as a speaker who maintains that position and, at the same time, the patient interacts with the analyst holding the session and from which he gives response to his comments, interventions, interpretations or constructions. We should not talk about "the analyst and his patient" because that shows a state of personal belonging that excludes the analyst from the couple or group that defines them both.

The classical concept of transference serves as a back-drop to new ideas on interference. This is based on several ideas, beginning with subjectivity and the relationship between subjects based not only in what is similar and different but in what is alien or foreign. What is different should be seen as radically different. Two related subjects show ways of being, feeling, and thinking that disturb and unsettle the other. This stems from alterity (otherness) and alteration. It is not possible to foretell what comes from the other person. Surprise has to do with alteration. This constitutes an obstacle that transference tries to side-step in order to avoid unsettling what the relationship with the other should be, and this is what is conveyed by analytical work. The concept of interference facilitates working with the obstacle, its acceptance, its non-expulsion, and its possible change in joint work. This means that both participants will be modified.

Before transforming it into a technical tool, interference was used to include obstacles that came from the external world, to render them at the service of patients' resistance, to rationalise their difficulties in free association or letting unconscious productions emerge, showing a way of access to internal conflicts, presented through lateness, absence, or other outside obstacles that prevented the patient from behaving consciously appropriately. Since the analyst is "always" supposed to be in the session, his presence opens the possibility of infantile unconscious or projective meanings of his own world of inner objects. The criteria for the analyst's "stability" in the psychoanalytical setting comes from the modern conception of "stability" present in early links and its organisational value in the infantile mind. It also comes from links with other people as well as things such as work relationships. Unexpected changes produce great anxiety, but since they cannot be foreseen, they compel us to include novelty, since stability includes various forms of repetition.

Resistance can be formulated as if something or someone is not allowed to reach a place, fulfilling his unconscious desire to frustrate or deprive whoever is represented by the analyst. It is equivalent to "I am not allowed to get there". Step by step we are able to find out that the "obstacles" that appear in every session have to be taken into account not only as an attack on the stability of the link due to the emotions of envy, jealousy, or rivalry derived from infantile experiences, but also because they cause anxiety because unexpected. Both analysts with patients and patients with analysts in their dimension of alterity (otherness) need to give space to explore similarities and differences.

Confronting the other

Interference takes place when two (or more) presences confront each other, recalling previous moments, and other, internal places. This "face" is present from the first moment of confrontation with the other. Two situations occur, difficult because of their simultaneous or consecutive existence: the projection of unconscious representations conveying previous fantasies that put transference to work. In that moment of newness, an emptiness is quickly but unsuccessfully occupied by various identification mechanisms through projection. These identifications attempt to match previous internal aspects of the subject present right now and here. Second, the newness and uncertainty of this stranger is a feature of how we regard the other. New emotions are superimposed, some conveyed by transference, such as love and hostility. Others are conveyed by interference and range from surprise to denial of novelty, either allowing its existence or evacuating it completely.

In the first case falling in love is a possibility; in the second, knowledge. A good question is: how can novelty or uncertainty have space in a relationship that takes place several days a week for many years? We could say that transference is appropriate to links, while interference is something external that has to be suppressed to allow the transference to evolve. That would be equivalent to saying that the ideal relationship should evolve without interference. But interference is the defining characteristic of every link between two subjects, appearing to be external to the degree that the link appears external. Since interference is inevitable, we can ask the consequences of thinking of it as inherent to the analytical relationship, so that we can work with it wherever it appears.

The emergence of the unpredictable

A patient comes regularly to sessions. Absences are unusual, planned for, and replaced during the same week. Unexpectedly, his wife contracts a chronic, debilitating disease. Medical consultations, tests, and lab exams occupy an important part of their lives. After a while his children tell him that he looks weakened. I see this too. He has lost several kilos, his skin is pale and yellow. He cannot move from his wife's side. He feels like "moving away" from any moment having to do with the couple or family life unrelated to his wife's illness. He starts missing sessions without notice or asks to reschedule late in order to be with his wife in a specialist's office. The session and the therapeutic link now seem to interfere in the relationship with his wife.

After penetrating his wife's body in order to control it and transform it into a link with a helpless, dependent object, we see that his own weight loss and pallor occur in identification with her. My interpretations interfere with his identification. As two subjects, we try to process our projective distance and our differentiated closeness, interfering in the transformation of myself as analyst into becoming helpless too. The patient has incorporated the suffering object and placed the analyst in the omnipotent position of modifying the hours and the actions—or of failing too. This interferes with the continuity of the analytic link that will require modification and confrontation of loss of the previous relationship. This interference in the session has to be put into words, since it hinders both his mission to save his wife and the analyst's mission to "save" the patient. In every link between subjects, what is foreign impedes the accomplishment of the desires of one subject, be it the patient or the analyst. The action of interfering belongs to the structure of the link. Belonging to a link means facing the other, confronting with, dealing with the other. Interference is consonant with the notion of misunderstanding between two subjects, with disagreement in the presence of the agreement, with the sense of being out of place that is present when one person tries to understand another. It is the opposite of empathy.

When we look for the causes of interference, we see two subjects who, besides their similarities and their differences, have to deal with their foreign aspects. Their inherent differences cannot be taken as a similarity. Nevertheless, others are compelled by the link they set up, be it marital, social, or analytical. They have to find a way to do something different with it. Analytical work gives a chance for analysing its impossibility. Once part of the link, you are able to confirm that the other cannot be erased according to your desires. Both subjects of speech are able to speak of the differences in their relationship, even while subjects of identity and searching for similarities. Power relationships take place in which each subject tries to impose his way of understanding. Interference means that work between subjects needs to occur, work that people try hard to avoid by finding spurious coincidences. For example: when I go back home I notify my wife that I am arriving; I want my desires to be accommodated, for example, to have my meal ready. That morning I left a sticker on the fridge notifying my "other" where I would be or where I could be found. This has to do with social insecurity. The security of coincidences suppresses the insecurity of not meeting the other. The sophistication of contemporary technological life has created lots of tools that intensify our reliance on coincidence. Still, we have an illusion of autonomy from the other who participates in the link.

The concept of countertransference, developed only much later than transference, implies a splitting of the analyst. Part of himself reacts and responds in an equivalent way to the patient and another part is out of the transference although within the session, in order to interpret the relationship between the patient and himself.

I suggest that it is not a question of finding a term to denote one of the subjects in the analytic situation, the analyst, but to give a name to refer to a fact in the relationship that does not take into account the specifics of identity that is desired by everyone. This has to do with the presence of the analyst and the patient, it indicates a difference of their internal objects established in absence and permanently, with each trying to make them present in the other, that is to say, with the purpose of cancelling the other's presence. This disturbs, it is a nuisance, it obstructs identification by imposing and interfering in their sense of identity. It opposes the desire of something else different to the presence of the other. Desire cannot desire the alien status of the other, it can only try to find possible identification, something that cannot be achieved but that gives hope that it can be accomplished by means of displacement into another person's qualities to represent subject's own identity.

As I said, interference differs from transference because it has to do with what is happening here and now. It is also necessary to differentiate it from the unfolding result of a displacement that took place in the present but whose meaning is present somewhere else. For instance, in the case of the "Rat Man", Freud tries to "force" free associations for good technical reasons when the patient is obstructed by ideas of the torture by rats in the story his colleague told. Freud tries to make his patient enter the mandate of free association, while the patient is trying not to do what his therapist is asking him to do. To call him, in that moment of confusion, "my captain", is part of the transference situation, of seeing him acting like the captain. The effort to resolve this obstacle between them is to take on an interference that cannot be suppressed but has to be treated. However, there is no need for this to happen since what Freud is trying to do is to conceptualise the transference rather than to conceptualise the interference.

Duplicity in the analytical relationship

Given the number of persons present in sessions (two in the individual session or three in the couple session or more in a family session), there is more than one record even in each person: the past in the present, that which is infantile in the present, the misunderstanding due to displacement from the inner world or the link to the relationship with the analyst that lets him understand what is "really" going on, being "really" the place where the effects are produced that are surplus to the session but take place during it.

However, the session, because of its special features, generates transference phenomena: the current situation in the actual moment which produces by its very presence differences between what is presented. It disturbs because it is unexpected, because it is not included and because it is contrary to identity. The scene of the origin coincides with the scene where it is taking place, because it comes from it. Therapeutic procedure points out the difficulty in processing the difference but not in finding coincidences. It is really difficult to "make a place to the other" and to "otherness".

For example, a family was dealing with the mother's irritation towards the daughter's demands, unable to distinguish the requests as if all requests were only one and the same one. They had eaten spaghetti with butter and cheese, but her daughter requested cream as she always did. They did not have cream at home and since it was already late there was no possibility of buying it. The daughter threw a fit and hit the plate with the cutlery and the mother raged at her. The daughter's irritation had the aim of making the mother feel irritated as well. In the paroxysm of the fight, the mother told her to leave the table and return when she calmed down. There is no space for the complaint, there is no possibility for showing what is lacking and there should not be any complaint about that. While the father tries to tell the mother that she should not have got irritated, she answers that he was not there at that moment and the couple argue. Should there be a space for the couple's argument? To give it a space means to open it up clearly, but this is not the only possibility since the rest of the members of the family group are there, not only in order to listen to what is going on. Decisions cannot be taken in solitude. All these actions are addressed to all those who are there in the session—those who are listening form the context for what is being said. It is not the same scenario or dispute for the one they had at home. The eldest brother and the father attend the session making no comments, as observers of this scene that is full of fury and of offers of advice to the mother. The eldest brother comments on what happened the previous day when he was with his friends at home. It was past midnight and he was listening to music and the youngest sister came up to them to ask them if she could play with them. The eldest brother said no. The youngest sister went back to her bedroom but after a while she came back to stay in the kitchen, where she could observe, although she was not participating. The brother says that this did not bother him because he did not see her, although he could have, but he did not send her away. As a foreigner she had a place in the periphery of the brother's play, accepted by him in that place. In this session, space is given to heterogeneity, to enter a complaint about what is lacking today. There is a possibility that as an analyst I am "not providing" and what is interfering is taken as a part of the transference, unifying it without giving a space to otherness, about the differences from one to the other.

The linking of interferences

The "lack of cream" is a fault the daughter attributes to the mother, which the mother does not accept. This interferes in the link between them and that interference is presented in the presence of those "thirds" that are there in person, not because they are there to testify the truth of what is being said, but because they give consistency to what interferes. Through speech, interference is produced: Does it come from another place? Is it a product of transference? I thought that it was not. It was produced there in the session, and it had to be solved there without any need of admitting that one of them is right or of splitting responsibility. A new space has to be built that considers everyone who speaks in the session. This means that they each have to detach from what is factually being said. "What is lacking" is not only the effect of a transference repetition. It is something that occurs in the session, due to a dissatisfaction of something that should be there and is not taking place there: an idea suitable for this situation and something that could produce it. "The cream", that thing that seems to have been lacking through maternal omission, and that fills the mother with guilt, covers up "an excess", a mother who cannot give space to another mother and another daughter, held by a father who thinks that his daughter's demands are permanently inappropriate, or that "she does it on purpose to show difficulties". In this way, he also occupies an "out of space" position. Each of them can question themselves about what space they should occupy. The mother may feel irritated as a consequence of not being able to understand what the daughter wants from her. The daughter may bring up: "What does my mother want from me when she wants me to eat the spaghetti without cream?" The father may ask himself what he should do, as there is a request for help to which no name has been given. The analyst could also consider this possibility: "What cream is needed here that is missing, and what am I supposed to make so that there is some?" If I ask this question, I would be achieving my place. It is not a transference place. Instead, it concerns an obstacle in our road. A solution is needed in order to keep on the trip, but most probably the road that is necessary to sustain the trip will be a new, unexpected one. What interferes is what impedes them from showing a desired functioning that is not possible, probably due to the presence of the analyst as a "presence". He is not only someone who makes interpretations but someone that establishes himself as a presence in the session.

Another patient comes in a state of "continuity", to tell us what he was thinking when something interposed itself into his preformed associative series. Again, it is interference that deprives him of the sense of continuity to his identity.

A family came to session, but before coming in they were surprised by an unexpected dispute that happened in the entrance to the session. They made it present as "dog shit" that their son stepped on just before coming into the analyst's house. Their first movement was to "clean" what was brought from "the outside" and interfered. A way of doing so was to interpret it. Here again, it is not what it is, but what it represents. Nevertheless, the bad smell still exists, an incident of no apparent significance, but if it stains the carpet it is a present that needs to be "cleaned" in order to gain access to its meaning. Will the analyst be unperturbed, not minding if the carpet is stained and a bad smell is present in the session? First of all there is a practical issue and after that there is interpretation of a meaning. These are two different moments that demonstrate that the analyst is a double person.

Interference provides witness that you are not on your own, and that you are not indivisible but are divided: transference and countertransference. There is no absolute knowledge: knowledge has to be built. It is not only an experience to be re-elaborated but through encountering the obstacle that every one of us turns out to be for the other, and which has to be passed through.

Perplexity as a basis for interference

If transference is linked to love (and hatred), interference is linked to perplexity.

How can it possibly be that the other has a word that does not correspond to the supposed correspondence of the loving word or to discordance in a relationship of hatred? If you have a word that is another type of word, what about identity? What about continuity? Nowadays we face situations in which perplexity is constantly on the scene. When the other is registered as excessive, he is transformed in an absence, a non-existent. He is declared missing, but the non-existent comes back as a threat. The idea of a wall, extended back in time like the Berlin wall or the wall that separates Israelis and Palestinians, the Mexicans trying to enter the United States illegally, also comes to constitute a "no word", a no "other", a no one with whom to talk, a no one with whom to deal. If the other does not talk then I don't have words either and my word is not a word. This severs "intersubjectivity".

Perplexity is a kind of oddness, of astonishment in the presence of what is supposed not to be produced or happen. It can have a paranoid drift but it is an attempt to recreate that there is an only way to see things, an only way of thinking, my way or that of the community to which I belong.

A patient gets to his session ten minutes late. He lies down on the couch and announces that he had several dreams. He only remembers one in which a patient of his from a prepayment company comes to see him. He told his wife and remembered that he does not want to assist any more patients from the prepayment company. I notice that he makes a passageway from the dream, from inside the dream to a scene presumably real and outside the session. He starts a track that I register as going away from the space that in the session is called "dream", where a character that did not want to assist or pay attention is present. The wife is introduced as a third character, a present-absent.

I tell him that he does not want to assist that patient and that this could be his own self asking and not receiving attention. The patient was making his way and my intervention brings in an obstacle and puts him at a crossroads. He stays in silence for a while. He then answers that yesterday a patient came to see him after nearly ten years and that he belonged to a prepayment company, he only came a few times. He was a psychotic. The patient said, "I did not like him. I told him I could see him after the holidays and he said no, that he wanted to be attended now."

It is convenient to differentiate two actions that look as if they are one: the transference action, that allows the displacement of an unconscious knowledge that is not tolerated by him to take place and therefore appears in a character as the representation of a dream, of a previous time that takes us back to an infantile situation of non-acceptance of the father. The other action interferes with his keeping at a distance in the session. I step in and tell him that it is preferable not to go through there. Is this transference or is it an action that is usually used and given a name, such as interference? What is its effect? To make present what I call "to be alien", or, in a bit different sense, "the third person".

In what looks like a transference field, there is an intersection of two paths: one has to do with the dream, the other with a description told as though real, not belonging to the dream and therefore less unconscious and more personal, nearer to common daily meaning. The patient is one person. The other person, represented by the analyst, opposes or tries to oppose, interferes with the direction the patient intends, and proposes another direction, saying "Let us take a look at the character in the dream and how he expresses himself when talking about what is going on within himself (the dream) and between us. Do I want to assist him? Or I don't want to assist him? Do I think he is psychotic? Do

I obstruct him?" The analyst that is supposed to interpret is opposing. This deviation interferes with the patient's intent, and imposes a new direction within the session and in the analysis.

Uniqueness or multiplicity

These categories give us an idea of the relationship that exists between transference and interference. We can characterise the first one as two people who talk about one, the patient. His unconscious is represented in his words and in those the analyst states things, accounting for the words of the patient as he restates the patient's words. There are two ways of thinking about the link between two persons. In the first, the relationship is thought of as originating in one of them and the second person reverberates with the identity of the first. In the second, and usually in the life of couples, one person tells the other that he is only answering the other, being unconscious of his own involvement and how the link introduces something new between them. Interference accounts for the multiplicity that is put into play in the link and in the session. It may seem that they are not the same and they are not, nevertheless the power (much has been said about the excess of power of the analyst), and the possibility of establishment of power relationships is something that both can exert. Hobbes has written that the weakest man has enough strength to kill the strongest man through secret machinations of confederation with others. Thus a patient may not associate, he may induce an interpretative line in accordance with his defences, he may be silent, or he may produce dreams that only serve to please the analyst.

The analyst can take the patient through a sector related to his theory, he can try to demonstrate the patient's defences and confront him with his conflict. It is difficult not to evoke Copernicus's theory that the sun, not the earth, was the centre of the universe. The change of celestial bodies did not modify by itself the criteria of centrality. Changing who is in the centre does not mean that centrality will give up its uniqueness. To explain the circular movements of different celestial bodies, Copernicus had to turn to the criteria of eccentricity or of epicycles, adventitious hypothesis that would enable him to solve the unsolved problem. With Kepler's First Law, and the substitution of an eclipse for a circle, thus allowing more than one focus of centrality, he questioned the idea of a single centre. Kepler had to give up the idea of the circle and all that was in it—the idea of the perfection of the world. He then admitted that the orbit might not be circular and perfect. Galileo (1564–1641), living in that period, had to renounce his fundamental observations of the universe when he was seventy years old, giving us an idea of just how powerful the interferences are between scientific ideas and religious and political forces.

To summarise

From a descriptive point of view, the presence of the two members of a couple that want to be together, and a third one that does not allow it—a child, a lover, a parent—the activity of any of them can be registered as interference, a hiatus in that space between two that are altered by something or someone unwelcome. The model of the Oedipus complex brings in the subject of a link of two with an intrusive third, a place that can be occupied by any of these characters. In the transference, a relationship of two, the patient and the analyst, the emergence of something coming from outside the session such as the patient coming late, forgetting the hour, an obstacle on the road—all these bring in the idea of interference. In such examples, the ideal situation is to take all those "thirds" back to their external place, away from the couple, to exclude the external reality so that it will not distress the transference relationship. Seen from the point of view of the subject, the unexpected and unwelcome third one introduces itself between the two of the couple. From the point of view of the link, interference inserts itself into the space between the members of any couple.

PART II

CASE EXAMPLES AND DISCUSSION

Contributions to the link perspective in interventions with families: theoretical and technical aspects, and clinical application

Elizabeth Palacios (Zaragoza, Spain) and Alicia Monserrat (Madrid, Spain)

A brief introduction

Working with families creates opportunities for thinking theoretically about how to address this type of group in clinical treatment. It also enables us to formulate hypotheses about how such a group works, psychoanalytically speaking, and how psychic change can take place. Nowadays, we know from within contemporary family and couple psychoanalysis that there are multiple ways of thinking and many theoretical concepts that need to be thoroughly understood, in order to build a more substantial methodological and theoretical corpus of knowledge and practice. We seek in this article to convey to colleagues the changes that we have perceived in link theory concerning contemporary family structure. We hope this exposition may help us to figure out a series of issues concerning changes that have occurred in family structure and, in particular, how this has affected links between family group members.

The concept of "links" offers a closer view of many of the phenomena we want to approach. Psychic life is a by-product of the way we link with each other in primary bonds. Link structures can be considered as having their origins within the organisation of a group, a dynamic that can be thought of as a "drama". Meeting the differences present in others is intrinsic to being a member of a group. The space for encounters and non-encounters, and of subjects having to make links in order to be able to work together, is a privileged setting in which to witness the changes that we have been able to perceive in clinical situations in contemporary families. It is also a special place in which we can facilitate processes of transformation that will help a family group confront new problems.

Many authors dealing with pathology often pay attention to links that they consider have become rigid. We prefer to use the concept of the "stereotype" as a defensive structure that hardens family links, and produces various stages of morbidity within family dynamics and symptoms that appear as emergent forms of the suffering in family groups that we meet in our consulting room.

Psychoanalytic theoretical models that aim to explain our links with others

We have been collaborating in a working group of family and couple psychoanalysis within The International Psychoanalytical Association (IPA) for several years. There we see that within psychoanalysis nowadays there are two principal models for understanding our relationships with others:

1. A group of analysts using the notion of British object relations, inspired by Klein, Rosenfeld, and contemporary Kleinian authors, holds a particular view of how unconscious selection of partners is made, as expressed in the work of Dicks (1967), Morgan (2005), Pincus and Dare (1978), and Ruszczynski (1993).
2. Another group, based in South America, uses new applications of the notion of "the link" in clinical work and technique (see for instance Bauleo, 1970a, 1970b; Berenstein, 2001a, 2001b, 2004, 2007; Pichon Rivière, 1985; and Puget & Berenstein, 1997).

The notion of "object relation" appears in Freud's papers on identification, with its first reference in his metapsychological work *Mourning and Melancholia* (Freud, 1917e). It is next referred to by Abraham (1924) and finally acquires its actual conceptualisation in Klein's work. The existence of an internal object implies the internalisation of experience with external objects in a personal way. From the Kleinian point of view, all psychic activity follows an unconscious phantasy, and experience takes the form of this object relationship. The unconscious phantasy establishes a logical structure that organises and codifies experience. The code followed within the internal world goes from a paranoid-schizoid to a depressive position. Conflicts can help us understand the status of this internal object and its tendencies to integrate or disintegrate. This internal object is the foundation of psychic reality. Interpretations of the external world will always come from this internal source, and the type of relationship that the ego will have with external objects depends on this.

From this point of view, the sense of life comes from this inner world. Each subject lives inside different characters in an internal family, and interprets outer world experiences in the light of internal object relations. Objects can be considered independent, and felt to have their own existence as part of an external world, after the depressive position has been achieved. However, they are then at risk of being lost or damaged. This theory of object relations is open to question, since it may be considered to be solipsistically focused on the ego's relationship with internal objects. External objects are conjectural. How a person deals with her anxieties determines how she is perceived as an autonomous person with needs to be known and to be taken care of.

The notion of a link or bond becomes significant when we need to understand how another mind plays a role in the development of a new mind. Winnicott's (1965, 1986) and Bion's (1962, 1967) theories attempt to address this. Bion describes the presence of the mind of an other as necessary in order to receive and metabolise an infant's emotions, so that they can be turned into psychic material that can help the new mind to think and dream. Bion describes a series of links—love, hate, and knowledge—that reveal the emotional quality of bonds and the reciprocal way in which objects nurture or destroy one another.

The idea that certain types of interactions can cause discreet mental illnesses such as schizophrenia is no longer tenable. It goes back to the 1960s, and was coined by practitioners such as Fromm-Reichman (1952) and Bateson (Bateson, Jackson, Haley, & Weakland, 1956), who were especially dedicated to work with very ill psychotic patients. Later, others studied the suffering everyone must undergo through shared links. "Suffering in the link" is a concept that tries to describe the psychic pain, distress, or affliction that results from being part of shared links in couples or families. Many authors, from both within and outside of psychoanalysis, have tried to investigate and explain how an individual person is shaped by the group to which he belongs (Pichon Rivière, 1985; Puget & Berenstein, 1997; Berenstein, 2001a, 2001b, 2004, 2007). Initially, they used this as an axis for their thinking about the notion of the third and thirdness, types of transference, and ideas derived from Lévi-Strauss's conceptualisations of links and laws of exchange as expounded in *The Elementary Structures of Kinship* (1969) and *Structural Anthropology* (1963).

Several authors (Berenstein, 2007; Kaës, 1987, 2007) have pointed out that we should not forget that subjects live in several worlds: an inner world with its representations; an intersubjective world in which the ego participates with others in intimate relationship experiencing emotions; and a third trans-subjective or socio-cultural world of belonging that determines our social identifications.

Many analysts nowadays try to understand what is happening in relationships with others from the perspective of the link. This runs counter to the idea of an inner world in which the ego with its object representations pays little attention to the presence of others, as though they were incidental, are seen only through the screen of our minds, and are confused at different levels with our inner world. If we consider the intersubjective world, as seen through the lens of the link, the presence of the "other" is inevitable and determines how the ego constitutes itself and obtains its shape as a subject. The other will not be denied. The other is a foreigner and in this sense cannot be incorporated into the ego. At the same time, the other contributes to the make-up of the ego. As a subject, we need to do something with the other's presence. The other behaves as an object of imposition. It should also be said that this is a totally different mechanism from that of projection and introjection, and that, in this way, the concept of the link is in contrast with, and complementary to, that of these central ideas of object relations theory.

The trans-subjective world of the link bears on our psychoanalytic work in ways that should not be underestimated. From this perspective, we can say that the subject has no permanent state. Subjects change according to age, and subjectivity evolves continuously with age. The changes that social realities impose on a person affect his subjectivity. Therefore, psychoanalytic treatment needs to make space for the other, the foreigner. With regard to identity, we are what we are able to do with others. Subjectivity is what is derived from our dealings with others.

Object relations emanate from what has taken place in another time and are brought to life in therapeutic sessions. The absence that they express makes its presence known through repetition compulsion. Some analysts think that their interpretations can convey a version of what has taken place in a session. Others believe that their interpretation communicates a new meaning that is embodied in the interpretation, something that is created between patient and analyst.

We are all inhabited by both object relations and by links with others. The analyst represents an internal object, and she also exerts the effect of a new presence, one who produces a difference. If there is any possibility of a new experience, it will be an outcome of the relationship between patient and analyst.

We have frequently considered family links as being determined by the individual destinies of each member of a family, as for example pathological mourning following the death of a father. Taking a new perspective, however, this group of links does not depend solely on individual destinies. Transference has an impact on the actual situation; the effect of its presence causes "interference".

The scenario of the clinical observation

In the following presentation of a clinical case we aim to assess whether an "alliance link" in the couple has been achieved, whether a psychic space for the children is possible, and, as a consequence, whether there will be a new possibility for them to acquire subjectivity.

Sequence of a family session

When working with family groups we generally see whether there is tendency for the internal group "to overpower" the external group, to paralyse it and prevent the necessary impetus for the reconstruction in each member of a unique internal group. The analyst has to consider the family link that has been constituted, reconsider the links between different members, and search out still unknown sources of suffering.

In the consulting room

The family came for treatment at the recommendation of the analyst of Javier, aged fifty-seven, the father, who had started psychoanalytical treatment three years earlier. The mother, Paloma, aged fifty-five, started psychotherapy seven years ago because of depression. Two years after Paloma started her therapy, Natalia, her youngest daughter, then fourteen years old, showed symptoms of anorexia. There are two other siblings: Christian, twenty-one years old, and Marisa, the eldest, twenty-two years old.

Natalia had trained to be a gymnast from the age of six, undergoing a strict diet and a stressful timetable. She started puberty rather late, or at least this is what Paloma thought. After her first menstruation she suddenly decided to give up gymnastics and began gaining weight. Paloma rather obsessively made her go on a diet, and the family's general physician sent her to a treatment centre for anorexia.

Marisa, the eldest daughter, presented no apparent problems. However, she was the one held responsible for many of the situations with which Paloma felt overwhelmed, in particular all the medical care Natalia needed. At the same time that Natalia showed anorectic symptoms, Javier had a heart attack and Marisa took care of him. Because of Javier's threatening levels of anxiety, his cardiologist was the person who recommended Javier should start psychoanalytic treatment. Two years after Javier started his analysis his emotional state became worse because his son Christian decided to give up his studies. It was said that Javier felt "great disappointment because his only son doesn't want to go on studying engineering". His analyst considered this situation so distressing for Javier and his wife that he recommended family therapy.

Javier and Paloma have been together for twenty-five years. When they first met, they thought that they would be together forever. Javier is an art designer and Paloma is an art teacher. They had worked hard to give their children education, so this situation was unbearable for them, because they had always known what they wanted for their children.

At the beginning of the treatment the family debated how they should describe their difficulties in communicating. The parents could not accept their son's wish to discontinue studying and to "see if he has more luck with music, leading a Bohemian life with no serious prospects ... . He thinks he could have a much better life and this is his choice ... . We cannot understand his position ... he could have a brilliant future as an engineer in my brother's enterprise ... . He could have such an easy path to the top ... . As Christian is already twenty-one, he could take charge of different family projects as an engineer as soon as he finished university." The father said with great pain, "I cannot understand why he makes this choice ... . I cannot accept his choice to be a musician."

Paloma oscillated between reproaching herself for her son's decision and believing that she had nothing to do with her son's choice. She said, "We have been on top of him too much most of the time, overwhelming him. He says that at times he felt suffocated, and now he decides something different."

Both Paloma and Javier put their son down, saying, "He is so inconstant, so inconsistent. He doesn't want anything that calls for great effort ... His options are always the easy ones ... Marisa, our eldest daughter, is already an architect and will soon have her own house ... She has started working in an office ... although this might not be the best moment to think of leaving the family because Natalia, with her anorexia, leaves no room for us to think about Marisa moving away from our home."

The family had been coming regularly to family sessions for nearly a year, recognising the analytical setting as an important space where they could express themselves. They were able to differentiate, disagree, and distinguish their different positions. This essential achievement allowed them to discriminate the internal from the external world in each family member, and at the same time, to feel part of a more cooperative family group.

In the first period of analysis, we could see a level in which the members of the family tended to "agglutinate" or join together to establish an idealised transference in which the family analysis was experienced as an ideal space. As such it was a refuge offering great relief, without the necessity to treat it as an actual analytic session—as if this refuge allowed a magical recovery, reconstituting a mythical family unit they previously had. This was expressed in terms such as, "The family united will never be defeated". At other times they brought biblical images on the same theme. The analyst felt that this feeling was in a way imposed in the countertransference. This defensive idealisation tended to obscure and deny the problems between family members and to prevent the emergence of difference.

Analytically, we worked together from within the transference-countertransference situation, helping the family to pass from illusion to disillusionment. One image the father brought stood out as especially helpful. In one session, he brought a biblical passage that explained "philoxenia". Three angels come to earth. Abraham and Sara welcomed them with treats, showing the religious duty of "brotherly hospitality" to these foreigners, sent by God. Javier's offering brought interesting associations about the conscious understanding of "the space given to their offspring". They began to understand that they actually had very different representations, that there was not "only one world" between them. There were many "different worlds". Feared images that only now came to light included Christian's "demonisation", and its polar opposite, that made Marisa into an angel. The parents generally functioned as a monolith, a "father-mother" figure, which Natalia called "the untouchables".

Session after Christmas

Christian was moving away from home to share an apartment with some members of his rock group. All the family members were on time except Christian. The analyst perceived an atmosphere of confusion, because everybody stood, not knowing which seat to choose. The analyst wondered whether they were referring only to their places here in the session or in their outside lives as well. They had just come back from a family event where they met relatives belonging to different generations and baby daughters belonging to their mother's sisters. They started talking with enthusiasm about the recent family gathering, but after a few minutes this enthusiasm dwindled. Again an atmosphere of confusion set in, felt in the countertransference as something incomprehensible. There had been other moments that felt like this. Then there was a deep silence.

ANALYST: It looks as if you are still waiting for someone to come in order for you to go on, could that be Christian?

JAVIER: I haven't been feeling too well lately. [He talks about physical problems for a short while—his stomach, back pain, possible surgery.] I have been told that a friend of mine recently died. We were very good friends at school and high school as well.

[An atmosphere of sadness invades the consulting room.]

PALOMA: This makes me remember my dad's illness and death.

[Just then Christian arrives, thirty-five minutes late. He interrupts his mother.]

PALOMA: You are always late. Once again! [She looks towards the analyst with disgust, as if to indicate, "You can see he is always away, off in his own world." She then goes on talking about her parents.] As a daughter, I would have never behaved like this. This would have been a sin. I never did to my parents what our son does to us! [A short silence.] My parents got divorced when I was five years old, because of an extramarital love affair my father had. My mother couldn't stand it and that was the end. I'm sure Christian is taking dance lessons instead of coming to therapy.

MARISA: It's me who goes to dance classes. I love when I can make my body move with rhythm and harmony.

ANALYST: Javier started taking about problems in his body and the death of an old friend, and about those who are absent. Paloma went on to say her father is no longer here, their divorce when Paloma was a child and finally Marisa has talked about her body, but with a very different meaning.

CHRISTIAN: I'm sorry, but I had things to do. Since I'm living on my own there are many things I have to do by myself [in a tone of complaint].

JAVIER: I don't do anything all day long! I rest all day long! [This is said in an ironical tone, showing a devalued image of Christian.]

The analyst feels that an atmosphere of resistance is obliterating the possibility of productive exchange. She tries to show all of them that Christian's late arrival is aside from a new aspect. New things are taking place now, while old ways of linking between the family members are repeated. In this session, it is difficult to put into words the meaning of these events for each of them in their inner worlds, and how each of the changes that have taken place in the outer world have been dramatised in this session.

The next session

Natalia started by recounting her dream from last night about the family being at the beach, as happened when the children were young.

PALOMA: When Marisa was three, she wasn't potty trained.

JAVIER: At that time I had my first surgery.

CHRISTIAN: I never noticed that dad had surgery then. I was only eight.

[The analyst felt that the group atmosphere was more dynamic.]

MARISA: I am able to understand now why I am always helping and taking care of others. Although I feel like being taken care of and I feel I need affection, I don't want my mother to confuse me with Christian, as she sometimes does.

JAVIER: [Jumps in] I also had a dream last night about attending a football match and meeting a group of my friends there. My father was there and my friend who recently passed away. I see them and I start crying. I get confused in the dream with my father. There is a scene in which I am the one in hospital and another scene in which it is my father who is in hospital. My father and my dead friend hug me to try to comfort me.

[Other associations appear during the session: Javier says that the dream makes him realise that he is here in a sort of "hospital" where everybody is a little damaged. Christian says that he has been thinking a lot what would happen if his parents got sick and died. The analyst tries to say something, but Paloma interrupts her and says that what Javier said about his father and his dead friend made her think that she could not live alone with her son and daughters if Javier was not with her. If that happened, she would die.]

ANALYST: It sounds as if each member of the family turns out to be a different person gaining autonomy. But this situation in which you differentiate is felt as if it is a mortal loss.

JAVIER: When I was a child I lived at a great distance from my parents, because I had so many siblings. I lived with my grandmother in her house until she died when I was an adolescent. Then my parents told me that I would have to come back home. I felt I had to comfort my parents because of their own parents' deaths.

ANALYST: And who comforts you? Or how can we comfort you here?

NATALIA: [Quite surprised] That means then, that the dead one was your grandmother-mother, and you were abandoned in her house! Was it like that? So that means that when your grandmother died you lost your real mother and you had to comfort our grandparents …

PALOMA: When I was a child I couldn't understand where the dead lived.

CHRISTIAN: [Ironically] It depends on whether they are baptised or not! If they are not baptised they are in limbo.

ANALYST: It looks as if today you fluctuate here between a "family hospital" and being in limbo. In a hospital, you can be taken care of. In limbo, you are without a God to look after you—like Javier who was left in his grandparents' home like an angel with no God.

  [Then Paloma and Javier start criticising their own parents, saying they were authoritarian, their mothers demanding and possessive, although internally cold. Both refer to experiences of abandonment. Paloma and Javier both felt guilty because they always felt that they had caused the painful circumstances their parents had to undergo. Marisa, Christian and Natalia look intently at their parents. Javier and Paloma notice this and look at one another in surprise and comfort.]

MARISA: [In a worried tone] Poor Mum and Dad, they have often been very lonely.

ANALYST: If children grow up, they have to leave their parents. Then the parents have to undergo a situation of abandonment similar to what they experienced when they were young.

JAVIER: [Puzzled] Life is full of paradoxes, I came here thinking that my children were ungrateful and now I realise that my parents were the ones that abandoned me by sending me to my grandparents. In our family nobody is abandoning anybody. This is a totally new situation.

ANALYST: A new situation that hurts.

Discussion

What we wish to show in this session is the movement from the external family group into the therapeutic group. Confusional anxieties emerge.

The projection of the inner world brought into the analytical situation (that represents the external world) shows a group of family members who are not able to figure out where they are because it is a different world from the one they have continually imposed from their conjoined inner worlds. In family analysis, there is a superimposing of different worlds: the external world *vs.* the internal world. The present family group in the clinical setting *vs.* the projections of phantasies linked to internal objects of members of the group onto other members of the group, making those other family members act out roles and links that represent the imposition of internal objects. Therefore, the ways of functioning in which they had behaved without differentiating between them, began to give way to new ways of being, both at home and in the analytic setting. This change was created by the acknowledgement of the "difference of the other" modelled by the analytic treatment.

We have often seen family groups in which a change of structure is necessary because of new situations in life that have to be faced. New paths emerge that facilitate discrimination between ego and non-ego structures, between inner and outer worlds, between the internal family group and the external family group. We then see how each member can be the receiver of contents from other members, and can act out roles corresponding to links with and internal objects of those other members. What is projected in the family group structure is not only a mental content or a feeling, but a series of links, each with emotional atmospheres attached to them. The recognition of different spaces and roles is often heralded by feelings of disorientation. Where are they? Where are we? In which group are we now? Are we with our children, with the grandparents, or with our own parents? This is the first step when the idea of family group breaks up and needs reorganisation.

In the first session the preverbal communication did not allow memories to appear. Thoughts and ideas were not able to flow in the dialogue. The analyst functioned then as "the memory" and tried to make the history of the family understandable by linking feelings of sorrow, suffering, death, and dancing, thereby establishing a relationship with the father's history. This way of proceeding functioned for the family group as a background group of constant elements that facilitated change in family dynamics. The family group then continued to elaborate as they were able to bring dreams and acknowledge change. The blocked interaction between the members of the family group gave way to co-operation.

In the family group, the analyst initially participated in an idealised scene (like being in heaven) where the objects are supposed to be protected from phantasies of abandonment. Family members began to feel that to be a family they needed more differentiation (to be baptised) in order not to remain trapped in the limbo of non-differentiation. New subjectivity, new ego organisation, became possible for each individual. In the group transference, a maternal relationship was initially exerted on the analyst in support of the family repetition of the avoidance of abandonment. Working through analysis, we saw that the future prospect of each member would not be recognised if they were not consistent with the father's ideals. We focused our work on the recognition of the desires and projects of each member of the group, not only those of the parents. Each of the members slowly began to recognise his or her "alterity"—their otherness to each other. Natalia, the anorexic youngest daughter, began to improve her social performance and her weight stabilised. Marisa, who wanted to move from the family home, was able to do so, and Natalia's pathology was no longer an impediment to this. Natalia decided to start an individual psychoanalytical treatment with an analyst outside the family circle, finding a space free from parental intrusion.

After a year working together, Paloma and Javier could recognise a space for their children. The intrusive link with the children—and with the analyst—underwent a process of transformation. The slow recognition of differences improved the relationship, in particular, with the son (who was the original reason for requesting family analysis), now happily a musician. Intrusiveness began changing to a more receptive link, in which they became interested in their son's achievement, both parents talking with pride about Christian's music. At the beginning, Christian's house was described as a "complete disaster". They could later describe Christian's "fantastic house, much like he is", with artistic details, and with a special studio, designed both for his musical practice and for everyday life.

Some conclusions

One function of the family group is to offer a container in which primary links can undergo needed transformation, giving way to new possibilities for mental growth. This function of the family group is facilitated during analytic treatment. The group has to be able to tolerate this new construction of possibilities between its members. What we are able to see in this family is that the parent and sibling roles gave permanence to narcissistic object relations of their internal world, passing on impediments derived from the family's history. The past, as seen through the lens of the present family group, made the family function with rigidity. Under the pressure of this past, a new future had to be constructed together with the analyst. The function of analysis is to transform this apparently "natural" and immutable history into a new history built within this new group. This constitutes psychoanalytic family work.

Discussion of "Contributions to the link perspective in interventions with families: theoretical and technical aspects, and clinical application" by A. Monserrat and E. Palacios

Janine Puget (Buenos Aires, Argentina)*

Where does the discussion of a paper lead?

Discussing a paper triggers a dialogue that stems from sharing ideas, from the space between two or more minds, from the time that elapses between writing the essay and reading it, and from the compelling world opening up when two or more subjects meet and take advantage of the potential of difference. This potential originates in the space between us and others, a space we often try to close when it seems that making and maintaining contact require hard work. A way to avoid this work, then, is searching for similarities and complementarities, which do not necessarily exist but are expressed in our scientific milieu by phrases such as "I thought the same thing" or "So and so says the same thing". By contrast, this "inter" space between writer and reader should give rise to new texts that enable us to find enriching interstices and set in motion the work of thought.

The authors start their potential dialogue with their readers by stating their theoretical position and carefully reviewing some of the many theoretical perspectives from which we may ponder families, couples, and groups today. The theoretical framework discussed is quite broad:

---

*Translated by Judith Filc.

Freud, Meltzer, Bion, M. Klein, and Abraham coexist with Argentine thinkers such as Pichon Rivière, Bleger, Bauleo, Berenstein, Puget, and Moguillansky. It is interesting to note the place assigned to Argentine literature. I believe this recognition is well deserved. For many years Argentine analysts have been exploring this field and advancing innovative theories that have made it possible to develop new devices. Just as Freud created the analytic session device and Klein the play device for analytic sessions with children, others created group, family, and couple sessions when they expanded their theoretical frameworks. These frameworks, which are considered new in the psychoanalytic field, will maintain their freshness thanks to countless questions arising in everyday clinical practice.

I say that they are psychoanalytic devices because many of us working with link devices have had to expand so-called traditional metapsychologies at times, and have needed to create new, autonomous metapsychologies that coexist with traditional ones at other times. Those of us who have adopted this perspective tackle, each in his or her own way, what we call linkage suffering. This suffering is directly connected to the effects of presence, which always dislodge subjects from their narcissistic positioning. By following this path, we gradually introduced a new vocabulary that incorporated the results of research on the difference between being alone with oneself and with an analyst who opens the possibility for one's internal world to unfold, on one hand, and on the other, being, or slowly becoming, with two or more others.

It is here that practitioners part ways. Some may use the same theoretical instruments in both cases. Others, Berenstein and myself among them (Berenstein & Puget, 1997), believe that these two situations are different. Each has its own conflicts and hence requires its own theoretical–clinical tools. In a way, I agree with the authors of the paper when they stress the significance of making room for, and giving a specific meaning to, what we designate as "the other". This notion is probably the cornerstone of the disagreements that have developed among professionals dealing with links.

In the discussion of the clinical material we can see the different ways of approaching it. In my case, I address specific moments in the narratives based on a theoretical framework that focuses on the "gradually doing" and "gradually becoming" that unfolds from the potential of the between-two (Puget, 2012a). To follow this approach, we must distinguish the subject-analyst whose interventions are within the register of interference (Puget, 2010) from the analyst who is the object of the transference. In addition, we must acknowledge the effects produced by the overlap of a clinical practice of the One and a clinical practice of the Two, each with its own rules of communication and subjective formation.

Clinical material

The presentation of what we call clinical material offers a variety of possibilities. The way of presenting it doubtless reveals the presenter's theoretical background and goals. When we are dealing with link material, whether from a family or a couple, the possibilities multiply. Each type of presentation certainly shows the analyst's need to "introduce" the situation to those who are not familiar with it—to recreate it because it is already in the past. A family is thus introduced to us allegedly to enable us to "become familiar with the situation". One possible method is to provide what is traditionally called a background, that is, depict each member of the family, point to the designated patient, mention the conscious reason for seeking help, how they came to request treatment or why treatment was indicated, and so on. This information, which is certainly useful, corresponds to a way of knowing that may become defensive at times. Furthermore, providing these data involves the risk of developing preconceived ideas about what we are searching for, what we aim to find, and where to direct our attention during an interview. It is as though an essential way of becoming familiar with a situation could exist outside specific contexts (Puget, 2008).

Another way of presenting material is "narrating," "introducing" a session or interview right away. In this case, biographical data appear as the audience learns, from family members' attitudes and the ways in which they engage with the therapeutic situation, who performs what role and how family suffering develops.

In the first case, based on the information provided we search for elements in the material that we think may be of use. In the second, we gradually envision the family and learn how its members relate to each other, what type of narratives and emotions emerge, and what communication means to them … something like building a story (Puget, 2006). While A. Monserrat and E. Palacios provide a background, this does not prevent them from addressing the link products emerging in each session.

A possible approach to psychoanalytic work

Since I would rather omit the so-called background for now, I will start by commenting on the first interviews. The characters that create the analytic situation struggle in the face of what they refer to as their difficulty to communicate. It seems as though the parents thought that communicating with their children meant that the latter accepted their parents' ideals. Such a way of thinking is equivalent to believing that the role of parents is to impose a certain future on their children that they, the parents, consider suitable in terms of their own ideals. As a consequence, the son's enthusiastic involvement with music is defined as "not studying". According to the parents his choice has no future, and so they belittle his project by saying that it is not serious. Their only son should take on the family's projects. In this way, what they call "communication", and we, "communication impairment", slowly takes shape.

We can already identify a problem. The parents believe that communication happens by imposing one's ideals on others. When they fail to do so, they feel disappointed and claim that they cannot understand the discrepancy between their own and others' expectations. They equate understanding with suppressing the other's desires and establishing asymmetrical power relations. The phrase "I don't understand you", frequently heard in link analyses, usually denotes an attempt to impose the thinking of the One, and a difficulty building from the Between-the-Two. A way of overcoming this obstacle is reproaching oneself for not bringing up one's child properly. This attitude allows the mother to recover the role of significant person who determines her children's future. "Everything depends on her, even if it means that she failed." The son's fate depended on her plans for him, even if she did not know how to instill these plans in him.

One of the daughters, a professional woman, wants to live on her own, but her project is thwarted by her parents, who do not think that this is a good time for her to leave home. So far, in this family relationship those who have a project of their own are denigrated, and those who agree to give up their project are venerated. Furthermore, the argument used by the parents to frustrate this daughter's project is that given the state of the other daughter, disparaged and anorexic, this is not a good time for the first one to move to her own place. The designated patient is very demanding, and they must care for her. At the same time, the narrative is somewhat confused. Supposedly they came because of one daughter's anorexia but also in response to conflicts arising after the father became seriously ill. There were, then, different reasons for demanding analysis, to which we might add that communication among family members was anorexic; they could not receive what was offered to them.

In the therapeutic space tension decreases, according to the authors, thanks to an idealised transference. Without downplaying the power of this hypothesis, I suggest that the analytic space introduced a different kind of listening that allowed family members to be heard and to start a project. In a way, it gave them more air, expanded the space of the between-two and thus alleviated the feeling of paralysing suffocation or, to say it in the authors' words, the agglutinative relationship. A space was created where speaking meant being heard without necessarily generating fruitless recrimination, and this development was possible thanks to what Berenstein and I have called "interference effect" (Berenstein & Puget, 1997). In this case, interference produces new ways of communication. Perhaps they will thus be able to find a more suitable phrase to account for the implications of a link exchange than the one they proclaim: "The family united will never be defeated."

There are many ways of being together. Some are suffocating, others creative. So far, Monserrat and Palacios diagnose this family's unity as an invalidating agglutination. Perhaps, by way of analytic work "united" may come to mean the instatement of new rules of exchange whereby each person can be another. They would thus be able to develop projects that would not necessarily please all of them. This is what the authors think when they claim that the family's defence mechanisms served to prevent the emergence of difference or, in other words, to avoid performing the work needed to do something with difference without eliminating it. It seems that the family has achieved this transformation in analysis—respecting each member's presence and modifying the role of the parental couple so that the latter may appear as linked rather than monolithic.

How do we signify what we usually designate as the absence of a family member?

There is a detail from a session that took place after the holidays that merits discussion. The session starts without one of the family members:

The son is absent. I wonder if this need to wait until everyone is present and, if somebody is missing, to look at the session from the logic of the lack is a prejudice of ours. For a long time I myself would provide interpretations that were based on the meaning of absence, of lack. Yet lately I have revised this idea and think that the session is created by those who are present, and that it is somehow complete. The fact that someone is not there need not be equated to an absence. It can be part of the dynamics of the unpredictable, which imposes on us something unthought and sometimes new.

After the analyst's intervention concerning the wait for "someone", each family member expresses his or her pain. We can already identify signs of difference; each views suffering differently. The father suffers because of his body, the mother recalls her father's death ... And the absent one arrives ... The situation abruptly changes. Entering into a different link dynamics, they resort to recriminations directed at the person who is, they say, "late". The mother reaffirms her belief that her mother–child relationship should be a replica of her relationship with her own parents. She would not have been late. To express her right to protest, she denigrates her son by telling him that it is obvious that he thinks the session is a dance lesson. In the process she also belittles her daughter's pursuits, since the latter actually takes dance lessons. We can begin to see that the only occupation that satisfies the parents is being a university student.

Recrimination

From my theoretical perspective, recrimination is the paradigm of the difficulty to process the effect of presence, an effect that demands that we do something with what presences impose on us (Puget, 2012b). Recrimination takes the verbal shape of a demand caused by the fact that life, the other, or the situation is not what subjects envisioned or desired. Consequently, when the one who, according to the mother, should have been there earlier arrives, what started as a dialogue where participants talked about their suffering is interrupted in order to restore an illusion of unity.

How did the treatment evolve?

The old and the new coexist. On the one hand, the son has left home, and therefore has to manage his life while his parents keep trying to impose their own projects on him. The situation has opened up to some extent, and now parents' imposition does not bring about the stagnation of the link. In any case, the analyst stresses the meaning given by the parents to the new situation that is developing, that is, their children's embarking on their own projects. The parents experience this development as a deadly loss, and therefore cannot enjoy the achievement it implies for the family as a whole.

New situations unfold where family members resort to symbolic language. They relate their dreams, and listening no longer entails replicating what the parents say. The children express themselves from their own point of view. One of the daughters hears the mother's discourse in amazement and says to her, "But the one who died was your grandmother-mother, and you were abandoned at her place ..." and so on. In other words, a creative mode of listening emerged from the family's ability to take each member's alterity into account. The appearance of surprise is another indicator of significant therapeutic progress; it is the antithesis of recrimination. Surprise and uncertainty are creative (Puget, 2010), and are often cancelled by recrimination and complaints.

The authors' final comment clearly summarises their theoretical stance, which I share. Nonetheless, I thought it would be useful to add some hypotheses that value the potentiality of the space of the between-two. These hypotheses led me to punctuate the material based on some signifiers pertaining to linking difficulties. Nonetheless, we share the idea that "fate" becomes contextualised history and new paths emerge that bridge link chasms.

Discussion of "Contributions to the link perspective in interventions with families: theoretical and technical aspects, and clinical application" by A. Monserrat and E. Palacios

Monica Vorchheimer (Buenos Aires, Argentina)

Lévi-Strauss wrote that there is an unsolvable paradox concerning cultural communication: "If a culture has little communication with other cultures, it is also more difficult for the respective emissary of those cultures to be able to span the richness and the significance of diversity" (Lévi-Strauss, 1955). Thus could be the text given by these authors, the genealogy of the theoretical family that gives a frame to their clinical understanding. Although the authors value object relations theory in order to understand intrapsychic phenomena, they also take into account the solipsism of these models. They describe how others are seen through the screen of our own minds, being confused in different levels with our own inner world.

This perspective has not only to do with solipsism but also with the direction of meaning, coming from the inner world towards the outer world. As they say later, the extension of the theory of object relations to the understanding of link phenomena is not enough to comprehend the significance given to the actual existence of the other in the field of link interaction. We add that, considering this model, the present cannot be explained by transference of meanings that come from the past, for this gives a thin margin for the conceptualisation of experience as novelty.

The authors identify their thinking with the development of ideas that underline the effects of presence of the other in the constitution of links: the relationship of the ego with its objects cannot be considered as mere projections of the inner world. The meeting with the other has to be considered as producing effects with its presence; the other subject, has value per se in the constitution of subjectivity. The premise that "[w]e are all inhabited by object relations and by links with others" amplifies psychoanalytic metapsychology by introducing notions such as "presence", "imposition", and "interference". The clinical value of these concepts coined by I. Berenstein and J. Puget is illustrated in this clinical material.

The family is referred for family analysis by the father's analyst who considers that the suffering and loss of hope of the father and his wife are due to the fact their son has abandoned his studies of engineering. We are soon told that Natalia's earlier anorexia was not a sufficient reason for making them ask for family therapy. The strict diet seems to correspond in agreement with ego demands, ego-syntonic to family principles of which the mother is the representative spokesperson. In contrast, what comes up when Christian abandons his studies is the great disappointment for both parents: "Javier and Paloma think that they have worked hard to give each of their children good studies and that this situation is unbearable for them". We are able to see how "strict diet and working hard" are both signifiers that belong to the same field of meaning of family ideals embodied by the parents who "have always had an idea of what they wanted for their children" and they also believed that they would be together forever ("When they first met they thought that they would be together forever and ever"). We underline the idea "forever and ever" in this formulation since this conception of eternity goes hand in hand with the shared illusion of what they desire for their children. Christian had a future, within the parents' desires, a place in the family's business that would lead him to reach the top of success as an engineer. We will take a look at the importance given to success and to the continuity of the family through what they call "family projects". "We can't understand his position," they say, where what can be understood is put on the same level as what can be shared.

The authors tell us that the family needed a period of time in order to work on the subject of illusion and disillusionment, and to come to the understanding of how their children's adolescence is a request for psychic work on the family structure in order to work on the dogmatic foundation of the family links, of which the ideals of continuity without change, effort, success, and strictness are the inheritance.

It is interesting to highlight the figure of "philoxenia" recalled by the father in one of the sessions in which three angels are received by Abraham and Sara, the biblical parents. While this purports to represent hospitality in its positive sense, it emphasises unconsciously a Messianic atmosphere that organises this family in which the angels—in contrast with the devils—have no sexuality. We will go back to this point later on.

In the session after Christmas, Christian is moving from his parent's home and arrives late to the session. There is an atmosphere of confusion. They do not know where to sit. Why isn't Christian, the designated devil, present? They begin with enthusiasm which declines rapidly as confusion is followed by silence. The analyst interprets that they seem to be waiting for someone, Christian, in order to continue. Although nobody makes direct reference to the analyst's interpretation, an association follows by the father about diseases and death. Is Christian's moving out equivalent to death? This reminds Paloma of Javier's father's illness and death. Does she need to put herself on the same level as Javier because similarities give her a sense of belonging to the same family? Similarities dignify the space given to suffering, death, and sorrow; the atmosphere that joined them around the festivity has long ago been lost. Is this session, in which Christian has not yet arrived, different from others, since "the family" is all of them living together and believing that they are all together as the parents thought they would be? Do they need to find similarities at the expense of wiping out individuality?

Then we see Paloma's annoyance when her son arrives late: "You are always late. Once again!" "Always" she denies the fact that this session—and this being late—is new and cannot be understood as a repetition of times before. In this way, this specific lateness is deprived of its unknown aspect: Christian's motivations are left out, shrinking the space for curiosity and individuality. Once again what could be a circumstance "to be known" is given an already known meaning: being late as always. This is a fault that she would have never committed with her own parents she tells the analyst with disgust. This is a privileged moment in the transference in which Paloma includes the analyst in her world of meanings, believing that her way of looking at life will be shared by her, supposing there is one only way of understanding the world and that the analyst participates of this vision. Nobody seems to contradict the sayings of the mother. Is there an implicit threat of being seen as a devil if someone thinks different to Paloma, if her statements, expressed with total certainty, are questioned?

After a brief silence, associations come from Paloma. She remembers her parent's divorce due to her father's infidelity and she adds her conviction that Christian considers the family sessions as if they were dancing lessons. Through these associations, underlying matters enter the scene: the divorce comes in series with the infidelity, sexuality, and the pleasure that needs be suppressed in order to guarantee a marriage and a family that could last forever and ever. If Christian is late this is due to an extramarital affair: "dance lessons"; this is a fault, bad conduct towards the parental couple, and "divorce" is bound to follow: "You are dancing, having an affair while I am suffering!" Marisa, makes clear that she is the one that takes dancing lessons, claiming for the body the acknowledgement, as a scenario for pleasure, not just for diseases such as her father's heart attack or Natalia's anorexia. In this atmosphere, pleasure and individual interest convey the semantics of betrayal and carelessness, leading to irreconcilable opposites: if suffering and effort are signals of being involved and belonging to the family group, desire and pleasure signify exclusion and abandonment of the family.

We can understand the beginning of the next session in a similar way. Natalia starts the session telling a dream: The family is at the beach, as when the kids were young. Paloma and Javier do not pay attention to the dream, instead recalling that Marisa could not control her sphincter, and add to it Javier's first surgery. Once again, after the pleasure at the beach is recalled by Natalia's dream, the ill body is invoked along with a disciplinary dimension. However, when father brings his own dream in which he feels sorrow for the death of his friend, a dream of hospitals, associations lead to Javier's childhood, the death of his grandparents, memories of tragedy and adversity which give a reason for a life full of sacrifice. The analyst says that the session is a place where the atmosphere of hospitals is present in which all of them can be part of the same "creed", as the suffering baptised ones who prevent the expulsion to limbo of those with demonic creeds like dancing and sexuality. The analyst shows them that the growing up of the children is experienced by the parents as a repetition of the abandonment they experienced in childhood. The father replies that in this family no one will be abandoned, and that this is a totally new situation.

Psychoanalysis progresses through oscillation amongst the possibility of awareness and the lack of it, learning from the hard psychic work needed for working through family, always felt as failure of proper functioning. Belonging to a family, being part of a family, is part of our sense of identity, not only to each family member, but also to the family group.

Adolescence is a turbulent state for the whole family as a group, since it brings forward, once again, the family's myths of origin revealing the end of the family's original identity with its desires, ideals, authorisations, and prohibitions. The family's early alliance was built around the idealised idea of a union that would last forever based on sacrifice, and excluding sexuality felt as a threat to the family. Psychoanalytical work explores the dynamics of these ossified meanings from the past that have held the representation of the group as one that would always have latency children. This clinical work shows how the emergence of newness is dealt with. Working together, family and analyst give space to new representations of the group that can provide a new experience of being a family, even though this will never again be the family that they thought it was and would be forever and ever.

References

Abraham, K. (1924). Un breve estudio de la evolución de la libido considerada la luz de los trastornos mentales. In: *Psicoanálisis Clínico*. Buenos Aires: Hormé.

Bateson, G., Jackson, D., Haley, J., & Weakland, J. (1956). Towards a theory of schizophrenia. *Behavioural Science, 1*: 251–254.

Bauleo, A. (1970a). *Ideología, grupo y familia*. Buenos Aires: Kargieman.
Bauleo, A. (1970b). *Psicoanálisis y grupalidad*. Buenos Aires: Paidós.
Berenstein, I. (2001a). *El sujeto y el Otro*. Buenos Aires: Paidós.
Berenstein, I. (2001b). *Clínica familiar psicoanalítica. Estructura y acontecimiento*. Buenos Aires: Paidós.
Berenstein, I. (2004). *Devenir otro con otro(s): ajenidad, presencia y interferencia*. Buenos Aires: Paidós.
Berenstein, I. (2007). *Del ser al hacer*. Buenos Aires: Paidós.
Berenstein, I., & Puget, J. (1997). *Lo vincular. Teoría y clínica psicoanalítica* (The Link: Psychoanalytic Theory and Clinical Practice). Buenos Aires: Paidós.
Bion, W. R. (1962). *Learning from Experience*. London: William Heinemann.
Bion, W. R. (1967). *Second Thoughts*. London: Karnac.
Dicks, H. (1967). *Marital Tensions*. London: Routledge.
Freud, S. (1917e). Mourning and melancholia. *S. E., 14*: 239. London: Hogarth.
Fromm-Reichmann, F. (1952). *Algunos Aspectos de la Psicoterapia Psicoanalítica con Esquizofrénicos*. In: *Psicoterapia de la Psicosis*. Buenos Aires: Hormé.
Kaës, R. (1987). *Pacto Denegativo en los conjuntos trans-subjetivos. En Lo Negativo. Figuras y Modalidades*. Buenos Aires: Amorrortu Editores.
Kaës, R. (2007). *Linking, Alliances, and Shared Space*. London: The International Psychoanalytical Association.
Lévi-Strauss, C. (1963). *Antropología Estructural*. Buenos Aires: Eudeba.
Lévi-Strauss, C. (1969). *Las Estructuras Elementales del Parentesco*. Barcelona: Paidós.
Morgan, M. (2005). On being able to be a couple: The importance of a creative couple in psychic life. In: F. Grier (Ed.), *Oedipus and the Couple* (pp. 9–30). London: Karnac.
Pichon Rivière, E. (1985). *Teoría del Vínculo*. Buenos Aires: Nueva Visión.
Pincus, L., & Dare, C. (1978). *Secrets in the Family*. London: Faber & Faber.
Puget, J. (2006). The use of the past and the present in the clinical setting: Pasts and presents. *International Journal of Psychoanalysis, 87*: 1691–1707.
Puget, J. (2008). Cada vez nos conocemos menos (We know each other increasingly less). *Revista de Psicoterapia Psicoanalítica, 3*: 79–90.
Puget, J. (2010). The subjectivity of certainty and the subjectivity of uncertainty. *Psychoanalytic Dialogues*. 20: 4–20.
Puget, J. (2012a). "Transferencia, contratransferencia, interferencia" (Transference, countertransference, interference). In: I. C. Gomes, M. I. Assumpção Fernandes & R. Blay Levisky (Eds.), *Diálogos Psicoanalíticos sobre Familia e Casal* (Psychoanalytic Dialogues on Family and Couples) (pp. 85–94). San Pablo: Zagodoni Editora.
Puget, J. (2012b). Efectos de presencia, efectos de ausencia. Diversas maneras de pensarlo (Effects of presence, effects of absence. Different ways of reflecting). *Psicoanálisis, 34*: 385–399.

Puget, J., & Berenstein I. (1997). *Lo vincular teoría y clínica Psicoanalítica*. Buenos Aires: Paidós.

Ruszczynski, S. (1993). *Psychotherapy with Couples: Theory and Practice at the Tavistock Institute of Marital Studies*. London: Karnac.

Winnicott, D. W. (1965). *The Maturational Process and the Facilitating Environment*. London: Hogarth.

Winnicott, D. W. (1986). *Home is Where We Start From*. Harmondsworth, Middlesex: Penguin.

CHAPTER SIX

A couple case seen at Tavistock Relationships

Mary Morgan (London, England)

Joe and Lucy

When I met Joe and Lucy, they were in their late twenties and had been living together for just over a year. Both had previous relationships that seemed intense and quite passionate at the beginning but could not be sustained. They did wonder if this relationship was yet another to suffer the same fate. When they met, the feelings between them were strong; they felt they had a lot in common, wanted a lasting relationship and children. Despite their conscious aspirations to be together and have a family, they conveyed many difficulties about the ordinary experience of relating to each other, creating in each of them deep anxiety and a sense of despair.

The initial consultations

I felt Joe and Lucy's approach to me in the first meeting was tentative and anxious. Joe had a rather unkempt appearance; he was dressed smartly in a suit but also looked neglected. When he came into the room he looked around as if rather dazed and took time to make eye contact with me. Lucy was pale and understated. She sat anxiously on the edge of the chair with her head lowered, darting glances towards me. A few minutes into the consultation I realised she was quietly crying. When I commented on it she said it was just because they were here—it had been quite a process getting themselves here. She seemed exhausted and said they disagreed about many things and could not find a way of resolving conflicts.

We had three initial consultations. During them, Joe talked about a kind of unconditional reciprocal love he longed for with Lucy, but he felt they couldn't create the conditions for this. I understood him to mean that it never felt safe enough to get as close as he would like. Lucy shared the aspiration for a loving relationship but often felt things became too intense with Joe. She needed a bit more separateness. Joe's attempts to create openness between them seemed to feel threatening to Lucy who put up barriers and did not always share what she thought. This left Joe feeling anxious and mistrustful. He felt there were too many misunderstandings when they tried to communicate, and when communication broke down he felt a sense of despair. He also worried when he sensed Lucy becoming despairing as he then felt their relationship, or at least his dream of the relationship with her, would crumble. Joe acknowledged that sometimes instead of despair, he felt and expressed anger, and Lucy then withdrew, exacerbating his anxiety. Over the three consultations and later in the therapy I learnt something of their background and their relationship to their parents.

Joe was brought up in an industrial city in southern Europe, the eldest of three siblings in a "poor family". His father was alcoholic and violent, part of a frightening adult world Joe felt born into but could not identify with. As he got older his father gradually became an increasingly pathetic figure. He described a depressed mother who was distant and inaccessible. When he looked at her he felt there was "an invisible screen", and sometimes he felt anxious about what was on the other side. His parents divorced when he was six and, as the only boy with two younger sisters, he felt he had to take on a parental role and some responsibility for his mother. Joe's mother while being emotionally remote also related to him in a way that invited him too much into her sexual relationships with boyfriends.

Lucy was brought up in a more affluent family. Her parents separated soon after her birth and intermittently reunited for brief periods, but never for long enough for her to feel secure. The relationship between her parents continually broke down following verbal and sometimes physical hostility. Her father later remarried and she had two younger half-sisters. Like Joe, Lucy found her mother preoccupied. She felt her mother never heard her properly and distorted what she communicated, often implying they were in agreement about things when they were not. Lucy said that even now she found it hard to distinguish her own thoughts and feelings from other peoples, especially Joe's.

The therapy

At the end of the consultation, we agreed to commence weekly therapy sessions beginning two weeks later. As they settled into therapy, I noticed the couple were full of anxiety. I felt that they especially needed the experience of being heard accurately. They chose to take turns to give each other space to talk, not able to rely on me to take them both in but creating a structure in which they could feel surer of being heard. When it was either's turn to speak, if interrupted, they felt destabilised. I had to provide a careful reiteration of what each had said, but it became problematic when I tried to put these two accounts together, as if this would annihilate them individually. I was struck that neither felt that taking in what the other had said might be valuable, not only as a response to the other but also to themselves. Their state of mind was always different; the response from the other was often experienced as closing everything down, and an assaultive "statement of fact" that obliterated their own feeling of what was real.

I realised this lack of intercourse, curiosity, and creativity had an enormous impact on the couple's relationship. They felt unsupported by each other emotionally, each left alone with difficult feelings they could not contain. It was also extremely difficult for them to think through decisions because they could not explore what each other felt and bring their thoughts together. This linked to their presenting problem about when and if to start a family. When they tried talking about it, one of them might throw up a concern that the other would take as a negative rather than explore the concern.

Without the experience of the other's benign interest in their state of mind, they resorted in a controlling way to trying to tell the other and me how they felt. There was anxiety that the other would intervene and they would lose track of their inner experience and even their hold on reality. Similarly, they could not enquire about the other, as taking the other inside put their own experience under threat. In the transference they each wanted me to understand them, but when I focused on their relationship, things became tense and difficult because, in this parallel way, they feared me bringing them together in my mind.

Clinical vignette one: the primary object as willfully misunderstanding

A few months into the work, we could not do much about the sense of annihilation that came about with any kind of intercourse, but we were slowly able to begin to explore the way they felt the other got inside them and distorted their experience. They were talking about a shopping trip they had at the weekend, which seemed to have been frustrating and futile. As they tried to describe their experience, I could see that each felt the other was projecting their own experience, not allowing the other to have a separate experience. Their dialogue deteriorated and became confused, as each seemed powerless to keep the other's projection from threatening their own experience.

I had to stop listening to the account of the shopping trip in order to focus on this disturbing process. I realised that if I tried to talk about the shopping trip, I too would inevitably be pushing another view into them that they would experience as distorting. I felt that this countertransference illuminated something about the basic difficulty of their relating connected to their early experience. There was no container that could help organise their experience, only another object projecting into them and distorting their experience.

This can be such a complex problem in couples. Joe and Lucy were trying to get heard while at the same time trying to keep the other out. It became too threatening to take in what the other was feeling, as instead of being a loving thing, it felt like an attack—curiosity imbued with hate instead of love. Opening communication channels made them feel vulnerable to unwanted projections. At times it was even more directly persecutory, because each felt the other was willfully misunderstanding.

Clinical vignette two: a defence against being curious

In one session, Lucy said she felt I had been unfair to her the previous week when I had asked whether she could hear Joe. But, she said, I had not asked him if he could hear her. I reflected for a moment on whether I had been uneven-handed. Perhaps in this way I had. I then remembered that I had not addressed the same question to Joe, as I had felt aware of the particularly impermeable state of mind Lucy seemed to be in when Joe had been trying to describe something upsetting to him. I realised that what was important to them was that everything had to be "fair". Had I addressed the same question to him, it might have been "fair" but it would have taken us away from what felt important at that point and would have felt to me like a poor, uncreative couple therapy intervention. They felt I could not explore only one of their states of mind while retaining a "couple state of mind" (Morgan, 2001). When I said to Lucy that she felt it was more important that I was fair than that I convey what I really thought, it led to some understanding of this dynamic. Many times when one of them tried to talk to the other about something—for example how difficult one had found the other's anger—the partner would respond: "But *you* have to own your own anger!" Then the original anger, regardless of who expressed it, never got explored. It felt like the attempt was to put it back into the other rather than to own anything. To keep everything between them fair and equally poised was an unconscious action to prevent any exploration. In retrospect I think this cancelling out of each other's experience was what I was avoiding in the hope that if we understood more about Lucy's impermeability this might elucidate a couple dynamic.

With some couples, the therapist's secure "couple state of mind" allows this kind of exploration, as they have the experience, both lived in the therapy and in relation to the therapist, that a temporary focus on one partner is in the service of understanding the couple. But for Joe and Lucy, as in this instance, something I had said or not said felt like an attack. It put me in touch with how most often they were not after developing understanding. Instead they needed to take control of their relationship so that it would feel safe and still. They constantly sought validation rather than enquiring into things, unable to engage with an interpretation by agreeing, disagreeing, elaborating, or associating. In this way, their feeling that curiosity and learning injured rather than helped, impeded the work.

Clinical vignette three: lack of safety

In another session after a break, Joe accused Lucy of denying things she had previously said. This made him mad. He also accused her of not responding to him when he told her he was upset. There was a crisis at work and he feared losing the job he had only just acquired. Lucy said she actually did not hear Joe sometimes, that he might say the words while she was distracted with something else, like cooking dinner. She also realised that when upset she sometimes said things she did not mean, and then became defensive and denied saying them. This session illustrated that in their unsafe atmosphere, things said in the heat of the moment could not be retracted. The more Lucy felt pinned down, the more defensive she became. Words, once spoken, could easily become "things" that threatened and injured. When they tried to listen to each other, they quickly became anxious, and it was almost impossible to listen to the other's worries. Sharing anxiety felt like an attack, forcing unwelcome feelings into the other, like the mother Bion described who "could not tolerate experiencing such feelings and reacted either by denying them ingress, or alternatively by becoming a prey to the anxiety which resulted from introjection of the infant's feelings" (Bion, 1959, p. 313).

In this therapy, I had to try continuously to establish the setting as a safe place. It felt important to attend to breaks properly, and to take up any impingement on the frame. Progress in sessions could easily fall apart after a day or two. I linked this difficulty in taking in and retaining things to their problem with curiosity, not only about the object and about themselves.

Clinical vignette four: the primary object—the experience of evacuation

The couple's level of anxiety was illustrated in the following session. They began by discussing how hard it was to talk. They felt so vulnerable if they turned to each other for understanding that they had to "meet" and "check in" before they could begin. Joe felt Lucy did this by getting him to agree that they would talk at an appointed hour, sitting at the kitchen table without the radio on, as it was most of the time. Lucy felt Joe would then try and move around the kitchen, making coffee or attending to something else, which made her feel as if she did not exist. She was left sitting by herself, trying to listen to him but unable to hear him properly, feeling she was some kind of "listening machine" or "listening bucket".

Lucy's expressions further illuminate the couple's difficulty taking something in. One was subject to the other's evacuation as if they were a bucket. This also reflected a dynamic between them and me. They wanted me to take their experience in, but they were not at all sure about the process of me giving it back to them, whether it could be more digested and understood, or whether it would be returned attached to my own projections or with malign intent. Both Joe and Lucy seemed to have experienced a lack of ordinary maternal containment. Joe felt he could not penetrate his mother's mind and was fearful of what lay behind her "glazed eyes". Lucy often could not get the response she needed from her depressed mother, and when she did get a response, was not sure what belonged to her and what belonged to her mother. Later in therapy she described the disturbing experience of feeling her boundaries dissolving and no longer knowing what she thought or felt or who she was.

With these difficulties in relating, having an emotional "intercourse" did not feel safe. They were thus unable to build up an idea of a relationship as a symbolic third, or as a third position to help them process differences, disagreements, frustrations, anger, and hatred, with the hope that understanding might eventually come out of these struggles. They did not have the vantage point from which to see themselves with curiosity. A lot of the time they felt in a battle for survival, trying to find space to articulate their experience before the other took over. In this state of mind, in which each felt desperation about being heard properly, it was difficult for them to hear, or be curious about what was going on between them. Such couples have difficulty seeing each other as separate, because one partner tries omnipotently to control the other in order to make them into the kind of object they need them to be. Or they try to impose their own version of reality on the other as if it were the only possible version. In these couples, for life to be bearable, the individual tyrannises the other to ensure certain forms of behaviour. That Joe and Lucy were missing a fundamental belief in relationships as potentially benign and creative, affected not only them as a couple, but also the therapeutic endeavour based on such beliefs.

Conclusion

This couple quickly became dependent on the therapy because, in a healthy way, they knew they needed a container and were able to respond to the therapist's offer. Initially they may only have sensed my being able to hear each of them reasonably accurately, despite also experiencing me as mishearing, unfair, or projecting into them. Nonetheless, therapy enabled them, over time, to build a less fearful, less paranoid view of the other's interest. Therapy itself offered more safety than they had previously felt. Gradually they were able to take inside a more benign experience of my curiosity about them, in other words to allow and slowly appreciate a non-intrusive exploration inside themselves and their relationship.

Discussion of "A couple case seen at Tavistock Relationships" by Mary Morgan

Lia Rachel Colussi Cypel, Eliana Riberti Nazareth, and Susana Muszkat (São Paulo, Brazil)

We first thank Mary Morgan for sharing with us so richly the intimacy of her psychoanalytic practice and the theoretical–clinical orientation which guides her. She reveals herself, as we have long known, as an especially sensitive psychoanalyst, of great ability and serious commitment to her function as link analyst.

As a result, her comprehension of the complex case, her presentation and elaboration of the main unconscious psychic elements in the couple's conflict, seemed to us not only to be valuable in relation to the concepts, but also flawless in her understanding. Nevertheless, much can be said usefully about approaches to psychoanalytic links, due to the rich potential of psychoanalysis to transform, and also to its expansion into new areas of work.

We believe the construction of the clinical situation begins in the mind of the analyst, in the theoretical model he or she adopts concerning the functioning of the human mind (in the individual or link context), which, in turn, determines the cross-section that will be taken of elements of the clinical situation that are considered analytically.

Implicitly this depends on the analyst's unconscious internal position as a real person, on his internal setting, which also defines his idea of the field of link psychoanalysis and the way he relates to his analytic function. This defines, finally, his way of being a psychoanalyst in relation to life, to himself, and to the other. As there are many variables, there are many ways to build a link-oriented clinical situation.

Are situations less or more correct? Less or more efficient? Each situation must have its conceptual assumptions that sustain the vertex adopted, each with its personal truths and truths of that moment. All this has to make sense to the analyst in a process of "personal recital", which, after all, is the most fundamental and indispensable element for genuine clinical encounter.

Here we aim to highlight some aspects and to expand our reflections on the link field, in order to promote opportunity for discussion, and to favour an exchange of experiences around the diversity of ideas that characterise and enrich psychoanalytic work. Therefore, we propose a few questions for reflection:

1. How much importance do we attribute to the past of the patients?
2. How necessary is it that we know beforehand the past of each one and/or the past of their links?
3. How would such information interfere in our way of positioning ourselves as analysts and of approaching and experiencing the link process?

These statements point to two important theoretical/clinical directions to be considered, in terms of the very conception of the link:

A. Link analysis could be taken, essentially, as a process with linear and sequential temporality, with the prevalence of understanding psychodynamics in a logic of cause and effect—the individual determining the link. In this case, the analyst would occupy the place of valuing knowledge which he can offer patients about how their conflicts arise from their individual pasts in which the respective projective identifications act on the current link, as transferential re-editions of their primitive object relations.

Or:

B. Link analysis could seek to value, apprehend, and tolerate the relative nature of the multiple dimensions and of continual, ineffable movement between them, pertaining to the nature of the psyche. The result is clinical practice as a basic analytical position of permanent and indispensable investigation about what is observed, felt, and thought, the analyst conscious that interpretation made on the basis of emotional experience is always only what is possible at that moment, a partial aspect of a whole that is always inaccessible and unknown.

What justifies this clinical understanding is the notion that psychic reality and its manifestations are characterised by unpredictability, uncertainty, probabilities, and contradictions, although also having invariant aspects. It means conceiving of the mind, and therefore the links that emerge, as a complex, multidimensional, and multifactorial system with infinite possibilities of transformation in relation to its internal reality (intrasubjective) and external reality (intersubjective).

As a result of these ideas, analysis is conceived as a dialectic model, in constant alternation and transformation between analyst and patient(s), building together partial and temporary theses, antitheses, and syntheses, in a successive spiral movement in which everyone learns from the emotional experience in the "here-and-now" of the session.

The analyst imbued with this vision would no longer be one from whom to expect interpretations/interventions spoken as if by someone who asserts the truth. Rather, this analyst pursues meaning, not causes, all in search of psychic expansion. In place of explanatory conclusions, conjectures, and possible hypotheses, he would establish relations between clinical facts, bring together psychic events, always investigating, dealing with doubt, and, therefore, questioning himself and the patient(s), leading them to also question themselves and their truths, which until then were thought to be inalienable. Such an analyst allows for a reflective attitude about the patient's participation in the resulting conflictual link. This questioning position of the analyst expresses his personal awareness of "not knowing" and the capacity to tolerate uncertainty. Through this vertex, the development of the capacity to think about the "singular unconscious emotional experience of that link happening now in the session" is the focus of analytical work. It aims for the new, the unknown, happening in the present.

What definition of link could be valid in this context?

We believe that individuals and links construct themselves and determine each other continually and mutually, alternating between movements of search and opposition between participants, in a permanent power struggle between narcissistic individual demands (thereby denying the existence of the other as a subject) and the acceptance of otherness, making space in their lives to fit this disturbing other who generates turbulence by dislocating them from their centre of identity, even though this identity is, at the same time, so necessary and indispensable for the expansion of subjectivity.

This conflict also includes the possibility that the symptomatic difficulty of the current moment due is alive due to the forceful action of projective identification, which leads a couple to imprisonment in emotional experiences of the individual's or couple's past. This past difficulty is specifically revived by characteristics of the psychodynamics of their link. It therefore floods the present in the form of repeated distortions of the other and of the link. These overarching invariants in the link analytic process demand repeated reframing. They are manifest as traditions, with the feel of permanence and pertinence. At other times, they offer resistance against change and against contact with what is new and creative in the present. They require different technical interventions depending on whether the analyst is dealing with experiences of absence or of presence of the old objects and old links.

In the clinical case that Mary Morgan offers, we understand that the couple organised itself predominantly around the narcissistic area of each member, which justified the need for the analyst to focus often on the primitive object relations present in the transferences in the couple. Would it be interesting to think of ways of expanding this couple's functional understanding? For instance, could it be useful to the development of the therapeutic process to identify which types of unconscious alliances both of them experience, the specific product of that "in between" they both build at every moment, which would be responsible for triggering certain specific aspects of each of their pasts? Our concern with their historic past has to do with certain aspects of their history, which can be identified as they appear in their present dynamic. This would allow us in the present to reframe the past, and rather than the past continuing to frame the present.

Considering these things, we suggest three questions: What? How? What for?

What is happening in the session? Which psychic elements of the current link are involved? Which loving or aggressive feelings, fantasies, desires, or fears, are released that belong to that particular link?

How does this happen dynamically in the link. How does it appear in the current situation? Is this experienced in a constructive or destructive manner?

What for? For what cause? Related to which unconscious link configurations, trickeries, alliances, and pacts? Is it promoting the evolution or regression of the link between the pair?

These elaborations and discoveries, when present, would be a *sine qua non* for the most genuine learning possible about the current emotional link, in other words, of the possibility of psychic change by means of "becoming different through the link". These questions offer possibilities towards apprehension of the singularities of the subjects of the link, in which the new might have specific place in the present.

It may no longer serve us to think of transference as only the updating of a past in the present, except when dealing with the kind of transference that reproduces the past rigidly in the present. In these cases, links predominantly function through projective identification.

Furthermore, we believe that we must take into account other manifestations of the unconscious beyond the expressions of a repressed unconscious. Or rather, what is the place of preconceptions that are actualised in present emotional experience that had no previous registration?

These considerations open up new questions to be discussed more broadly as we examine the use of transference and of interpretation in the link situation. Would such analytic work focus on working in transference, or working the transference? Do we interpret or not? If we do interpret, what, when, and how do we interpret?

These are some considerations that, in turn, could generate new investigations compatible with the inquisitive position of an analyst who asks himself indispensable questions in search of enhancing his capacity to think about the meaning of emotional experience.

With these ideas, we hope to contribute to an enlarged consideration of family analytic process.

Discussion of "A couple case seen at Tavistock Relationships" by Mary Morgan

Diana Norsa (Rome, Italy)

Mary Morgan has given us the opportunity to examine interesting issues in her paper on her couple.

I will organise my discussion around the following points:

1. What indications lead us to choose between an individual, couple, or family psychoanalytic treatment for our patients?
2. In psychoanalytic psychotherapy of the couple, the patient in analysis is the link.
3. Last, I would like to propose reflections on curiosity and adolescence.

Mary Morgan dwells upon the absence of curiosity in the relationship between Joe and Lucy due to the difficulty of reciprocal listening. Quoting Bion to validate her thesis, she refers to early negative experiences, for instance, a primary object inappropriate to answer the needs of being listened to; a distorted introjection, the presence of anger and disillusion rather than love, as far as the object of libidinal cathexis is concerned. I would like to add some thoughts on Joe and Lucy's adolescence, and on adolescence in general seen as a second opportunity to transform (beyond the repetition compulsion) the primary experiences of curiosity.

To what extent is the decision to treat a couple in therapy based on the couple's specific request? Sometimes the request for a therapy of the couple comes from fear of facing uneasiness alone: in these cases an intervention with the couple can help one or both face an individual therapy. At times one member of the couple is already in analysis and the analyst suggests a parallel couple therapy, aware that the collusive link is blocking the analysis.

At other times, uneasiness is generated within the couple even though it is a relationship with a good foundation and has potential for growth. In these cases a psychoanalytic psychotherapy of the couple link can help to recover the resources, contributing to a more satisfactory relationship and to further individual growth.

Mary Morgan presents us a classic case of difficulty in the couple's link, where disillusion, anger, and frustration are continually exchanged, whilst neither partner is prepared to admit the failure of a common project. We are not talking about the disillusion which follows the intense love phase described by Freud, where passionate desire is gradually displaced by a healthy link based on reciprocal trust, solidarity, and sharing. The link between Joe and Lucy functions as a defence against states of personal uneasiness. Even though it generates despair, it also protects against breakdown, which both fear facing alone.

Morgan describes how each member of the couple felt there was an absence of closeness, limiting their feeling of love and of being held. Joe was frustrated because he felt Lucy excluded him from her emotive life, so he felt alone. Lucy, on the other hand, felt Joe's attempts to express his sentiments were an intrusion, and perhaps it was. But Lucy also demanded the right to express her frustrated needs of how she felt, often feeling overpowered by his needs that negated hers. To all appearances it seems there was no room for two in this couple! Both admitted that communication between them was intermittent and conflictual.

Lucy found it difficult to resolve disagreements and conflicts with Joe as communication broke down easily, which Joe confirmed. In these cases a psychoanalytic couple psychotherapy is the indicated treatment in order to allow the patients to decide if each is to go his or her own way, to live his or her own life, and eventually continue with individual psychotherapeutic work.

The description of this couple gives me the impression of an anti-libidinal link (according to Fairbairn's definition), which generates frustration and despair, and strengthens the negation of having a libidinal life.

This introduces my second point: in a psychoanalytic couple psychotherapy, the link is the patient. People suffer individually from psychic suffering. However, relationships can generate suffering, or reinforce an existing suffering, or else relieve it, thus producing a beneficial effect. When we perceive that personal suffering is reinforced by the relationship, as in this case, we need to intervene therapeutically on the relationship. I am talking about the same consideration we make when we see families that generate suffering in their children and cause individual therapies to fail. With adolescents, we need to begin with family therapy in order to create a psychic space that allows the adolescent to move on to individual psychotherapy or analysis. If, on the other hand, the children are young, I prefer to follow the tradition of the Winnicott Institute in Rome and Psychoanalysis of the Couple and the Family (PCF), Rome, commencing with two parallel therapies: the child and the parents with separate therapists. In a family with very small children, a joint session is the preferred setting.

I would like to refer to some passages in Morgan's presentation that illustrate clearly how the task of a psychoanalytic couple psychotherapy takes on the suffering of both patients by intervening in their link.

In the first vignette Morgan gives us two elements on which to reflect:

1. The state of annihilation experienced by the analyst in the session faithfully mirrors the state of annihilation of the couple.
2. A shopping trip recounted by the couple shows clearly their incapacity to share their individual wishes or face conflict.

The analyst tells us she finds it more worthwhile to deal with the distorted way of communicating between the couple rather than the conflict generated by the shopping trip itself. Intervening on the modality of communicating is what I was referring to when I underlined the importance of considering the link of the couple as the patient: the state of annihilation felt in the countertransference addresses the analysis of the couple (the same way as it addresses the analyst in the individual setting), showing the degree of suffering and anger. Here we are not dealing with a conflict between two individuals generated by contrasting opinions or wishes, but with an extremely oppressive experience which is expressed by a modality utilised by both partners that cancels the possibility of existence of the other. Annihilation implies self-suffering.

In the second vignette we witness transference: Lucy involves the analyst in a problem of being "fair". The analyst's analysis of this as a couple collusion is crucial, because even though Lucy gives voice to the remonstrance, she is speaking for both partners who are convinced that to be "fair" is more important than to be themselves. In my opinion this is the crucial point of the whole therapy. We witness an unconscious pact between Joe and Lucy that shows how they utilise reciprocal control to withhold their anger, which on the contrary becomes intensified, but also allows the possibility to be curious, to express themselves freely, and to be alive to sex. This interlocking control causes a regression to pathological dependence, thus annulling the capacity for development in the individuals.

Now I will comment on the relation between curiosity and adolescence.

We have observed the difficulties Mary Morgan met with this couple. Each demanded to be listened to individually. Morgan cites Bion, who refers to curiosity as a tangible sign of wish that goes far beyond the need for survival, stimulating libidinal cathexis onto the mother and onto other objects, including the father. Curiosity, therefore is a sign of free libido. I found Morgan's thoughts on curiosity stimulating when she connects the lack of curiosity in this couple to the difficulty communicating with each other and their refusal to accept a third person, including the analyst.

Curiosity is not a psychoanalytic concept, but it evokes important elements, including the libidinal experience between self and object, becoming particularly important in adolescence, concerning the peer group and the opposite sex. The adolescent experience in relation to others constitutes an important possibility for transformation thanks to the widening distance of the link within the family, and because in adolescence curiosity stimulates a sort of self-therapy.

In a previous paper entitled "Intimacy, collusion and complicity in psychotherapy with couples", Baldassarre and I wrote:

> A couple can reach an affective and libidinally dynamic stability when it can build a bridge between the unconscious need for intimacy in the service of the self, to collusion as a socially necessary dual defensive organization. We define this bridge with the term complicity; some couples in treatment prompt us to highlight the adolescent subjectivization process, as an area of the adult mind that plays an important role in the dual dynamic process. In our opinion, the possibility that in time a couple can mutually acknowledge itself as a libidinal object for satisfactory sexuality can be ascribed to adolescent complicity. (Norsa & Baldassarre, 2007, p. 87)

It is important to pay attention to the adolescent phase when we are working with couples, because the adolescent process determines whether the individual is able to correct some aspects of childhood experience—in this case the aspect dealing with either abandoned and/or intrusive primary objects.

We ask ourselves, therefore, why Lucy and Joe chose each other: probably because they both identified with each other's problems, seeking self-therapy in their mirroring. Falling in love implies regression, which in turn gives each partner the possibility of accessing deeper levels of the other. When a valid experience of subjectivisation in adolescence is lacking, nothing can oppose the regressive dynamic. Instead of a healthy conflict between "me" and "us" we are dealing with fascination and/or terror of getting trapped one inside the other.

Joe's attempts at self-therapy in adolescence must have failed miserably. Joe's previous relationships were probably failures. What did he gain from those painful experiences? In what way did that experience unconsciously influence Joe to choose Lucy?

Lucy's adolescence, on the other hand is underscored by two important elements: her aunt and the new wife of her father. The aunt seems to be a negative model, unable to liberate herself from a chronic psychic illness, in spite of much assistance from her sister, Lucy's mother. Of the father's wife we know very little, only that she was able to do the opposite of Lucy's mother: maintain a stable relationship with the father and have children. Indirectly we learn that these experiences may have been important for Lucy, because her first job was to be a mother's helper, where she was able to identify with positive female aspects, until the father of the family started getting interested in her, so that she had to leave abruptly, once more in crisis.

In a paper on families and couples with history of previous marriages and relationships, I underlined two basic reasons why people tend to get married again: the repetition compulsion and the need to repair internal relationships (Norsa, 2014).

> The desire to remarry, despite the suffering caused by repeated separations, can depend both on repetition compulsion of previous traumatic situations, and on an increased self-awareness—what we normally call: "learning from experience", that drives us to a new sexual, romantic relationship … . Kernberg (1995) reminds us that divorce and a new marriage is a way of giving us a new opportunity to reach maturity: people share a period of their life with a partner and the following with a different one in a satisfactory way.
>
> Nonetheless, despite the desire to have new opportunities to grow, some couples are motivated by the urge of repetition compulsion. (Norsa, 2014, p. 110)

As Enid Balint underlined:

> Over and over again people come back to their failures in an attempt to remedy them … we could say that in marriage we unconsciously hope to find a solution to our intimate and primitive problems, particularly to those that we cannot communicate socially. (Balint, 1968, p. 41)

In Morgan's couple, repetition compulsion dominates. If earlier there was a libidinal tendency that sought to cathect the new object in the hope of transforming the internal relationship of this couple, there is no remnant of that hope here.

References

Balint, E. (1968). Unconscious communications between husband and wife. In: S. Ruszczynski (Ed.), *Psychotherapy with Couples* (pp. 30–43). London: Karnac, 1993.

Bion, W. R. (1959). Attacks on linking. *International Journal of Psycho-Analysis*, 40: 308–315.

Kernberg, O. (1995). *Love Relations: Normality and Pathology*. New Haven, CT: Yale University Press.

Morgan, M. (2001). First contacts: the therapist's couple state of mind as a factor in the containment of couples seen for initial consultations. In: F. Grier (Ed.), *Brief Encounters with Couples* (pp. 17–32). London: Karnac.

Norsa, D. (2014). Transformation through repetition of female and male representations in reconstructed families. In: A. Nicolò, P. Benghozi & D. Lucarelli (Eds.), *Families in Transformation* (pp. 109–129). London: Karnac.

Norsa, D., & Baldassarre, L. (2007). Intimacy, collusion and complicity in psychotherapy with couples. *Revue Internationale de Psychanalyse du Couple et de la Famille*, No. 2. www.aipcf.net.

CHAPTER SEVEN

Parental couple therapy

Daniela Lucarelli and Gabriela Tavazza (Rome, Italy)

As psychoanalysts of the Italian Psychoanalytical Society with interests in couple and family psychoanalysis, we present a clinical case here in order to promote the project of sharing theoretical approaches and examine ways of meeting patients and our methodologies so that our work with couples and families can improve.

Case illustration: Lidia and Paolo

We present clinical material from a family treatment conducted by Gabriela Tavazza. This family of divorced parents came to analysis requesting urgent help after Luca, their twenty-year-old second son, was hospitalised for a delusional outburst. For six months this young man had been perceiving his friends, and then his parents, as dangerous, able to enter his mind and steal his thoughts. The mother, Lidia, is a manager in the NHS and the father, Paolo, a high school teacher, both in their late fifties. Their eldest son, Sandro, lives with his mother, Luca with his father.

First interview

Lidia and Paolo arrive deeply upset. Luca has just been forcibly hospitalised following intervention by the police when he locked himself in his father's flat. They are overwhelmed, feeling they have done violence to their son. Suffering pervades the meeting. Both parents are almost paralysed, in a sort of stupor, annihilated by something previously unthinkable. Mother seems to need to contain her anxiety by providing, as if evacuating, a detailed description of the events. Father's gaze and body are immobile.

They say that in the past months some difficult events have affected Luca: the break-up with his girlfriend for alleged infidelity with a childhood friend of his, and his difficulties starting university. They admit they have undervalued Luca's persecutory way of seeing things, considering it a *"peculiar"* trait of his personality. They describe him as a sweet, silent child who never caused problems. They cannot recollect any meaningful negative events. On the contrary, Sandro, two-and-a-half years older, is described as difficult and demanding, and recently even more aggressive. In their narrative Luca stands out as *"lacking presence"*, for being quiet and undemanding, while Sandro stands out as *"excessive presence"*.

The analyst is struck by the guilt expressed mainly by the father for taking recourse in a damaging hospitalisation. He says: *"I would have never imagined I could do this kind of thing to him."* The session is filled with the loneliness of each member and the distance between them. Deep emotion emerges from Father's deep identification with Luca, while Mother controls her emotions.

The initial request for help seems unusual given that this couple separated over ten years earlier. Each had a new partner, suggesting questions to the analyst concerning the status of their psychic separation, the nature of their unconscious alliance, and, most of all, the quality of their relation to their children. What struck her in particular was the shared denial of warning signs in their son, and their difficulty in assigning a meaning to an event not representable in their minds. She feels that no parental couple able to give form to a "shared parenting capacity" was in the room, but rather two lonely persons, each talking of their son as if talking to themselves. Meanwhile the content of their son's delusion—aimed at both of them—seems to call them into question as a parental couple.

Luca's delusion was characterised by the idea that his parents could read and steal his thoughts. This made the analyst wonder if there was a colonisation of his self. Perhaps during adolescence, this situation highlighted Luca's inability to create individual psychic space.

Considering the unresolved situation of the parents' relationship, despite their divorce, the analyst suggested weekly analytical couple therapy, considering that Luca's psychotic symptoms related to the psychological relations with significant figures of his life and with the parents' fantasies. His pathology could be viewed from a transpersonal standpoint in addition to the intrapsychic one (Nicolò, 2005). Therefore she privileged work with the parental couple as requisite to Luca's recovery. Meanwhile, Luca was discharged from the hospital with medication, and started twice-weekly individual psychoanalytical treatment. The decision to propose couple therapy left the analyst in some doubt because the couple was separated. This concern remained in the early treatment until subsequent developments reassured her. The couple accepted immediately the proposal for conjoint treatment which lasted two years. The material below refers to the early treatment and illustrates the couple's collusive organisation and narcissistic appropriations from their children, while highlighting aspects of psychic transmission.

From the start, sessions were characterised by their concerns both about their parenting experience and their personal histories. Both engaged readily in self-reflection. The analyst's simple listening triggered reflections and narratives—more from Lydia—that occupied whole sessions, as if both had been waiting for someone to listen.

Progress of the couple therapy: a session from the second month

Lidia starts talking, and floods the session with emotional memories. During her first pregnancy, she prayed to God for the baby not to be a girl. The analyst learns that a baby girl would have recalled the tragic experience Lidia had with her own mother, who suffered the onset of schizophrenia right after the birth of Lidia's younger brother, although the diagnosis was made much later. Her mother's delusions led her father to separate and move with his children to another city. Later Lidia chose to return with her mother. Lidia recalls how she tried to help her mother and how she had always been considered as the cause of her mother's illness. Mother often said, "*It's your fault, you are evil.*" Lidia recalls fighting not to be overwhelmed.

> I carried on this commitment all my life. I was a rebel. I protested all the time but this was my way to feel alive.

Lidia associates her rebelliousness with Sandro's attitude—contrarian from the beginning. Sandro was named after his paternal great-grandfather, the first boy in his generation for both families.

Paolo, usually more withdrawn, now recalls how proud they were of the baby:

> He was mythical. We always took him along. He was always with us. He was an extension of us.

Later it emerges that Sandro was born nine months after his paternal grandfather's death due to a car accident that was later proved a suicide.

In early sessions, Paolo and Lidia were shy, cautious in being together again. They communicated mainly to the analyst, with little exchange between them. Their politeness masked fear of the re-emergence of the conflicts of their early separation. Their caution caused the analyst to wonder how much they needed to "sound out" her capacity for listening, and how difficult it would be to get near to their emergent infantile needs and the anxiety that they might drive their analyst-mother crazy.

Further development of the couple therapy: a session in the fourth month

After Lidia's first son's birth, she did not want more children. Despite using an IUD, she became pregnant with twins, but one foetus died at two months' gestation. She was afraid the other foetus might have been damaged, resulting in a malformed child, so she considered abortion.

> I was not willing to spend my whole pregnancy in bed, nor to change my life for this child. I did all I could to lose him.

Only in her fifth month, when the baby was declared normal, could she accept this new son. Luca was born normally but did not grow. For six months, breast feeding was not enough. But because the child was quiet, it took time to realise he was seriously undernourished. Lidia's narrative made it seem that Luca's birth was a biological accident in which his father could not play a protective role and she too failed to make him grow.

The analyst was struck by Lidia's lack of awareness of the emotional implications of what she said. She felt she better understood how difficult it was for Lidia as a new mother, and how this confronted her with identifying with her own mother with each of her sons. Lidia felt unable to maintain a maternal function because of her identification with a "crazy" mother, afraid to end up in a situation of need and dependence on an intrusive and persecutory object that would take her over, a persecutory internal object she still deeply hated. Therefore she could not identify with her sons' needs because this would put her in contact with her own infantile, angry, deprived aspects. Her experience of motherhood had been characterised by the presence of "not wanting a child", a wish that had been transferred to her by her mother and then transferred to her sons.

In a subsequent session Paolo suggested a similarity between Luca's quietness and himself as a child.

> I could sit still for hours in my mother's armchair listening to the classical music that she adored. Now I understand that this was pretty odd, but I didn't want to disappoint her.

Paolo discloses that his mother too was schizophrenic. His father hid this from him until one day he had bought the Rolling Stones single "19th Nervous Breakdown". This provoked a delusional fit in his mother, who accused Paolo of ridiculing her and humiliating her. Only later did Paolo learn that his mother probably started to break down right after his birth.

The scenario outlined by the couple's narratives allowed the analyst to identify a transgenerational dimension from three areas of inter- and intrapsychic functioning: first, the relation of each with internal parents; second, couple collusion; and third, transgenerational mandate in parent–child relations.

The couple based its unconscious link on unresolved psychic problems in each family of origin. In this phase of treatment, the analyst assumed a couple collusion concerning the denial and rejection of split-off emotions that could not be worked through at the level of disconnection. Each partner seemed to search in the other for resonance to his own family and individual traumatic "unthought known".

Now better understanding the parents' relation with their children, it seemed to the analyst that Lidia made narcissistic use of both children. Sandro represented her demanding and evil aspects fraught with aggression, while Luca, rejected in pregnancy and later in feeding, represented herself as rejected by her mother. Paolo also experienced his sons as narcissistic objects inseparable from himself. He said Sandro was *"their extension"* and that Luca was similar to him in being blocked and annihilated in front of his own mother's illness. The analyst speculated that the choice to have a baby right after Paolo's father's suicide could have corresponded to Paolo's need to quench the pain of a difficult mourning. Sandro represented a declaration of life, continuation of his kin (he was named after his great-grandfather) but being "mythical" he could not be seen as an individual.

The first signs of therapeutic change appeared in the relation between analyst and couple, then between the patients. They started talking to each other, thus integrating their memories, suggesting explanations of their past histories, and creating a new narrative as a couple and as individuals. Their communication became more straightforward in talking to the analyst. They seemed more certain that she was paying attention to them and more able to fend off infantile anxieties related to a lack of internal listening objects.

The narrative of their stories

In the next period of treatment Paolo and Lidia felt their worry for their children was contained. They began to own previously disavowed stories. In sessions, the narrative of one member triggered similar memories in the other. Now the analyst witnessed lively mutual exchange as they helped each other find themselves. Each was surprised to see similar aspects in the other. Each acknowledged psychic and sometimes physical violence in their families of origin. A memory of violence emerged as Lidia remembered that her mother had locked her up for a month, preventing her from seeing Paolo, then her fiancé, perceiving him as threating her relationship to her daughter. Her mother pressured Lidia, controlling her daily life and her thoughts. *"She came inside me,"* Lidia says. Similarly Paolo recalls how he was forced to leave his hometown for two years by his father who opposed his marrying Lidia, saying she was unfit for him. Their lives are portrayed as dominated by unforeseen events and delusional contents.

After a comment by the analyst on the presence of phantasies in both families that associated their births to psychosis in their mothers, they acknowledge the presence of unconscious experience of damaging their mothers by being born, and their own damage from the birth of their sons (Aulagnier, 1976, 1984, 1992). The sense of pending threat was also expressed in their description of the violent deaths in both families. Lidia's brother committed suicide by jumping out of a window shortly after Luca's birth, and Paolo described his father's suicide. This acknowledgment of similarities in their lives emerged along with the progressive lessening of collusion in their relationship. Only after the first year of treatment could Lidia and Paolo see the affinities on which their marriage was unconsciously based. Not even divorce had changed their unconscious link, despite each having new relationships.

At the beginning of the second year, Lidia began to consider deeper meanings related to the anxiety she felt during Luca's outbursts, and to acknowledge how this anxiety expressed her ever-present fear of going insane, damaging her children, and being damaged by them—all contributing to her fear of identifying with her crazy mother. Thus she began to build an independent self.

Paolo expressed having felt shame in his adolescence for his alcoholic father, and the humiliation of having to rescue him drunk and lost. He said:

> I always thought that I would never give my children the impression that I was fragile and needy ... so I did not want to talk of my experiences because I would have been moved. I did not want them to see me in that state. Even my mother's illness is not well known to my children. They only think their grandma is a bit weird. My sons don't know much about my family also because I did not want to tell stories I was ashamed of.

He had overlooked, disowned, or repressed aspects of his life, while Lidia had looked for "explanations" with an evacuative approach to painful aspects of her life, such as her mother's illness and her oddities, her brother's suicide, her own divorce. They had shared secrecy and not telling. The couple had always managed life through denial. An example was their divorce, which their children still did not understand. Lidia had told them: *"It is my fault, because I fell in love with another man."* With this answer she identified with the guilt assigned her by her mother. She had used a similar explanation with the analyst in an effort at being truthful, but actually blocking a search for more complex motives. The analyst kept an open mind because Lidia's statements seemed to block her thinking, making it similar to Lidia's and preventing more profitable reconstruction of events. On the other hand, Paolo's silence had seemed to indicate his wish to avoid his wife's pressure against letting his thoughts emerge.

The couple's relationship was based on a reparative consoling link. As Paolo said: *"We could only comfort each other."* Together they had fended off aggression and hatred while enabling each of them to leave their problematic families of origin.

The first dream in therapy

After eighteen months, Lidia acknowledged the changes achieved by family members. Sandro had left home and was more stable emotionally, and recently had asked to start treatment. Luca continued analysis and medication, showing more self-reflective capacity. The parents enlarged their parenting capacity. Appearing basically depressive, Lidia recounts her first dream in this treatment.

> I am on a totally upturned road, a dirt patch full of potholes and stones. Walking slowly, I realise the road ends on a chasm into which I risk falling. I feel suspended, dangling over the empty chasm. I look around and notice that on the side there is a wide, recently renovated tarmac road, looking as if no one has used it yet. I wake up deeply anxious about the risk of falling in the chasm.

Then she cries silently. Paolo tries to comfort her, saying the dream has a happy ending, but life is full of hurdles and one is often alone facing them. He recalls dreams where he felt he was falling but always woke before actually falling. Falling is associated to losing control, the impossibility to be "held", the fear of going insane. He associates the wide road to the therapeutic path and thinks that this means the possibility of a safer "road". Lidia listens in silence, then says she feels blocked by anxiety. Maybe it's true that today she has different options in facing her own and her children's difficulties, but her fear of falling into a chasm is still intense.

The analyst considered this dream as a couple dream due to the associations activated in both members, and representing the mood of both, on which their collusion was based (Anzieu, 1975; Kaës, Faimberg, Enriquez, & Baranès, 1993; Nicolò, 1994). It shows a common shared experience of traumatic lack of support, of feeling "not held", non-existence because of lack of support, risk of insanity and of "break-down" (Winnicott, 1963) that already has taken place.

The dream also shows Lidia's psychic state as changes in family relations deprive her of the defences she has used. The waning of couple collusion and progressive differentiation of the sons highlight the internal situation previously required by the defaults, excesses, and unpredictability of old maternal and paternal functions, and by the detachment Lidia induced to defend herself. She had previously protected this fragile and inconsistent internal state, a non-integration of the ego (Winnicott, 1965), through recourse to intrapsychic and interpersonal defence mechanisms. Paolo employed similar ones in the unconscious couple link and the narcissistic identification with the children. Now both parents could see much of this.

The road to therapeutic process provides a chance for subjectivisation that is, however, quite difficult to achieve. The work of linking and dependence on analysis puts the patients in contact with the original traumatic experience in which the interfering environment led to unthinkable anxiety (Winnicott, 1965). These defences were re-enacted in the transference, where they feared damaging the analyst-mother by driving her crazy and inducing her breakdown. The fear of falling into a chasm evoked the primitive agony of the failure of the primary maternal preoccupation they both had suffered, which was re-enacted in relation to their sons. This dream marked the birth of new capacity both at individual and parental couple levels.

Conclusion

Treatment ended by general agreement after two years. Lidia and Paolo felt they had been able to re-think and re-narrate their story, acknowledging its collusive aspects and the affinity of experience, such as the mutual comfort of their relationship at the expense of libidinal aspects. Things that had been impossible to say about their experience as children and impossible to think for their children, found a place and a narrative so that they could build a new parental "we" that had seemed absent at the beginning: *"we think, we feel, we suppose"*—a "we" that could acknowledge difference and give rise to otherness. Luca acquired reasonable emotional stability while continuing both analysis and pharmacological treatment, re-initiated his adolescent development process, and was able to graduate and begin living on his own. Sandro decided to start his own therapy. Two years after ending couple treatment, the analyst learned that Paolo had remarried, and Lidia started individual analysis and had improved her career.

Discussion of "Parental couple therapy" by Daniela Lucarelli and Gabriela Tavazza

Anna Maria Nicolò (Rome, Italy)

I wish to offer a model of psychoanalytical work with families and couples, using the case history presented by Lucarelli and Tavazza. I will consider 1) the psychotic family; 2) the dream in the couple session; and 3) the treatment model.

Our observation is not solely of the subject's internal world or of object relations between subjects and their projections, but also relations between persons that emerge in various forms during sessions. We see function based on intertwining mutual projective identifications, and on the relations these members build in time. Links are a third element co-constructed by members through interaction. Each member is at the intersection of links capable of influencing her, but at the same time she contributes to shaping these links. We focus particularly on the relation between the intrapsychic and the interpersonal, and on the convergence and interlacing of these two levels (Nicolò, 2003).

The psychotic family

Psychotic pathology is intrapsychic and transpersonal. We have to study links in psychosis at both interactive and fantasy levels. The features most in evidence are prohibition of thinking, absence of boundaries and of private space for the self, difficulty in subjectivisation and individuation/separation, and alienating identifications organised over several generations that characterise the original patient and the parents. This functioning allows the subject to by-pass her own conflicts by using the other person. These conflicts originate either in the subject's childhood or in transgenerational transmission, due to inability to elaborate and think about traumatic losses, persecuting experiences, primitive agonies, and to difficulty accepting devaluation and disappointment. When these cannot be expressed in open symptomatology, they find expression in types of relations that become indispensable for life, while the person attempts to balance issues of death, hate, and lack. The other person—child or a partner—then performs the economic and dynamic work the subject is unable to perform for herself, but then the person can never separate or become autonomous (Nicolò, 2006a, 2006b). In the fascinating case history here, each partner married in the unconscious hope of accepting and healing the traumatic sense of devaluation and disappointment caused by their relation to their mothers through the other. This prevented separation from their mothers, and had kept the marital relation in suspended animation, preventing both partners from constructing a sense of we-ness as they experienced the impossibility of separating or of talking to each other.

Such families are constantly suspended between the psychic and physical death, as for instance in the history of suicides. Hate for one's infantile parts is massively projected onto children who are not differentiated from oneself. We thus identify another feature of psychotic functioning: the presence of alienating identifications, those maddening objects (Badaracco, 2000) that enslave and parasitise patients' personalities from within. We hear that Luca's delusion is characterised by the idea that his parents can read his mind and steal his thoughts. Among other aspects of psychotic families, untold secrets typically determine contradictory communication between official and unofficial versions. Such double communication attacks children's identity by generating paradoxical situations in which each communication level opposes the other. We can picture this when we hear father saying: "*My sons don't know much about my family also because I did not want to tell stories I was ashamed of.*"

Dreams in family sessions

In couple or family therapy, we often hear dreams presented by one or more members. Then we not only have an expression of the internal world of one person, but we also witness a vehicle of collective functioning. The dream of a family member or a partner demonstrates one person's elaboration, and also allows identification of various modes of function, and of intrapsychic and transpersonal defences, showing how each person reacts differently according to their circumstances and capacity.

There are multiple uses of the dreams in couple sessions (Nicolò, 2010; Nicolò, Norsa, & Carratelli, 2003). Among them are 1) One partner may dream on behalf of the other, or to illustrate actions of the other; 2) Sometimes dreams presented by both partners in a session show complementary aspects, or collusive levels between partners; 3) One partner may dream the same problem brought or dreamed by the other, that, however, shows different defences, as in this case; 4) Dreams can also highlight rejected, dissociated, or split-off aspects in the dreamer or her partner, and in the relationship. The dream of a family member or partner can reveal content unknown to the other or to the dreamer.

In the session presented, we see one aspect common to Lidia's and Paolo's dreams: the fear of falling, losing control, becoming insane, and being annihilated. The fact that neither partner had had proper holding explains their unconscious motives for choosing each other. Lidia can dream because both she and her husband have found containment and reverie in the therapeutic setting. The dream itself provides a sort of dream-holding especially useful for psychotic families, as other family members lend their alpha function to the psychotic member, allowing him to symbolise unmetabolised beta experiences (Bion, 1965). Support to the psychotic patient who lacks the ability to mentalize, allows this function to emerge in an unconscious family matrix. It is as if the dream provided a boundary and can repair the dream screen to restore the inadequate function of a weak preconscious (Nicolò, Norsa, & Carratelli, 2003).

The treatment model

In such clinical situations, we have to decide on the best setting for effective treatment. It is difficult to engage these patients because they attack relations both in their internal world and in the therapeutic relationship. In some cases we might be forced to provide preliminary management designed to reach towards therapy. Patients do not always accept individual treatment, nor do families and couples always accept conjoint treatment. So we have to decide what setting is most viable and acceptable. These dimensions include the family's individuation/ separation capacity, the existence of some form of private space for the self. Individual or family treatment can be a first step for the other mode. I believe that an integrated treatment model is best. The core of integrated treatment is the creation of a working team, a third space made up of two analysts working on the same case with functions of integration and reparation. Referring to the case Tavazza and Lucarelli have given us, when the main mechanisms are colonisation, control, and parasitisation of the other's psyche, the creation of two settings—an individual one and one for the parental couple—can be useful independently from the creation of a third integrated setting. An individual setting allows for the creation of a private space for the self, free from intrusions, with a psychic skin for the individual patient. A couple setting allows for the establishment of healthy generational boundaries, and for work on existing transgenerational ghosts and psychosis-inducing relationships. In such situations we see a monstrous primal scene with a pre-oedipal, anti-oedipal, and anti-depressive incestuous functioning. The presence of an analyst for the patient and one for the family allows for the transfer of projections and investments from inside the family to a new unknown object, the analyst. Fortunately, this was not experienced by this patient or the couple as violating an unconscious deal with other family members.

Discussion of "Parental couple therapy" by Daniela Lucarelli and Gabriela Tavazza

David E. Scharff, MD (Washington, DC, USA)

Daniela Lucarelli and Gabriela Tavazza have given us the rationale for the work that the analyst Gabriela Tavazza conducted with the couple. This non-standard case is a couple psychoanalytic therapy of a long-divorced couple who sought help because of their younger son's psychosis.

My first consideration for discussion is the question of taking a divorced couple into treatment. The analyst made a decision to treat the couple because she thought the son's psychotic delusional system was aimed at both parents. She focused on intergenerational transmission of elements of trauma that had considerable impact on each parent, and on the couple, with the assumption that their interpsychic disturbances had influenced and continued to influence twenty-year-old boy, Luca, as he still lived with the father. It may be that the son refused treatment, so that treating the parents was the only option.

I would agree with the idea that the multiple traumata (the history of two suicides of the parents' parents, the boy as a replacement pregnancy for a father who committed suicide, the psychotic maternal grandmother who blamed Luca's mother for the grandmother's illness, and the parents' difficulty in wanting and loving Luca) all must have influenced Luca and been important in his character formation and acute psychosis.

However, from a family psychoanalyst's point of view, I wonder if the analyst might have considered seeing the son or both sons with the parents. Although Luca received both medication and, eventually, his own therapy, the treating analyst did not seem to consider the idea of a conjoint family approach which, it seems to me, might have been a better option. I find that when there are multiple and interlocking traumata, a family group approach is often most effective and psychologically economical. The authors think that Luca is affected by the interpsychic processes of a family that still maintained malignant links despite the ten-year marital separation, so the living link, the interpersonal unconscious ties in this family, are likely to reverberate among the four of them. That means to me that while the parents, separately and together, influence Luca, he and Sandro must also influence the parents through a mutual, complex group unconscious system of links. A family group approach would be more likely to place all these vectors in the room with the analyst.

Now, accepting that the analyst decided on a mode of treatment validated by the good outcome after two years of treatment gives us an opportunity see how she sees the progress and what interventions and ways of working seemed central to couple and family growth. I agree with the authors that the couple is the foundation of the family, at the cross-hairs of the generations before and after, and the link to the wider family and world. Therefore, it is often effective to treat the couple as a means of leveraging help for children, even grown children. The vivid description of the evolving process was compelling. From the beginning, when Ms Tavazza felt that the younger son Luca "lacked presence" and the older son Sandro showed "excessive presence" to the growing understanding of the parental couple, we come to see a portrait of a family in which two parents could not form a psychological parental couple because they were so narcissistically preoccupied. They could not "see" Luca (or presumably Sandro) because they were so caught up in dealing with their own intergenerational trauma and traumatic internal objects. This led each of them to intrude into the minds of their children with their own worries, and with the transgenerational imposition of alien introjects that they also carried. Lidia, the mother, had a schizophrenic mother who blamed Lidia for her illness. As a result of being hated and unwanted, Lidia was so afraid of damaging a child and being damaged by him, that she tried to "lose" or abort Luca. He failed to thrive in early months, and although no longer living with his mother, is still failing to thrive psychologically. She sees him as a new version of the mother who hated and blamed her.

Lidia's history and internal world join with Luca in a destructive interpersonal unconscious link. But it is not only with her that he has a malignant link. Paolo, the father, although less articulate in the early part of the treatment, has painful identifications that haunt him and his relationship with Luca. As the treatment continues, it emerges that Paolo also had a schizophrenic mother. This is revealed, as the authors tell us, because the provision of a holding space by the analyst (a crucial technical provision of the treatment) enables the couple to build new individual narratives. As each tells more about herself and himself, the other finds new parts of their history. We see that the parents' original bond must have been formed partly on the basis of unconscious identifications concerning suicidally depressed fathers and crazy mothers who blamed Lidia and Paolo as children. The authors tell us that this overlapping relation to each of their internal parents led to couple collusion and transgenerational projection of malignant objects into their children.

The term "couple collusion" implies that parents have destructive motivations. Generally parents do the best they can, even though they falter. I prefer to say these parents shared persecuting internal objects, and in attempting to defend themselves from feeling destructive, they project destructiveness into each other and into their children. Often the children projectively identify with the persecuting object, and through a combination of attempts to defend the parents from the harm children feel they might do, and attempts to defend themselves from fear and hatred, children enact destructive patterns. If we employ "because clauses" interpretatively, we could say, "You projected out the hate to defend yourself when you were unable to defend yourself against the hateful and fearful parent, and your child has had to do the same." This line of interpretation might have usefully augmented other helpful interpretations Ms Tavazza employed.

As treatment continued, the analyst saw how the couple's relationship viewed their children as narcissistic objects, and as she did so, the couple began to change. As the analyst grew a richer image of the couple in her mind, their capacity to work grew, because her mind became a container for growth that the couple took in. Then each of them grew an expanded mental container. This is a central element of psychic growth. Now, as one partner remembered previously split-off traumatic elements, the other was enabled to do so. In the place of a traumatic shared organisation, a generative organisation developed in the space shared by the couple. In couple analysis they grew a capacity to be a parental couple even in the absence of being a marital couple. More traumatic memories emerged, but now they became memories with meaning rather than being unrepresentable traumata. Now elements of more conscious secrecy also came into the work; guilt could be acknowledged and shared.

The paper culminates with the report of Lidia's dream, which I agree is a product of the couple (Scharff & Scharff, 2011). The couple then worked to associate together and to give the dream rich meaning.

This is the first time in the paper that the authors mention transference to the analyst. This is a crucial element in the healing power of analytic couple therapy. While I agree with the authors that "at the transference level there is the fear of damaging the analyst mother, driving her crazy and repeating the breakdown", I would have liked to hear more description of the transference elements of the whole treatment. For me, the contextual transference, the unconscious attitude of the couple to the analyst as an analytic parent, is central (Scharff & Scharff, 1987, 1991). It is in this crucible that early issues of trust in the environmental mother emerge for reworking. It seems to me that the contextual transference early in the treatment must have been quite fearful, echoing the couple's projective identifications of blame into each other. Reading between the lines, I see the growth of a sturdy, trusting contextual transference by each of the parents, and by them as a couple. This interactional growth of an unconscious link in the treatment itself, of the container it forms, has to be worked out in the transference/countertransference matrix.

Finally, the authors tell us "a parental 'we' emerged that had seemed totally absent at the beginning ... that can give rise to otherness." This elegantly summarises the growth of a process in the couple that is fully comparable to the growth of a sturdy internal container in individual analysis. The authors tell us that each of the family members showed signs of maturation and growth. It is such growth in families that encourages us all in the difficult work we do.

Discussion of "Parental couple therapy" by Daniela Lucarelli and Gabriela Tavazza

Timothy Keogh (Sydney, Australia)

Daniela Lucarelli and Gabriella Tavazza's paper represents a highly complex piece of work aimed at improving the matrix of relationships in the family and assisting in the recovery of the parent's psychotic son, Luca. It is transformative work, which allows new linkages among family members previously compromised by defences aimed at unthinkable anxieties.

The couple's presentation suggested to the therapist that the psychotic symptoms in their son Luca had relevance to unmetabolised experiences in the family and in the parents' families of origin, having transpersonal as well as an intrapsychic relevance (Nicolò, 2005). I would also like to consider the work from the perspective of Bion's ideas regarding psychotic and non-psychotic aspects of the personality, in the family as the patient. Such psychoanalytically oriented interventions should be able to take their place alongside others used with families in which there is a psychotic break in an adolescent (Asen & Schuff, 2006; Dixon & Lehman, 1995; Doane & Becker, 1993).

Bion suggests that the psychotic part of the personality arises from "a minute splitting of all that part of the personality that is concerned with awareness of internal and external reality and the expulsion of these fragments so that they enter into or engulf their objects." As a consequence, the psychotic personality constructs a universe of bizarre objects in which the person is unable to think and suffers existence in a state of hallucinosis. There are a number of psychic pre-conditions to this structure, including: "a preponderance of destructive impulses ... a hatred of reality, internal and external ... a dread of immanent annihilation, and, finally, a ... precipitate formation of object relations, foremost amongst which is the transference, whose thinness is in marked contrast with the tenacity with which they are maintained" (1957, p. 266).

In this couple I suggest that we see splitting and expulsion of fragments into the children in the form of narcissistic appropriation of the children by the parents, and projective identification into them as defences against unbearable realities, the preconditions which foster the type of psychic structure that appears to have existed in this family. The authors say that the couple cannot think and operates by "evacuating" unprocessed bits of their experience—what Bion would describe as evacuating non-metabolisable beta elements. The couple felt potentially annihilated by unthinkable internal experience. The parents have not been able to face the realities from their own families of origin, projecting particularly into their second son, Luca, who has lived with his father since the marital break-up and who, because of what he seems to carry for the family, has been seen as having "no presence". Luca's persecutory thoughts concerning his parents—especially ideas of being robbed of his thoughts by his parents—also give clues to the difficulties with individuation and separation in the parents and in the family.

The therapist ultimately discovers the detailed shape of the intergenerational trauma when both parents begin to be able to tell their stories of growing up with psychotic mothers and feeling responsible. The therapist comes to understand that they still live with this situation in their internalised self-object relationships. For both of them this has impacted their identifications with their children. Consistent with the need to manage unwanted realities in the couple's two children, there also appears to have been a split between the children: Sandor has an "excessive presence" and is aggressive and demanding, while Luca has been quiet and unproblematic until his psychotic break. The couple's, and particularly the father's, sense of melancholic guilt about Luca highlights the presence of unacknowledged damaged internal objects and associated realities that were too difficult to face.

In the early session material, we see how each child carries something for the parents with respect to unresolved traumatic histories. Sandor reveals his mother's rebellious characteristics which she developed as a means of surviving the blame for her own mother's psychotic illness (because she is "evil"). Sandor was also born in the wake of the unresolved loss of his father's own father. These factors shed some light on how he was seen by the parents as "mythical".

Later we find an ocean of disturbing experience dealt with by evacuation and projective identification. An intergenerational ghost in Luca has become the repository of this unwanted experience. Sandor, born after the death of Paolo's father, is also used to avoid the painful loss of Paolo's father's suicide. The authors add that the parents' lacked capacity for symbolic function. With the realisation that Paolo also had a psychotic mother about whose illness he carried unconscious guilt, it became clear to the analyst that a key issue in the transference was how to facilitate the couple's infantile neediness linked to a fear of driving the analyst-mother crazy. Referring to Bion's model, it is important to recognise psychotic and non-psychotic manifestations that needed to be understood and interpreted differently. The dominance of projective identification in the operation of the psychotic aspect of functioning is crucial to understanding these differences. The lack of symbolic functioning evident in the couple further alludes to the "developmental level" on which they operated. One aspect was their impoverished capacity to operate as a couple, as "we" rather than "I". Their omnipotent state of mind worked to keep at bay the experience of separateness. The intergenerational transmission of an inability to separate replayed in the marital relationship, and then in the parent–child relationships.

From this perspective, the decision to privilege couple treatment appears to have been vindicated. I nevertheless believe that it would be helpful to have heard more discussion about the nature of the therapeutic focus and the specific actions that allowed this couple to move from their initial psychic position. I wonder how the links to annihilation anxieties were managed.

It would also be helpful to know more about the assessment of developmental levels of the couple and the implicit match of treatment to levels of functioning. Such issues bear on matters of the identification of therapeutic action at different points in treatment. At first, in their most undifferentiated state, it appeared that the parents needed the help of the therapist in order to provide a psychic skin, or "*le moi-peau*" (Anzieu, 1985). At other times their presentation had a persecutory feel, which suggests the need for interpretation of splitting and projection that characterised family functioning. More saturated interpretations were presumably left until later when there was more ego function in the couple. Once the therapist was experienced as a solid container, the couple were able gradually to face their fear of the breakdown. The unthinkable became thinkable and individuation began. From the vertex of attachment theory, the family also could be thought of in terms of the unresolved losses and trauma that shaped disorganised or unresolved attachment styles.

I also wonder whether family sessions may have benefitted the children. We are told that Luca received psychoanalytic and psychopharmacological treatment, but would it have been helpful to Luca to hear about his parents' history and struggles to understand the legacy he carried. This also raises the issue of how we assume that changes in the parental relationships are translated into the parent-child relationship in older children who no longer live with their parents or live with one parent, or in a new situation.

In this case, because of the amount of raw, undigested trauma, both in the current family presenting and the family of origin, the facilitation of the holding and containing therapeutic environment represented the bulk of the early work. The transformative work moved later to a process of taking back projected aspects of internalised self-object relations.

In conclusion, this case eloquently presents a case for the utility of family and couple therapy when there has been adolescent psychotic breakdown. The case illustrates many of Bion's concepts and, in particular, his views about how a psychotic part of personality can form as a means of protecting against unthinkable realities. It demonstrates the relevance to the quality of thinking in a family in which a psychotic aspect is split off and located in children. It is important to collect such cases and to study their outcomes in a manner that forms an evidence base for this important type of intervention.

References

Anzieu, D. (1975). *Il gruppo e l'inconscio*. Borla: Roma.

Anzieu, D. (1985). *The Skin Ego*. New Haven, CT: Yale University Press, 1989.

Asen, E., & Schuff, H. (2006). Psychosis and multiple family group therapy. *Journal of Family Therapy, 28*: 58–72.

Aulagnier, P. (1975). *La violence de l'interprétation. Du pictogramme à l'énoncé*. Paris: PUF. (*La violenza dell'interpretazione*. Roma: Borla, 1994).

Aulagnier, P. (1976). Le droit au secret: condition pour pouvoir penser. *Nouvelle revue de psychanalyse, 14*: 141–157.

Aulagnier, P. (1984). *L'apprenti-historien et le maître-sorcier. Du discoursidentifiant au discour délirant*. Paris: PUF. (*L'apprendista storico e il maestro stregone*. Bari-Roma: La Biblioteca, 2002).

Aulagnier, P. (1992). Voies d'entrée dans la psychose. *Topique, 49*: 7–29.

Badaracco, J. G. (2000). Psicoanálisis familiar: los otros en nosotros y el descubrimiento del sí mismo. Buenos Aires, Argentina: Paidós.

Bion, W. R. (1957). Differentiation of the psychotic from the non-psychotic personalities. *International Journal of Psycho-Analysis, 38*: 266–275.

Bion, W. R. (1965). *Transformations*. London: Heinemann.

Dixon, L. B., & Lehman, A. F. (1995). Family interventions for schizophrenia. *Schizophrenia Bulletin*, 21: 631–643.

Doane, J. A., & Becker, D. F. (1993). Changes in family emotional climate and course of psychiatric illness in hospitalized young adults and adolescents. *New Trends in Experimental & Clinical Psychiatry*, 9: 63–77.

Kaës, R., Faimberg, H., Enriquez, M., & Baranes, J.-J. (1993). *Transmission de la vie psychique entre générations*. Paris: Dunod.

Nicolò, A. M. (1994). A chi appartiene il sogno del sognatore? In: *Richard e Piggle 2*. Pensiero Scientifico: Roma.

Nicolò, A. M. (2005). La famiglia e la psicosi. Un punto di vista psicoanalitico sulle patologie transpersonali. In: A. M. Nicolò & G. Trapanese (Eds.), *Quale psicoanalisi per la famiglia?* Milano: Franco Angeli.

Nicolò, A. M. (2006a). The family and psychosis: transpersonal pathologies. In: J. S. Scharff & D. E. Scharff (Eds.), *New Paradigms for Treating Relationships* (pp. 63–76). Lanham, MD: Jason Aronson.

Nicolò, A. M. (2006b). Folie à deux as a model for transpersonal disorders. In: J. S. Scharff & D. E. Scharff (Eds.), *New Paradigms for Treating Relationships* (pp. 77–85). Lanham, MD: Jason Aronson.

Nicolò, A. M. (2010). The dream as a bridge between levels of functioning in both the family and the couple. *International Review of Psychoanalysis of Couple and Family*, 7: 2010–2011, www.aipcf.net.

Nicolò, A. M., Norsa, D., & Carratelli, T. (2003). Playing with dreams: The introduction of a third party into the transference dynamic of the couple. *Journal of Applied Psychoanalytic Studies*, 5: 283–296.

Scharff, D. E., & Scharff, J. S. (1987). *Object Relations Family Therapy*. Northvale, NJ: Jason Aronson.

Scharff, D. E., & Scharff, J. S. (1991). *Object Relations Couple Therapy*. Northvale, NJ: Jason Aronson.

Scharff, D. E., & Scharff, J. S. (2011). *The Interpersonal Unconscious*. Lanham, MD: Jason Aronson.

Winnicott, D. W. (1963). Fear of breakdown. In: *Psychoanalytic Explorations* (pp. 87–95). Cambridge, MA: Harvard University Press, 1974.

Winnicott, D. W. (1965). Classification. In: *The Maturational Processes and the Facilitating Environment: Studies in the Theory of Emotional Development* (pp. 124–139). London: Hogarth.

CHAPTER EIGHT

A complex couple case*

Barbara Bianchini (Milan, Italy)

Giuseppe and Noemi

Stefano Bolognini writes about couples who seek therapy: "According to Bion, projective identification is the result of the child's need to rid himself of beta-elements which he is unable to metabolise and which, in order for them to be transformed into alpha-elements, require the presence of a containing mind that can accept, give meaning to and return them in a tolerable form. In this light, the request for therapy made by couples can also be read as an implicit request for a mind into which to evacuate, a container that can serve its primary function, that of containment." He continues that in such cases, there is a need for "a preliminary phase of constituting a container which can meet the couple's needs of evacuation and which can tolerate containing tension and excesses, allowing above all the experience of a receptive space" (Bolognini, 2008, p. 174). I will illustrate this process in the following case.

---

*This case was reported in *Couple and Family Psychoanalysis* (2014) 4: 56–68, and is reprinted here by permission.

Giuseppe and Noemi are about sixty years old and were sent to us by the two analysts who, in collaboration, treat their two adolescent daughters; the elder had developed a serious eating disorder in recent years and the younger presented psychotic symptoms that led to a breakdown and admission to psychiatric care. The girls' therapists had observed deep conflict between the parents, manifested in mutual destructiveness and a family environment of great confusion. They are both graduates with degrees in physics; he is a university professor, she a successful manager. They have been married for many years and had their children late in their marriage. It is immediately striking that two such intelligent and professionally successful people are so ill-equipped to understand and cope with such terrifying aspects of their daughters (anorexia and hallucinations). Noemi comes from a family that, before the war, was forced to flee its country of origin, causing a traumatic uprooting and a loss of identity and ties. This event represents very well her own identity: fragile and dependent and in search of a safe haven in which to finally find refuge. During the first years of their marriage she suffered from quite severe depression and was prone to panic attacks. Since then she has been taking medication for her condition. Giuseppe tells us of a childhood of poverty, marked by sacrifice and strict rules. He and his parents strove to acquire a better social status and he eventually graduated and pursued a good career. He presents a rigid personality of an obsessive nature, expressed in outbursts of anger and excitation. They are both only children and have invested in education and culture. Their relationship seems to be the result of mutual hope—for Noemi of the security to be found with a self-made man and for Giuseppe of the potential he saw in a woman from a different culture and the new stimulus she could bring to his life, a sort of compensation for all his previous efforts. Noemi was therefore profoundly disappointed to realise how uncompromising her husband was, and Giuseppe to find that Noemi suffered from depression.

When their daughters began to show signs of being disturbed they felt completely alone and unequipped to cope. Their disappointment in a relationship that had not lived up to their expectation was intolerable. When they came to us it was evident that their relationship generated only pain, from which Giuseppe defended himself by getting into a rage, and Noemi by isolating herself. The initial period was marked by Giuseppe's attitude of extreme disparagement and refusal towards the therapy and towards all those who were caring for his daughters ("*They*

don't understand anything, they're only in it for the money"); by Noemi's
continual denigration of her husband; by her sloppy appearance when
she came to therapy sessions; by references to a dirty and untidy home,
where nobody had his own bed but slept wherever there was the need,
where there were no fixed meal times. All these factors contributed to
an atmosphere of hopelessness, great worry, and preoccupation with
practical matters in the therapy session. The therapists felt impotent and
belittled, as if with frightened, hungry wolves. The couple's relationship was a succession of emotional bonfires onto which each of them
poured petrol, the purpose of their mutual aggression being to keep
something older, more personal, alive. In one particular moment of
rage, Giuseppe expresses the desire to go and "piss" on the grave of an
old schoolmistress, so intolerable were her educational shortcomings.

As in individual psychotherapy, the function of containment in the
couple is primarily one of sharing the meaning of what is communicated by the patients, for as long as necessary and sometimes for a
long period of time. The therapist's main objective is to ensure that the
patients know that their message has been received. In working with
couples this task is made more complex by the fact that the therapist
must maintain a non-aligned status (Zavattini, 2006), a balance between
the partners when receiving conflicting emotional states. It has been
observed that if this balance is achieved and both partners benefit from
an experience of containment, then the levels of conflict in the couple
diminish considerably. Each partner's communication, his stories and
memories, must be given equal value while attempting to abstract emotions from them.

After one year of working together, Noemi brings this dream to a
session: She finds herself in a big, untidy kitchen and has to cook some
live prawns but cannot find a pot the right size. She is speaking in her
native language in the dream and, for the first time, also speaks it in
the session. The therapists stress that the dream is about both of them,
recounting the difficulties associated with never having the right-sized
pots. It is noted that it is necessary to find a more suitable pot, a bigger
one, in which to cook the prawns (coarse, raw elements, beta elements)
and find someone who speaks a "mother tongue" in order to be able to
prepare good food.

Developing Ferro's theory and technique (Ferro, 2006, 2007, 2010),
we have attempted, through communication in sessions with Noemi
and Giuseppe, to draw out their emotions in order to restore a "mental

life" and trust to these patients who felt themselves to be failures as parents and who continually put each other down. Ferro speaks of the course of analysis as an "open operation" that is not continually "marked", where the content brought to sessions by the couple can find a welcoming space and room for possible development. Rather than through a decoding type of interpretation, growth is achieved through micro-experiences of being on the same wavelength as each partner in the couple, in such a way that the threads of emotion in the analytic field may be woven into a stronger fabric and thus allow access to more intense content.

Over the three years of therapy, they renovated their kitchen, creating more cupboards and storage space. Their elder daughter allowed herself to be admitted into a state-run centre and subsequently to a community, where she began to learn to be more independent of her parents. She returned home after one year and went to live with her grandmother, where she had her own room, then enrolled at university, where she started dating someone. For their younger daughter, they engaged a trusted tutor. The grandmother then went to live in a home for the elderly in a caring environment. When her death came, it was greeted by the family with great sadness but also with serene acceptance. Giuseppe tells us that he is doing consultancy work again for a client who appreciates and values him.

In one of their sessions about a year before the end of therapy, they both look extremely sad. Giuseppe lets us know that Noemi is gloomy and depressed; she feels that her husband constantly criticises her. For this reason she thinks, angrily, that she is worthless. She tells us that now that things are going better she has begun to feel afraid. She has had her first panic attack in a long time. She feels tired and would like to be able to go away, but realises she would not be able to cope on her own. The therapists acknowledge her depression and fear, and comment on the anger that isolates her and makes her passive. Noemi admits that in the same way as her husband gives vent to his rage by raising his voice and railing against the world, so she expresses it by closing in on herself, for example, by sleeping all morning, and in a lack of involvement in life that leaves no hope for the future. She recounts the disorientation she felt at a certain stage in her life when she realised she could no longer count on the support of her parents and, if anything, she would have to support them. She recalls how uncomfortable she felt as a child when she herself had to write notes to her teachers since her mother could not speak or write Italian, and how anxious she was about the stability of the family when her father lost his job and she had to contribute to the family budget by doing translation work. Long before she was even aware of the fact, Noemi had to support her parents but she had also inherited from them an important resource in the form of another language, her mother tongue. Their daughters' progress has now attenuated the feelings of being failed parents, which had caused them so much anguish, and they can recognise and appreciate their efforts and hard work. At this stage Noemi tells a joke, which reveals that she is much more in contact with her anger that, until now, she avoided by projecting it into her husband and retreating into gloomy apathy. She tells the story of the man who complains to the waiter about the poor quality of his food but then refuses to accept any other dish prepared by the chef in its place, however exquisite and inviting. He says, "No, I don't want them, I prefer to stay mad." "That's how I feel," says Noemi. "I'm afraid that I would prefer to stay mad rather than accept that things might have improved." Giuseppe says nothing but smiles affectionately at his wife, implying that this story is about him too.

Giuseppe becomes aggressive and incensed when his usual defensive obsessiveness, which he expresses through constant control and continual efforts to stem his anxiety, is no longer effective. Noemi sinks deeper into fatigue and boredom when her narcissistically fragile personality can no longer cope with the emotional turmoil caused by her pain. Their mental coupling can be represented as a hypertrophic content of beta-elements seeking to interact with an inadequate container that is unavailable because overwhelmed and therefore unable to function. During the course of therapy we tried to develop the relationship between the containing function and the emotional content that the couple brought to each session. Being aware of the imbalance between the capacity of the container and the excessive content, we realised just how closely related they were, coexisting in a state of mutual dependence. "[T]he function of the container can be seen generically for an individual ... to be able to *share* their emotional experience with another caring individual whose very act of *caring* acts to *circumscribe* the emotional moment ... the container's act of containment also presupposes that it not only translates emotional communication and transduces emotional volume or valence, but it also *withholds* some of what it contains, sometimes indefinitely" (Grotstein, 2007, p. 157, original emphasis).

We may see that within couples, and particularly in this couple, partners seek a receptive containing mind in the other that is able to accommodate proto-emotional states that cannot find a place or significance in their own mind and thus cause suffering. When this expectation of containment is continually met with disappointment because of proto-emotions that are too violent and/or an inadequate container, the therapeutic experience becomes first and foremost an opportunity for both patients to avail themselves of a receptive, containing mind. The transformational function and the development of the container-contained relationship come about in the presence of a therapist whose mind can communicate with the patients by using their own language as a "vector" (Ferro, 2006, p. 33). Through the observation and description of the facts, the therapist is able to highlight the emotional experience. Consequently, the connections, similarities, and differences observed help us to shift the vertex of each partner's personally lived experience to that of the other partner, to the ultimate benefit of the relationship. The therapists' intervention modulates the interaction between the two and aims to find the right "temperature" between the thoughts and feelings derived from the emotional experience of each partner. Through dynamic development of the emotional threads that constitute the container, space is created for new content. Noemi now has a more profound awareness of the emotional significance of her depression. When faced with difficulties, Giuseppe is better able to tolerate doubts and expectations without necessarily looking for reasons and solutions. They are both more aware of the complexity of their emotions. A greater capacity for thought and containment allows the development of new thoughts and an awareness of one's own emotions, benefitting the container, which, thanks to being so enriched, can now expand. We concur with Ogden (2004) in maintaining that this is what constitutes the development of the therapeutic function. Noemi and Giuseppe are more able to tolerate each other's need and to accept a partial and mutual dependence and consequently to grow in their capacity as parents.

Discussion of "A complex couple case" by Barbara Bianchini

Elizabeth Palacios (Zaragoza, Spain)

Our colleague's paper tries to show us the way she works analytically with couples following a post-Kleinian and Bionian theoretical point of view. Technically, she shows us how she tries to deal in the example she gives us of Giuseppe and Noemi following the notions of containment and types of projective identification in the transference and counter-transference field.

Giuseppe and Noemi show a narcissistic type of interaction. The unconscious election of partner seems to have occurred when the notion of thirdness was not installed. In this sense it is difficult to think of there being room for new subjectivity. Thus when new minds try to develop, they encounter important difficulties. This is what happens to the two daughters in this family, the elder having to cope with a serious eating disorder and the younger with psychotic breakdown.

The clinical material presented by the analyst is not fresh material in which we can see the interaction between the two members of the couple. It is an elaboration of the analyst. This makes it difficult for us to see how the interaction actually occurs in this case, and how the analyst has to deal technically with this narcissistic organisation, although we are told of these difficulties beginning in the indication of couple treatment because of the daughter's individual treatment, and after that when we are told of Giuseppe's and Noemi's refusal of couple treatment or any other version of treatment. All these indications make them aware of their incapacities. Their narcissistic woes are nearly unbearable.

Giuseppe and Noemi, both coming from difficult backgrounds, gained positions in life by means of a shared culture that functions as a means of supporting their pathological narcissism. The analyst describes how the couple kept together because they "mutually gave hope to each other" and felt their marriage as an opportunity to compensate for failures in their previous efforts in life. Nevertheless, the analyst feels surprised that these two well-educated people are not able to perform well in the emotional aspects of building a family. There is an implicit theory or ideology of the analyst (we all use them most of the time) in which good cultural performance and intelligence in this field makes us think that it should help in our emotional performance. Of course, this has nothing to do either with capability in the emotional field nor in bringing up emotionally healthy children.

The fact that Giuseppe and Noemi were together for a long time before having children shows us that children were not needed in the structure they initially constructed. This "mutual dependence on one another" shows us how they tried to complement each other from a narcissistic point of view with little possibility for thirdness. The narcissistic illusion of being one had already been challenged when they could not find completeness in one another, as, for instance, in Noemi's severe depression and panic attacks, which Giuseppe was unable to tolerate. The pathology in both girls and the need of many therapeutic interventions showed them that this narcissistic reward was unfulfillable, dashing their narcissistic illusion of completeness. The difficulties showed by the daughters as well as Noemi's depression gave them finally the conviction that the structure and phantasy they needed to survive was beyond their reach.

The analyst shows us in a first approach how she tries to build a container (the mind of the analyst) into which this ill couple can put their mental function, and where they can find significance for their primitive narcissistic functioning. As I understand the analytical process in these types of narcissistic structures in couples it is necessary, as an initial step, to build a new psychic space that can let us operate. If this is not possible, analytic therapy turns out to be another nuisance to the couple, and they do not accept the complication that interferes with the fulfilment of their illusion of narcissistic completeness. In this case, the analyst shows us how the therapists strive to build this new space, in which to be able to give birth to new psychic functioning: a container, a big pot, in the language Noemi brings in her dream (the analyst's mind), in which to give new status to their emotional complexities. The appearance of dreams as an outcome of the analytical work, and the possibility of using them to show what is going on in the couple's functioning, validates the idea that the analyst is accomplishing a good deal with this difficult and ill couple.

Discussion of "A complex couple case" by Barbara Bianchini

Karen Proner (New York, New York, USA)

Barbara Bianchini presents clinical material to illustrate the preliminary phase of a "transformational therapeutic relationship". She draws upon many models to conceptualise her work with this couple: Bion, Ferro, Zavattini, Ogden. She begins with Bion's model of the mind to understand the impasse in a couple in a family crisis, impelled to find a container to evacuate overwhelming emotions.

Giuseppe and Noemi were sent by the analysts of their two daughters. Both daughters had serious disorders and one daughter required psychiatric inpatient care. The parents were said by the children's therapists to "manifest mutual destructiveness and a family environment of great confusion". The parents are educated professionals, but emotionally "ill equipped to understand and cope with such terrifying aspects of their daughters' anorexia and hallucinations". We are told of their mutually traumatic backgrounds: mother as a child refugee, suffering loss, and father suffering the rigid fear of poverty (loss) as a child. Mother presented as more fragile and dependent, seeking a secure object. She suffered from panic attacks. Giuseppe held his panic together by the use of rigid obsessive defences that would break through with outbursts of anger. They were both drawn to each other's anxieties and defences and both disappointed when they did not help with this family crisis of their daughters' emotional problems. The fear and pain, and, no doubt, guilt, of this family crisis brought the couple's characteristic dynamic to the surface: Giuseppe's rages and Noemi's withdrawal. In the beginning of treatment with Bianchini, Giuseppe denigrated the therapists (therapist and therapists seeing their daughters). Noemi denigrated Giuseppe, and neglected her body and family responsibilities. The therapist writes of the parents' preoccupying need to perform parental functions, seen as working out practical matters. However, hopelessness and impotence were conveyed in the transference. My own thought was of refugees overwhelmed by a new place or parents overwhelmed by the impotence of poverty. The primitiveness of these parents' anxieties came through when Bianchini writes of her countertransference: "the therapist felt impotent and belittled … as if with frightened hungry wolves." She understood further that their relationship of emotional bonfires onto which each of them poured petrol was employed in order to keep something personal alive—something from infantile days. The primitive nature of both Giuseppe and Naomi's anxieties are felt as a pack of frightened hungry wolves by the therapist. The emotional tenor of this couple is manifest through their aggression, the purpose of which is to keep something alive. This reminds one of Rosenfeld's ideas of "destructive narcissism". How, then, can one create a container for both members? The couple's intractable infantile need to keep the status quo may be the first task of understanding for the couple's therapist.

Bianchini turns to Zavattini, who brings some technical light to this situation. Non-alignment suggests that the therapist's balanced identification with both partners conflicting emotional states will result in diminishing the levels of conflict. She also emphasises that for the container to function it has to have a quality enduring "for as long as necessary which can be a long time".

I have another thought that played a part even more than the balanced listening and receptivity: the therapist's awareness on an unconscious level of how their shared primary need was for things to "stay alive" by staying the same. I think this understanding of how overwhelmed, impotent, and useless these parents were feeling with both daughters problems contained their deeper anxiety. Dr. Bianchini' became aware that the family crisis had stirred up their individual unconscious infantile and childhood anxieties. The therapist was in an emotional "den of wolves" and "movement was dangerous". Bianchini emphasises that the therapist of a couple, as with an individual, needs to ensure that the patients know that their message has been received. I believe that if she did not receive this clear projective identification (in the transference and countertransference) and consciously understand the depth of their anxieties before knowing more about the content, perhaps Dr. Bianchini would not have been able to contain this situation. It would be interesting to hear how she responded to the couple's and individuals' communication during this time of negative transference—or perhaps one might call it a "preliminary impasse" which I think has a different quality from "resistance". Here we are in the realm of pathological organisations of Steiner and O'Shaughnessy, and the fear of change of Bion.

For the first year, Bianchini contained this couple's internal and external anxieties. Then Noemi had a dream of an untidy kitchen and has to prepare live prawns. She feels ill-equipped. There is no pot, that is, no container, and the idea that she does not have the right size is relevant to her speaking in her childhood tongue in the dream. One could understand that she felt like a young girl herself trying to mother her daughters. Bianchini understands how what has now found a way through to Noemi's symbolic capacity in a dream is her need for a container to process (cook) beta elements which are "raw", that is, infantile unconscious anxieties. The work Bianchini has done in providing a container has had its effect in Noemi's clarifying awareness of what she needs. I always believe these dream images come when they are already in the process of being established. Needless to say, the need for something comes when you have allowed yourself to begin to have it. I believe Bianchini has established a link between herself and

Noemi's internal maternal object. This, in turn, provides a prototype for a connecting couple who provides a space for their emotions to be safely felt, heard, and contained. Bianchini states that the best way to achieve this is through "micro-experiences", rather than the use of classic de-coding interpretations. These responses express incremental understanding.

It is interesting to note that as this couples' kitchen became modified and enlarged, the daughter was able to decide to separate and seek residential help. The couple is then able to work through separation and even the death of a grandmother. Father, in his new differentiated state, is able to value himself and to notice Noemi's depression, her withdrawal that expresses despair reaching back to her earliest days. In this new couple and family configuration of differentiation and separation, Noemi expresses a loss of internal support and, worse, that she now realises it is up to her to provide for both herself and her objects. She was aware of the loss of the old defensive pathological projective identification in which she managed to provide herself a kind of parenting based on resentful hatred of the inadequacy of her parents. This gave impetus to her ego in what may have been precocious development. A link is made to her anger with her husband. Then comes the profoundly relevant "joke". Now, years after the seemingly intractable beginning of treatment, she expresses her need to stay mad rather than to accept improvement. She would have to eat the good food. Does that mean she would have to give up her revengeful holding on to "bad objects"? One can make a meal of bad objects and the (preconscious) energy from revenge. This constitutes a moving moment of emotional understanding between Giuseppe and Noemi.

Finally, Bianchini speaks of the violent proto-emotions that are too much for the container. She understood that Noemi and Giuseppe both had violent unprocessed parts of themselves from "early poverty" and "loss" of the objects of their internal world, which generated unthinkable aggression. They maintained a primitive form of a container made up of intrusive identifications, rather than projective identifications, which have violence at their heart. Such a primitive mechanism does not seek a container in its entirety, because it is complicated by early states of frustration, envy, and rage. It damages the capacity of the container to function, while maintaining a kind of rigid intractable status quo, which Meltzer calls a "claustrum". I am left with thoughts and questions: Why was it Noemi who dreamt the dream for both of them?

She seemed to precipitate the move of the couple out of their rigidly held structure. Does this have to do with the way her defences were manifest? She seemed to use splitting off of her own destructive rage to remain in depressed, split-off, withdrawn states alternating with attacking through denigration. Perhaps this is a more controlled form of attack than her husband's attacks. His manner of explosive rage and relentless rejection seemed to act out and disseminate the violence in a wolf-like way that was not conducive of thought or symbolic function. He embraced Noemi's moment of truth about her rage and resentment. It seemed as if he were experiencing a "total situation" of being understood. I wonder if what Bianchini emphasises at the end of the paper is key in this movement in the couple. That is to say that this constitutes the "presence of the transformational function of the analyst" who can modulate the anxieties, as differences, similarities, and connections become clearer and more meaningful.

References

Bolognini, S. (2008). *Passaggi segreti Teoria e tecnica della relazione interpsichica*. Torino: Bollati Boringhieri (English translation: *Secret Passages: The Theory and Technique of Interpsychic Relations*. London: Routledge, 2010).

Ferro, A. (2006). *Tecnica e creatività. Il lavoro analitico*. Milano: Raffaello Cortina Editore (English translation: *Mind Works: Technique and Creativity in Psychoanalysis*. London: Routledge, 2009).

Ferro, A. (2007). *Evitare le emozioni, vivere le emozioni*. Milano: Raffaello Cortina Editore (English translation: *Avoiding Emotions, Living Emotions*. London: Routledge, 2011).

Ferro, A. (2010). *Tormenti di anime Passioni, sintomi, sogni*. Milano: Raffaello Cortina Editore (English translation: *Torments of the Soul: Passion, Symptoms, Dreams*. London: Routledge, 2014).

Grotstein, J. S. (2007). *A Beam of Intense Darkness: Wilfred Bion's Legacy to Psychoanalysis*. London: Karnac.

Ogden, T. H. (2004). On holding and containing, being and dreaming. *International Journal of Psychoanalysis, 85*: 1349–1364.

Zavattini, G. C. (2006). Lo "spazio triangolare" ed il setting nella psicoterapia psicoanalitica di coppia. *Psicoanalisis e Intersubjetividad, 1*, www.intersubjetividad.com.ar/.

CHAPTER NINE

Trauma and early enactment in couple therapy

Félix Velasco Alva and Delia de la Cerda Aldape
(Mexico City, Mexico)

Clinical material

As Freud said of chess, it is difficult to predict what is going to happen after the first move. That was our experience in working with a couple who attended analytic couple therapy. Suddenly, after four months, the woman cancelled by letter and did not respond to her therapist's telephone inquiries.

We will report on this couple's evaluation and brief treatment. We have selected sessions from different moments of the case, including the analyst's revelation of his fantasies and emotions in relation to the material as it shifted from session to session during the brief time that the treatment lasted. We held joint sessions, and sometimes individual sessions with either of them, most usually with the man who was willing to attend regularly but sometimes with the woman alone when she had changed the agreed appointment time.

Juan (age forty-seven) and Rosa (age forty-two) are of low socio-economic status. Juan is a plumber who has lost his job, and Rosa works sporadically when a job turns up. They came for therapy with Felix Velasco once a week, for a forty-five-minute session. We videotaped the vast majority with the couple's consent, and so we have reproduced the selected written material verbatim. At the end of each session we filmed the analyst's immediate impressions and have included those at the end of our description of each session in this case report.

The beginning

Rosa and Juan sought help in December 2012. Five months before then, they had separated when Rosa left the house after a big argument that ended in violence. Two months later, they divorced. Juan has openly expressed his wish to reconcile so that they can recreate their family life with their two children, Petra (age twenty-three) and José (age nineteen). Rosa, however, has been hesitant to return to live with Juan and rebuild their family.

In the initial interview, Rosa reported that, in recent years, Juan had been jealous and controlling. He continually questioned where she was going and accused her of having another relationship, because, he said, "she was more distant and remote". Their frequent arguments escalated until Juan began to attack Rosa verbally and physically, hitting her in the face in the presence of her daughter on a couple of occasions. This is what led Rosa to leave the house.

Since she left home, however, the same arguments continued constantly, now by phone. Juan pursued Rosa, insisting that she return. He accused her of having another relationship, and reported this as a fact to both their families. On one occasion he went to her house and broke the television and the phone and tore her clothes. On another occasion, Juan went with his daughter to ask Rosa to come back, but an argument ensued, and again Juan attacked Rosa physically. Their daughter had to intervene.

Juan said that ever since Rosa left him, he had lost his desire to work or even to live. Because he has stopped working, his economic situation has broken down. He said that he might as well take his own life. However, he has never attempted to do so, and so this appears to be only a threat.

In her individual interview, Rosa told us that she was the last child, with eight brothers. Their alcoholic father frequently beat their mother which resulted in several separations. During one of these separations, Rosa's mother got pregnant with her, and her father doubted that he was the father. She had been treated like a stranger. Both her mother and father beat her frequently.

Shortly before she turned fifteen, when her father was drunk, he forced her to have sex with him. He penetrated her with violence. She never dared to say anything because he threatened her. She and he kept this traumatic event secret, and to this day no one in her family knows. A year after this event, she met Juan and escaped for a life with him. She has told Juan about the beatings, but not about the sexual abuse.

I said I was surprised that something so traumatic had been kept hidden from everyone. To my further surprise, Rosa's affective tone suggested to me that she had dissociated and was not listening to me. I asked her if she had ever thought about how the rape might have affected her relationship with Juan. I added that it would be important to talk about it in the upcoming sessions. I was talking to myself because she was far from listening, much less addressing the issue in therapy.

Rosa's thoughts turned to the early years of the relationship which were often good. They were in love and sex was satisfactory. They went to work in the United States. There, their first daughter was born, and then they returned to Mexico with their daughter, and after a time back home their son was born.

Rosa said that about ten years ago Juan had a relationship with a younger woman. At that time he had thought of separating from Rosa, but this woman was murdered. So Juan returned to Rosa and told her what had happened. Because of this upset, Rosa went to individual therapy for a year, and during that whole time she still did not tell her therapist about the traumatic event with her father. She decided to continue the relationship with Juan. Another time, she caught Juan petting with a neighbour with whom he had said he had gone dancing. Even though he did not take her complaints about this seriously, she finally agreed to continue the relationship.

Juan said that, in contrast to Rosa's family, he comes from a well-functioning family. He had four siblings, a brother who died of a lung tumor, a sister who does not have much to do, and two brothers who live in the United States. His parents are the owners of the house where Rosa and Juan live. They reside in a city close to the capital, visit frequently, and stay for a few weeks in the house, because it belongs to them. Juan is the least successful child, and so his parents help him financially.

During the Christmas holiday, Rosa and Juan got together and later went out, had sex, and returned to discuss their relationship. She was ambivalent. She decided not to return to him. Nevertheless, they still communicate frequently by telephone.

Analyst's first impressions

In the first interviews, I gathered information about gaps in their different versions of their life, trying to be neutral, warm, and empathetic, and giving space to both of them. Although Juan was sorry for the violence to Rosa, he insisted that the reason for her departure and the breakdown of the relationship was that she had been with another man. She insisted there was no one. In sessions, she was firm in her decision to not return, but outside the sessions she used flimsy pretexts to look for Juan.

I had contradictory thoughts and feelings. On the one hand I felt angry hearing Rosa's description of Juan's aggression. I did not like the image of the jealous man who kept watch on his wife and assaulted her on two occasions, and justified his aggression. I doubted she ever had another relationship. I also thought about her ambivalence. In words, she did not want to return to be with him, but in action, she accepted his invitation, went out with him, and had sex. And they had involved their children in their fighting. He had allied with the children and had made them believe his version that Rosa had "abandoned" them by going with another man.

Initially I recommended they separate and no longer involve the children in their disputes. In my countertransference I wished they could return to being an integrated family, but I also thought that the degree of violence would preclude that possibility. When I was seeing them, I could not stop thinking about the fact that Rosa had been beaten and raped by her own father, and that Juan did not know this. Undoubtedly this played an important role in their conflict. Rosa recognised in individual sessions that Juan's aggression reminded her of the girlhood attacks, but when Juan was present, she kept the secret, so it was unavailable for couple reflection. Privately, I thought that if Rosa opened up on the topic of her violation in a couple session, it would help us all understand their current relationship.

Some representative joint sessions

Joint session of 25 January (almost two months after starting treatment)

T: What happened in December? I gather that you went dancing and had intercourse. Rosa, did you want it or not? Do you think of going back to Juan?

R: Well, I wanted to have sex because I was with him ... but then came the accusations of all kinds, like if I danced, how come I dance better than I used to, and why am I listening to that music? He annoys me. He pushes me.

T: So, you had to think again about going back?

R: Accusations and more accusations. [To Juan] So then forget about me.

T: [To Juan] What do you think of this?

J: She takes everything the wrong way. Everything sounds like an accusation to her. "Hmmm. You're dancing better." I was just making conversation.

R: So you didn't ask me who I was going dancing with?

J: It was just small talk. If you had been angry you would not have had sex with me. Well, hate me or love me, let's settle this. I don't want to be just your lover. She said to me, "Don't be surprised if I decide to have a new relationship" and before that she had denied having one! I thought she wanted to come back to me. *She* had looked for *me...*

T: Rosa, did you go looking for him?

R: I did not have money to buy medicines or food.

J: She is all about exploiting me. I know that there is no chemistry. She told me, "I don't want anything to do with you." Then, why go out dancing with me, if you hate me so? She sent me a message: "You treated me like a whore." So I took back my money, so she couldn't think that.

R: He didn't even give me the money.

T: [To Rosa] What did you mean by "another" relationship?

R: No, I did not tell him that. He simply asked me if I was with someone, and I said, no. He twists the words however he wants.

T: However, you did use the words "another relationship". There would obviously be jealousy about that.

R: Too much jealousy.

T: Don't you think that saying that would tend to be misunderstood? Juan, if you give money and things, you give them, but you cannot give and take away. But here's the main thing: These questions that you ask, like "Where did you learn to dance? Why are you listening to this kind of music?" and so on, lead to misunderstanding.

J: If these things about dancing bothered her so much, then why she was with me?

T: Ok. [To Rosa] Do you want to be with him?

R: [Smiling] Yes. I wanted to be with him, but then the criticisms began.

T: It's one thing to see Rosa wants to have sex with you, that she still likes you, and desires intercourse with you. But it is quite another thing to think that means that she would now return home.

R: Yes, but *he* said he wanted to end it.

J: No, I said definitively I do not want to play the role of "lover".

T: Ok, Juan. But then why do you invite her to have sex?

J: Because I want to know how she will react to the invitation.

T: Rosa, I understand that you are alone, and you were sick at Christmastime. Okay there was an invitation, but if you just say yes, it can be misinterpreted. Instead, you can say, "I am going to have sex but I am not coming back." Then he can say, then I don't want to have sex. Any move towards each other has to be clear.

R: Eight days ago, I went to see my daughter at Juan's house. I was talking with her. When I got home, Juan called me on the phone and bugged me with his questions, "Where are you? Are you at your house? Why didn't you say hello to me, and wish me happy birthday?"

J: You just ignored me.

R: He said "Where are you?" because he wanted me to see him and kiss him.

J: Why else would you go to my house?

R: To see my children!

(In this session, Juan and Rosa communicate as if playing a game of "telephone" where one repeats what has been heard in a distorted form. They each "understand" what they want to. Rosa provokes Juan's jealousy and he responds aggressively. I tried repeatedly to clarify the confusing messages. Countertransferentially, I felt more identified with

Juan, whom I perceived as the victim of Rosa's unconscious hysterical seduction leading to total confusion. She had been causing jealousy by concealing information, telling half-truths, giving double messages, suggesting and denying another relationship. On the other hand, I had a sense of powerlessness while trying without success to clarify and achieve some insight. I am starting to ask what role I play in all this).

Joint session of 1 February

T: Tell me what do you each want to do?

R: I want my children, I want to be close to them. As for him, I do not know. After his physical and verbal attacks, I don't know.

T: Juan, what do you want?

J: My family. To return to how we were: a whole family, living together. Everything is breaking up and it hurts me.

T: Each of you gives different versions of what happened. There are doubts, distrust, and confusion. You do avoid swearing and insulting each other now. We should work on clarifying the mixed up facts. I still do not understand why or when things go wrong. Rosa, the relationship that Juan had with another woman twenty years ago hurt you deeply?

R: It did. I was deeply in love with Juan. I went to therapy because of it. I was on my own [Rosa becomes very emotional]. I was in pain, but he was, too, at the death of this woman.

T: [To Juan] Was that so?

J: I felt guilty; I thought that she died because of me. I was cheating on Rosa, and on this other girl. It got very bad.

T: Rosa, do you think that he intended to leave you for the other woman?

R: Of course, I said that to him.

J: No. She will not believe me but, the most important thing to me is my family.

T: [To Rosa] Did you ever meet the other woman?

R: She worked in a bar. They met at a family party. A neighbour invited her. They liked each other, got in touch, and started to go out.

T: You have overcome a lot. You started living together quite young. You went to the States. Then you had the problem of the affair and got over that. Five years ago you got married. When did the relationship break down?

R: I worked hard along with him. I was helping him, and that was
    moving us forward. Then two years ago he told me to get out of
    his house. I thought, "Why should I make such an effort if he might
    kick me out at any moment?"

T: Juan, you say that she started to change.

J: She already had changed. My children and I asked ourselves, if she
    was not taking care of the house, not cooking, if she was unhappy,
    sad, and weepy maybe she was in menopause. We said, "What has
    happened?"

R: He said I changed. Supposedly I gained confidence.

J: Oh she had confidence. [To Rosa] Did you go out with those girl-
    friends? Did you go drinking?

T: See Juan, you apparently agreed.

J: I told her, "To me you are beautiful. You should go out with me,
    wear a nice dress …". She wore it, but to go out with her friends.

T: [To Rosa] It is undeniable that you like him,

R: [Laughs]

J: [To Rosa] Don't go with them, come with me.

R: My girlfriends and I were getting ready to go to the theatre, and
    at that very moment, he told me not to go. He was obviously
    jealous …

J: Then everything fell apart.

T: [To Juan] You and Rosa used to have a strong relationship. As far
    as I know, she was never jealous of you. But after your affair, you
    started being jealous of her.

R: He began to ask me where I was going, who was calling me.

T: Tell me more about what happened the day you were going to the
    theatre.

J: I said, "Do not go with them. Come with me."

R: Well I said, "Fine, we will go tomorrow." I stayed home and we
    began to talk.

J: She went nuts.

R: He grabbed me at that point.

J: No, I did not hit her.

R: He took me barefoot out of the bedroom. Then, I became distant
    with him. He started with the jealousy, invading my privacy, and
    checking my cellphone.

T: This went on for how long?

R: For months. Even when my friend had an accident and I went to see a doctor with her, he got angry and jealous.

J: She came back at one in the morning!

R: When I got home, he had locked the bedroom door. He wouldn't let me in. I asked, "Why you are so angry? If you have something to say, say it." Then he hurt me physically.

J: She exploded and said, "It's my house too!"

R: Then he grabbed me. He used his fist to hit me, and he kicked me. You do not understand how it affects me, because when I lived with my parents as a girl, I was physically abused. My parents did the same to me.

T: Getting beat up by a person is sufficient reason to leave that person. I hope you understand that. So then what happened?

J: Four months later, she comes looking for me.

R: Before that, he came to my home and broke my TV and cellphone.

J: Everyone told me that she was with someone.

T: You took your revenge.

J: Well not, really. I only pulled her up by the ear, in front of my daughter,

R: Yes, he wanted me to explain who I had been with.

J: She is lying. I went with my mom to ask her to come back.

T: Why did you go with your mom?

J: Because, my parents like her very much.

R: Then he tried to date Marcela, a friend of mine.

J: It was for revenge. I wanted to show her that Marcela was not her friend. It was Marcela who told me Rosa had been seeing someone, and that's why I broke the television.

R: Marcela kissed him before he got out of the taxi.

T: [Energetically] Juan, look how much you try to justify your aggression and infidelity! I believe that there is much more to clarify here.

(In this session, I felt angry and upset at Juan's self-justification for beating her, at his increasing jealousy, and at the fact that he acts as if he were entitled to everything while she is not. The rules of the game are not clear. Rosa has already mentioned twice that she was beaten as a girl and that the violence with Juan recalled this for her. I see her ambivalence. I begin to doubt that they will continue in treatment. I emphasise that this is only one chapter and that we can try to clear this up and move on to the rest of the narrative. Juan keeps justifying his jealousy. I am amazed at my countertransference response of scolding him).

Joint session of 8 February

T: Have you seen each other?

J: No, I have given her space. I believe it is already all over.

T: [To Rosa] What do you think?

R: Well, it is not true that he has given me space.

T: [Trying to reconcile] Well, I think as I mentioned the book is not closed. You just have to give her space.

R: Well, I miss my children, and I also miss the many years when we were living together and it was good [She is moved to tears].

T: What were the good things about living with him?

R: He was happy, he joked.

T: Do you feel that he changed much?

R: Yes, he changed a lot. [To Juan] I also have changed.

T: In what way have you changed, Rosa?

R: Not in the way he says. I used to go out alone on my own.

T: Did you go out together?

J: When I proposed marriage five years ago, we started going out together, and then she began to change. I began to depend on her to go out with me. I could not move one foot out without her. She was a very good woman.

R: He did not get along with my girlfriends' husbands.

J: We had a different kind of marriage than them. We got married young. Their husbands were elitist and talked about money. I don't have a profession.

T: [To Rosa] Do you see it that way?

R: No. He did not want to join me with my friends and their husbands.

T: [To Juan] Were you jealous of her at that time?

J: No, I did not feel jealous. She went out alone, and so did I.

T: Then why did you become jealous?

J: About her going out alone. I felt I was not her priority anymore. Then she stopped doing things in the house, so it exploded.

R: I did do the things around the house, but his mother and his sister took over our house, and I was not willing to tolerate that. I complained.

J: I told her: the house belonged to my parents, and they lent us money. They have their own bedroom there, and come once a month. My sister came every day to help when they were there. Rosa did nothing to help.

T: [To Rosa] Did your family visit you?

R: They hardly ever came to see me. I told him that his sister helped too much, but he did nothing.

J: My parents truly love Rosa. My father cried when she left.

R: I have seen my father-in-law as a father since I was sixteen years old.

T: Is there no get-together for your family?

R: No, really, they do get together. My parents are separated but living together.

J: It's bad when they are together—I feel it. They envy me. They think we have more money than they do.

R: I defend you, Juan.

T: [To Rosa] Your father-in-law loves you and you sound emotional when you speak of him, and [to Juan] your mom loves Rosa as well. How do you explain that?

J: I have been good with her mom.

T: Do you get support from your families during the separation?

R: Not really. His parents and my mom all supported Juan, because he told them that I had another relationship. My family did not approve. Now they are closer to me again.

J: When it came out that the accusations were false, her parents returned to see her, but she did not tell them where she lived.

T: Was that out of pride?

R: That's already changed. Now they come to see me.

J: They never see her, anyway.

R: I left my family to be with him. Now they are more calm about that, and I do see them. At first, they did not want to see me and only supported him. He just told my brothers a lot of bullshit. I resent them. I told my mom, "Although I deceived Juan, I was your daughter."

(This session seemed more productive, more reflective, with some signs of emotion from both. They were able to stay separated, but she was still clearly emotionally connected to him. For a moment, I had the fantasy that she could talk about the sexual abuse that happened with her father because in my countertransference I felt touched by both of them).

Juan came alone to the next session. Rosa sent me a message telling me she had to work, asking for another appointment. I tried to call three times, but there was no answer.

(After that, I reflected on my insistence on reviving the treatment and appealing to Rosa. I felt closer to her, eager to keep helping her, even though she was hiding things or blocking me from access to her private thoughts and memories. She was unconsciously "teasing" her husband and now me, using projective identification, by appealing for help, affection and concern and then rejecting it in order to make us feel guilty or helpless. Rosa saw my interest in her. Most likely in the transference she saw me as a man who, by showing interest, was threatening like her father. Similarly, her husband's approaches were initially accepted then quickly rejected, followed by her rapid getaway that repeated the escape that she made after the father's sexual assault).

Discussion of "Trauma and early enactment in couple therapy" by Felix Velasco Alva and Delia de la Cerda Aldape

Jill Savege Scharff (Washington, DC)

Many thanks to Felix Velasco and Delia de la Cerda Aldape for detailed process notes on a challenging case—one that ended in disappointment. It is not often the case that a presenter is generous enough to present such a case. Yet this one provides vivid material for our learning. The presentation details a joint and individual assessment process, and three sessions (25 January, 1 and 8 February) from a brief analytic couple therapy conducted over four months by Felix Velasco with Juan and Rosa, a separated middle-aged couple with grown children living in the family home with their father. As a teenager, Rosa had left her family of origin where she was abused physically and sexually by her violent father in order to be with Juan and enjoy a better life. Rosa and Juan were in love, their relationship was good, and so it continued while they conceived and raised their son and daughter. Ten years ago, Juan had an affair which ended when the woman was murdered, and yet Juan and Rosa's couple relationship survived this betrayal and its traumatic ending. Five years ago, Rosa and Juan married, and a few years later Juan became increasingly jealous, suspicious that now Rosa was the one having an affair. Rosa neglected her household duties, and Juan became increasingly controlling and violent, turned her family against her with unsubstantiated accusations of infidelity, and threw her out of the house.

Since then arguments continued, often with violence, because Juan wants Rosa to come home as his wife again, and Rosa remains apart. Rosa is ambivalent: she wants to be home with her children, but she cannot accept Juan's criticism, control, jealousy, and violence. Rosa had sex with Juan at Christmas, which proved to him that she was not angry with him, and he thought that if she could be his lover, she should be his wife again, but Rosa had sex with him only because they were together at that moment, not with the intention of reconciling, and she believes he is flirting with other women anyway. When Rosa visits their home, Juan thinks she is looking for him, but she says she is there only to see her children or to get money from him for food or medicine. In their therapy sessions, they say that they are separated but outside their sessions they pursue each other. After each of the sessions, Felix gives his countertransference responses and his thoughts about the couple and the therapeutic process.

The co-authors first direct our attention to the problem of abrupt premature termination of treatment. I will address the premature termination and the countertransference moments that seem most significant to me, and then turn to a few other issues concerning dependency, trauma, secrecy, and confidentiality.

The therapist, Felix, did not see the sudden ending coming. He was surprised when after a good session Rosa cancelled and erased his efforts to reconnect. However, there were already a couple of hints of a break in the commitment to treatment. In an early individual interview, when Felix learned of Rosa's rape by her drunken father, and tried to think about its being held as a secret from Juan, he felt that he was talking to himself, and concluded that she had dissociated. She cut off connection to him to avoid re-experiencing the traumatic memory—and the expected trauma of inquiry by a male authority trying to get close to her and penetrate her defences. This emotional way of leaving him stranded then got expressed in her more complete physical withdrawal from treatment, along with her retreat from Juan in unspoken ways.

In the session of 1 February, Felix deals with the doubts and confusion that stem from the couple's mutual accusations and ensuing violence and hurt. He becomes aware of their ambivalence about being together. He realises that this ambivalence may transfer to him, and threaten treatment. He already has the clue to the fragility of their commitment to treatment, but he must be erasing that from his mind when in the session of 8 February he is so surprised by the cancellation. I think this happened because his sense on 1 February that they might not continue with Felix is a reversal of his wish to be rid of them because they made him feel frustrated and powerless, so much so that he resorts to controlling the narrative progression. For instance, when Juan says calmly to Rosa, "What I do not understand is the relationship between my children and you", Felix does not join him in this inquiry towards deeper understanding, but asks "And then what happened?" and later he finds himself in a state of parental exasperation, scolding the couple, rather than confronting them with his helplessness and fears of being abandoned.

The influence of the secret

Over the months, the story of the beatings and rape by Rosa's father stayed on Felix's mind as key to the couple's problems, but he had learned of them in an individual interview with Rosa who cannot acknowledge their impact in couple sessions. Felix thought opening up that topic would relieve the couple of the need to enact it in their relationship, in which Rosa had sex with a violent man on whom she was dependent. But he could not find a way to do so, because it remained a secret (I will return to the problem of confidentiality in couple therapy). Although Felix did not open up that topic, Rosa may have held unconscious awareness of his interest in exploring it. When he pressed Rosa on the need for family connection, he encountered her resentment, and later her total elimination of him despite his attempts.

Shifting countertransferences

The co-authors describe the therapist's contradictory and shifting countertransferences, which echo the ambivalence and confusion generated in the couple. In the first session (25 January), the therapist recognises discrepancies in their stories. Felix usefully clarifies Rosa's message concerning her intentions towards Juan, but the couple's response to his clarification drives him to attempt greater clarity by prescribing words for them to speak. In identification with the couple, Felix wishes they could resume as a family (Juan's wish), but, worried about violence, he recommends separation (Rosa's apparent preference) and thus his actions belie his words (Rosa's mixed messages) and take the place of confronting the couple with the helpless frustration that they induce in him as they do in each other. In the second session (1 February) in response to the provocative and ambivalent couple, Felix has contradictory thoughts and feelings. He is partial to the wife as a victim of aggression, and does not believe she has been cheating on Juan, yet he is puzzled by her mixed messages and provocation of his jealousy. Yet Felix feels angry at Juan for being aggressive and for accusing his wife unfairly in order to justify his aggression. In what would be the last session (8 February), Felix helps the couple recall the goodness in their relationship, He reports sensing a warmth and connection. He was glad the couple was clearer and more reflective, and he experienced a positive countertransference equidistant to Rosa and Juan. When Rosa cancelled peremptorily, Felix was surprised and upset, as if he had not had clues previously. Like Rosa dissociating from her history, Felix momentarily blanked out on the history of the treatment, and found himself rather insistently pursuing the couple through contacting Rosa, just as Juan does. Felix is deeply engaged with and attuned to them, and now he has to bear the pain of not knowing why they quit. He may well be right in thinking that Rosa experienced his concern and her growing feeling of connection to him as a threat to her safety and a potential sexual assault from which she had to escape by cancelling further sessions, just as she had escaped from incest by marrying young into another family.

Dependency

From an American point of view, dependency is a major issue. Rosa is dependent on Juan for money to buy food and medicine because her work is casual. Juan and Rosa's adult children are dependent on their parents (who are not at all dependable). In Mexican culture this may be simply a matter of family loyalty. But the dependency issue runs deeper than that. Unlike his more successful brothers, Juan is dependent on his parents who own the house where he and Rosa have lived.

In the 1 February session, Rosa exploded with anger at being locked out of the house. She said, "It's my house too!" True, she lives there but it is not her house. She has no claim on it except through her relationship to Juan and his parents. Juan is so dependent on Rosa that he feels that without her he has no desire to work or even to live. Part of their mutual attraction is based on fulfilling dependency needs to maintain ego integrity.

Trauma, secrecy, and confidentiality in couple therapy

Trauma and secrecy are huge factors in the couple's difficulty maintaining a stable relationship. As a couple, Juan and Rosa have to bear the cumulative trauma of physical abuse throughout Rosa's childhood, the single shock trauma of incestuous rape in her adolescence, the secondary single shock trauma of murder of Juan's illicit lover, and the cumulative trauma of Juan's increasing jealousy-driven violence against Rosa. Violence and aggression have been conflated. Felix understands that trauma returns in current relationships, whether marriage or therapy, that safety is a fundamental need and right, and that trauma needs to be opened up, talked about, and the pain of it shared, or else it will continue to seek expression by being enacted. But he does not confront the couple with the need to do this, because he feels trapped in the secret. This is a problem often encountered when the assessment process includes individual interviews or the therapy is bent to meet with one member of a couple when the other does not show up.

If I need to see an individual, I make it clear to the couple that my commitment is to the confidentiality of the couple, not to its individuals. Then if someone tells me something that the spouse is not to know, I explain my commitment to them as a couple, so I cannot be party to withholding information crucial to their well-being. I do not, however, tell the secret. I give the individual time to come to terms with my position on this. I would work with Rosa on her blanking out when I am speaking, on her wish to dissociate from her history, on her fear of telling others about it. I would expect to prepare her for the revelation, and I would support her and them through dealing with the aftermath if she refuses, I would have to explain to the couple that I have information from Rosa that I am forbidden to share, and I would ask if Juan has any idea what it might be. Juan might think the secret I have been told is that Rosa is seeing someone, but I could honestly tell him that it is not. I believe Juan is correctly sensing Rosa's involvement with another man, and I would want to be able to show him that the man in question is her father as a traumatic object, continually rediscovered in Juan (only after the crucial change in their status from living together to being fully committed in marriage). But I would not want to "rape" Rosa by revealing the secret. If Rosa cannot accept my help to move toward discussing her abuse with Juan, while I know of it and can see it hurting them at every turn, I would feel disabled as their therapist. I would say so, and I would tell them with regret that, because of this, I am not able to help them (Incidentally I would not be surprised if Juan has suffered trauma too, and that he re-finds it in Rosa instead of dealing with his own history). I believe that speaking from inside one's own experience of therapeutic helplessness is paradoxically a powerful tool that is sometimes effective in re-establishing forward momentum in the treatment.

My approach to this couple in analytic couple therapy would be similar in some ways and quite different in others. Like Felix, I would listen and let the couple interact with each other and with me. Similarly I would talk with them about their daily life and make links to their histories. However, I would not make recommendations and teach them what to do. I would have to inquire more actively than Felix into the couple's culture and deal with my difference, not being Mexican. I would be more intent on gathering the couple transference to me and making interpretations concerning their feelings about me, and linking those reactions to their feelings for each other and their significant others. I would hope to use my countertransference as the basis from which to comment. I think I would come across as more confrontational as I aim to help them think about their experience of me, just as I will think with them about my experience of them. That said, it is hard to know if I would be able to work according to my ideal because I would want to follow the couple's lead and accommodate to their style of discourse and culture, and so I might find myself driving them away, and have to back off. I would, however, make that explicit. I would give a therapist-centred interpretation that I had allied with their defences because none of us is ready to do the hard work of thinking, understanding, and working for change. As a woman, I would have to deal with Juan's interest in flirting with me and Rosa's reaction to me as a representative of his other women (alive and dead). Now it occurs to me to wonder whether Juan was reacting to Felix's concern for Rosa and whether he told her to end the treatment.

Discussion of "Trauma and early enactment in couple therapy" by Félix Velasco Alva and Delia de la Cerda Aldape

Lin Tao (Beijing, China and London, England)

I appreciate Felix Velasco Alva and Delia de la Cerda Aldape's having offered such a detailed description of a clinical couple therapy, rich enough to promote deep discussion.

Before we start to discuss Rosa and Juan's relationship, let's make a hypothesis, a hypothesis about an oedipal wish which is kept as an oedipal secret. First, let's have a look at Rosa's father. Rosa's father always suspected his wife had sex with another man in conceiving Rosa. Perhaps we can think of this suspicion as Rosa's father projecting his unconscious oedipal wish to have sex with his mother onto his wife and an imagined another man. In the father's phantasy, the sex between his wife and another man symbolised the sex between his mother and him, and then he became the angry and punishing father, by which means he relieved himself of the fear of exposure of his own oedipal wish and he avoided fearful punishment. However, when he could not bear the intensity of his uncertainties, as well as his sense of being betrayed, he finally actualised his oedipal wish (and probably also Rosa's) by forcibly having sex with Rosa, which was so frightening that they both had to keep it as an absolute secret. We might find evidence for this hypothesis in the couple relationship between Rosa and Juan, through intergenerational transmission.

When Juan had an affair with another girl, we could see this as a kind of actualisation of their secret oedipal wishes (including Rosa's projection of her own oedipal wish). Then, the tragedy of the girl being murdered seemed to them to show how deadly it would be if the oedipal wishes were exposed and were secret no longer. Although we have less history about Juan, we still might see his fear of fulfilling his oedipal wish by the fact that he was unable to be successful, and needed his parent's care as though he were still a boy, as if he feared to show his phallic capacity, which he might treat as exposing his oedipal wishes. The death of the girl probably aroused deep anxiety in both of them in the area of their oedipal wishes. Juan seemed to project his oedipal wishes into Rosa, suspecting her of having an affair with another man. In this way, he put himself in his father's position, feeling angry at betrayal and carrying out punishment, relieving himself of deep anxiety of being punished (or even killed) due to the risk of exposing his own oedipal wishes. Rosa seemed to feel safer by continuously putting Juan in uncertainty, and by keeping secret her trauma of rape by her father. As a result, we can see that the shared unconscious phantasy of the couple seems to be the danger of the exposure of oedipal wishes. They tried to use defences of projective identification, keeping secrets and placing the uncertainty in the other.

After reading Felix Velasco's material, I also felt filled with uncertainty and even confusion, which seem to me to be the key words for understanding the material. For instance, after a period of a satisfying couple relationship between them, Juan's affair triggered a series of reactions between them. First, Juan had another woman and then he came back to Rosa after she was murdered, keeping Rosa in uncertainty. Then Rosa went out alone or with friends, danced, and planted uncertainty in Juan. It seems that if one carried the oedipal wish, the other is made to carry uncertainty. The couple could not contain this uncertainty as a couple. The failure of their defences might result from the unbearable intensity of uncertainty itself and the unbearable sense of betrayal. Then the one who is carrying uncertainty changes into a persecutor by rejecting or violent behaviour, just as Rosa's uncertain father changed into a violent and rapacious father. Therefore, their relationship was continually on the edge of breakdown even as they look for containment for these uncertainties and confusions.

We can also see how this couple projected uncertainty and confusion into the therapeutic space and into the therapist's mind, by means of which they defended against the exploration and exposure of their oedipal wishes). From the therapist's reflections on countertransference, we learn how he struggled. On the one hand, he tried to extricate himself by offering clarifications and questions. However the couple's answers always created more uncertainty. For instance, when Rosa answered the therapist's first questions at the beginning of the 25 January session, she said, "I wanted to have sex because I was with him", which is confusing to us as listeners. Again, when the therapist asked, "Did you go looking for him?" she answered "I did not have money to buy medicines or food". The therapist questions her relationship, but she answers about her relationship with money, medicine and food. Was she really looking for money through him, or was she really looking for him through money?

Later, when Rosa and Juan tell different stories, it is difficult to know who to believe. Facing the therapist's effort at clarification, the couple works hard to confuse him. The therapist reflects, "I have a sense of powerlessness, the more I try to clarify and achieve some insight. The results are poor, and I am starting to ask what role I am playing in all of this." Nevertheless, clarification remains his main line of approach. So it seems to me that there were two directions in the therapeutic room. The couple is spreading uncertainty and confusion, while the therapist is the one who feels uncertain and confused and carries on trying to clarify the confusion.

Rosa's sudden and unexpected dropping out surprises the therapist, who thought the session "seemed to be more productive, more reflective, with some signs of emotion from both". The therapist interestingly thought that she was "blocking me from access to her private thoughts and memories ... using projective identification, by appealing for help, affection and concern and then rejecting it in order to make us feel guilty or helpless ... she saw me in the transference as a man who by showing interest was threatening like her father, who beat her and raped her .... She repeated the escape that she made earlier after the traumatic event of the father's sexual assault." I agree with these thoughtful observations that Rosa felt as if she was being raped when asked clarifying questions. Such questions change the uncertain object into a persecutor. Finally, when the uncertainty became really unbearable, it appeared in the analytic transference-countertransference relationship. When Rosa felt she needed to put uncertainty into the other in order to defend against any exploration of her hidden oedipal wish, the therapist's exploration, questions, clarifications, and capacity to reflect were felt as a relentless attack on her.

At the beginning of the 25 January session, Rosa said that when she danced, she would get paranoid accusations from Juan. Here, it also seems that when Juan tried to get rid of those unbearable uncertainties through his questions, she had also felt attacked. So the therapist's questions had a similar effect on her. Therefore she defended herself by dropping out, thereby leaving the doubt and confusion in the therapist. When the therapist tried to clarify his confusion so as to get rid of his own uncertainty, she moved to avoid being exposed and attacked. We can see in this material how the couple provoked the therapist's uncertainty. His attempts at clarification had to be countered by the couple in order to maintain the situation dictated by their shared unconscious phantasy.

This prematurely terminated couple therapy gives a valuable example that enables us to see that our interventions—clarification, empathy, interpretation—cannot be treated as separate entities in clinical interaction, but should be perceived in the dynamic context of the therapeutic process. By making the therapist feel uncertainty and provoking him to ask clarifying questions, the couple recreated their destructive couple dynamics and deprived the therapy of time and space for understanding. This pattern constituted the couple's resistance through their forceful projective identifications.

Finally, I want to consider the effect of videotaping the sessions and of filming the analyst's immediate impressions. Based on the couple's history, I have inferred that one of the key traumas was continual damage through boundary intrusion. Videotape can form an intrusion into boundaries, especially in the early stages of therapy when the relationship is not secure. Videotaping makes unclear the boundaries between the inside and the outside of therapy. Things that happen inside the therapy can be accessible to others outside. In this way, taping might have meant to the couple a recreation of the traumatic situation. The unclear boundary between inside and outside therapy also might threaten the maintenance of secrets that is so important to the couple's dynamic. I also wonder whether videotaping and filming might have had some potentially difficult effect on the therapist as he prepared the case report. It might incite a wish to clarify, to get rid of uncertainty and confusion that was in parallel with the difficulties with this couple.

In this discussion, I have tried to understand how the couple's shared unconscious phantasies and defensive systems influenced both their relationship and the analytic relationship. The fear of the exposure of oedipal wishes, phantasies of consequent punishment or even being killed, the defence of projecting oedipal wish as well as keeping it secret, putting the other person into uncertainty and fear of a persecuting object—all these are main aspects of my understanding of this couple. Finally, I have conjectured that the very process of videotaping may have added another layer of boundary confusion and threat to the ones the couple already felt.

Discussion of "Trauma and early enactment in couple therapy" by Félix Velasco Alva and Delia de la Cerda Aldape

Caroline Sehon (USA)

Introduction

As through a camera lens, we access and bear witness to a cast of characters embroiled in a heated exchange between Rosa and Juan, a recently separated couple, along with their couple therapist, Felix Velasco. Many other players present themselves by their absence: Rosa and Juan's ancestors are embodied and expressed through their stories and unconscious dynamics. Delia de la Cerda Aldape is present as co-author; and the video camera itself symbolises a character in the field that captures evidence for an unseen audience.

We empathise with Felix, besieged by intense countertransference responses. The therapeutic setting threatens to collapse into a courtroom as Rosa and Juan hurl accusations, and render their non-guilty pleas before their therapist-turned-judge. Thinking about what each character brings to the couple bond generates hypotheses about each partner's contribution to their troubled relationship, and about their probable transferences to one another and to the therapist. We can then anticipate countertransference responses that may be induced.

Rosa

Rosa's traumatic history began when she was robbed of her birthright to know the true identity of her birth father in view of her mother's alleged affair. Hence, we would expect her internalised parental couple to be ambiguous and fractured. She witnessed physical battles between her mother and her alcoholic father that often led to separations. At other times, her mother colluded with the father, as they formed an aggressive parental unit and beat Rosa. Rosa was blamed for their strife and targeted as the cause of their infidelities. The only girl and the youngest of nine, and possibly illegitimate, Rosa perhaps represented an object of differentness in her family. At fifteen, after a lifetime of abuse, she fled her family and the father who had raped and threatened her were she to ever disclose his crimes. Rosa flung herself, like a child, one year later into the arms of Juan, who was only twenty-one.

This constellation would have etched in Rosa's mind a sense of self-perceived badness, recalling Fairbairn's discussion of the "moral defence" in which "it is better to be a sinner in a world ruled by God, than to live in a world ruled by the Devil" (Fairbairn, 1952) During the individual sessions, we learn that Rosa used dissociation to safeguard parts of her mind. A person who sustained this level of trauma would develop a more primitive personality organisation and have deficits in reflective functioning.

We could imagine how she likely formed an anxious, disorganised attachment to her parents with a complex, internalised combative parental dyad. Thus, she would have been deprived of a secure holding environment without opportunities for healthy development. Rosa would probably have left home invaded by countless encapsulated traumas that would be held in abeyance until they spilled into future intimate attachments. Therefore, a therapist would face considerable challenges and could anticipate that such traumas would later burst onto the therapeutic stage.

Juan

We know comparatively little about Juan's beginnings. We are told his family was more stable. It appears his parents remained together without an overt history of physical abuse or separations. He now has one sister and two brothers, and at some time lost one brother to lung cancer. An unemployed plumber, Juan was the least successful sibling. Juan, Rosa, and their two adult children, inhabited a house owned by Juan's parents. We might surmise that Juan remained childishly dependent in relation to his parents upon whom he leaned for financial support.

Such missing information carries meaning about unspoken life events, and inspires questions. We are not told about Juan's birth order, the nature of his relationship to his deceased brother, or Juan's age when his brother died. What can the unreported details of Juan's significant loss signify about Juan's own potentially split-off, unmourned, and traumatic loss? Why would a man from an apparently stable upbringing be drawn to an abused waif like Rosa? Might he have felt more substantial with her than with his own family? We are left to ponder unanswered questions about Juan's history, reflecting on the unconscious dynamics that possibly led Felix to refrain from asking questions or enacting a bias by under-reporting Juan's history.

The couple

Analytically, we are interested in the unconscious fantasies that attracted each partner to the other when they first met. Each partner would seek the other to contain repudiated aspects of the self. Through projective and introjective identification, the couple could hope to strengthen their mutual attachment and to repair their broken selves.

Underlying themes of violence and betrayal prevail within the sadomasochistic couple relationship. Perhaps Rosa found an opportunity to project her rejecting object relationships onto Juan as a way to salvage aspects of her mind and possibly heal from previous violent attachments. However, this could then lead Rosa to identify Juan as the aggressor through projective identification, and for Juan to enact the role of persecutor in relation to Rosa. Would he need to project his possibly unmourned loss of his brother onto Rosa as someone who will always be on the verge of leaving him, just as his brother "left" him prematurely and unexpectedly?

Juan depends for his very life on being with Rosa, conjuring an image of enmeshed dependency in which he cannot experience an autonomous, secure self, particularly at moments when Rosa expresses signs of individuation or separation. This dynamic would propel Juan to control her desperately and to accuse her of relationships from which he felt excluded. Complicating matters after their marriage, Juan suffered the loss of a mistress who was murdered, for which he blamed himself. His identification with the murderer of his mistress, and the projection into Rosa of his guilt could have left him at the mercy of Rosa as the aggressor or murderous object. This may be why Juan may have felt ever more on guard about Rosa's dealings outside the relationship prior to their separation.

Assessment phase

Prior to the treatment sessions, Felix conducted an assessment process in which he met individually with Rosa and Juan. This preliminary structuring of analytic couple therapy is an option often selected for high-conflict couples. However, this approach carries a risk that one partner may confide a secret in the couple therapist that will pose ethical and technical challenges as to whether, when, and how to make this secret known.

During an individual assessment session, Rosa confided in Felix that she had been molested by her father. In my view, this private revelation, held secretly, punctures the fabric of the couple therapeutic endeavour. The secret forms a private couple link between Rosa and the therapist.

Rosa might have had a split transference to Felix. He represents an idealised figure she could quickly entrust with her secret. Conversely, she might regard Felix transferentially as malignant, rejecting, and betraying. Felix would thus partially represent Rosa's father in the transference, leaving Juan to signify her abusive mother. Thus, Felix and Juan would form a perverse parental dyad in the transference.

This split-off transference confronted Felix with many technical challenges. He tells us that he felt constantly pressured to find a moment to support Rosa's unveiling her secret without betraying her confidence and retraumatising her. In the absence of finding such an opportunity, given the couple work's brevity, Rosa's parental transference to Juan might have been relatively unavailable for reflection.

At best, this secret represents a missed therapeutic opportunity. At worst, it poses a constant risk of an abrupt and premature end to the therapy that echoes the severing of Rosa's family ties. Somewhere in-between, we may view the unconscious split-off pairing between the therapist and one half of the couple as setting in motion a dynamic that continuously exerts a force in the analytic work.

Structuring the therapeutic journey

The couple therapy frame is firmly structured with a weekly and consistent, forty-five-minute session. However, the frame is also a flexible one—the therapist holds sessions even when only one member is present. Within the four-month couple therapy, individual sessions alternate with couple sessions. There is an unintentional bias in favour of Juan because Rosa often goes missing.

With such catastrophic trauma, departures from such a secure frame need to be judiciously selected and thoughtfully monitored, but flexible structure may fray the fabric of the couple setting, possibly inviting irreparable acting out, collusion between the therapist and one partner, and ultimate therapeutic rupture.

Video glimpses from the therapy

Through the ever-present camera lens, we gain glimpses into the couple five months after Rosa left Juan due to his unending physical abuse towards her. We witness couple impasse and frequent arguments. Juan's accusations concerning his wife's alleged infidelities had spiraled out of control, although we are told that Juan was the one with the actual affairs. Recently, he convinced his children that Rosa had abandoned them and him in pursuit of another man.

Rosa and Juan are adults in their early to mid-forties, yet we could just as well have been persuaded that they were teenagers. Time has collapsed: they were teenagers when they first met twenty-five years ago, when she was just sixteen, and he was twenty-one. Rosa says, "*He pushes me,*" and he counters, "*She takes everything the wrong way. Everything sounds like an accusation to her.*" Juan states, "*She is all about exploiting me,*" and she counters, "*He twists the words however he wants.*" Unable to listen and mentalize communication, each concludes with certainty that he or she knows what the other is saying. They are linked by sado-masochistic attacks—she torments him with seductive half-truths; he attacks her by controlling, forceful accusations and physically aggressive acts.

Two notable exceptions to this paranoid-schizoid mode emerge when Felix makes an interpretation to Juan: "*If you want to have sex, that's okay. What calls my attention is everything else ...*". About Juan's needling of Rosa, he says, "*You can ask anything whatever your intention, but given the circumstances, you're causing an argument.*" For just a moment, Juan could consider that possibility without perceiving the therapist as unfairly siding with Rosa. The couple momentarily assumes the depressive position and becomes more reflective in response to Felix's wondering about Rosa and Juan's families of origin, a brief reprieve from their entangled conflicts. We can see how the couple's violence induces feelings of impotence in the therapist. Although the therapist is aware of shifting identifications with each partner, he struggles to use this to serve the couple. Toppled from an analytic stance, the therapist is left often mediating, asking questions for clarification and giving advice about reducing ambiguous communication.

Rosa eventually abandoned the therapeutic venture, echoing her escape from her father and husband, re-enacting her life story of rupturing ties to bad objects. The therapeutic project was eclipsed before it began, in that the couple had not found a way to be and work together except through their aggression. The therapist's mind is plagued by unanswered questions, invaded by the trauma of Rosa's abrupt termination and by the immense suffering he witnessed. This premature ending evokes powerful feelings in us, as we resonate with Felix's loss of a couple who left before they could identify with their therapist's capacity to hold a couple state of mind on their behalf.

Reference

Fairbairn, W. R. D. (1952). *Psychoanalytic Studies of the Personality*. London: Routledge & Kegan Paul (With a new introduction by D. E. Scharff & E. F. Birtles, 1994).

CHAPTER TEN

Treating the family ramifications of sexual difficulty

David E. Scharff

M any years ago, Lars and Velia Simpson were willing to recreate their family life in the treatment setting, even in a video studio. Deeply concerned for their children, they brought an unusual capacity for looking at the interface between their own issues and those of the children. Lars and Velia came for treatment of their sexual difficulty, consisting of what she described as "I just hate sex", and what he described as premature ejaculation in which he lasted three to four minutes before ejaculation. Both had difficult histories. Velia's father had been emotionally abusive, and Lars' father had been discovered in a men's room trolling for sex when Lars was seventeen. He went to jail, and subsequently left the family for a homosexual partner and lifestyle. While Lars could remember almost nothing else of his childhood history, Velia described considerable sibling incestuous play and sexual longing in an atmosphere of family turmoil and deprivation.

In the initial evaluation, I asked about their three children. Eric, age seven-and-a-half, seemed relatively well adjusted; Alex, age five, seemed to be both anxious and hyperactive, with encopresis and enuresis both day and night; and Jeanette, age three-and-a-half, was not a concern. When I evaluated the family, I made a diagnosis of anxious hyperactivity for Alex, referred Velia for individual therapy for depression, and

Lars for therapy for depression following a life-long learning disability. The clinic was unable to provide couple or sex therapy, which was planned for later. Both Lars and five-year-old Alex proved to be rather refractory to individual treatment, while Velia's depression improved. Alex did however improve on stimulant medication.

A year later, I was now looking for a family to treat in the clinic provided they would agree to be seen in the video studio. I learned from my colleagues of the Simpson's continuing situation, and offered them both family and couple therapy, the family therapy to be done in the video studio. So approximately a year after I first saw them, we began with this arrangement while Velia continued in three- and then four-times-weekly therapy with the colleague I had originally referred them to.

I will give a brief summary of the course of therapy as background, in order to set the stage for the session that will be discussed by Drs Keogh and Moreno, and which they have viewed in the video version. In the first months of the family therapy, the oldest boy, Eric, now almost nine, was playing in a controlled way at being an "Incredible Hulk" with his brother and sister. Tension developed between Lars and Velia, and suddenly, in the children's play, Eric's Hulk lost all concern for others and rampaged. Velia immediately lost patience and lashed out verbally at Eric, saying she hated him for being like this. He collapsed in despair at his mother's anger. To my questioning, she was then able to say that his behaviour reminded her of her father, thoughtless and angrily abusive of others. But when she lashed out like this, then she hated herself because then *she* became like her father. Eric cried through this incident, but Lars was able to reach out for him and give solace, and yet to allow Velia to explore her own position of reading into Eric's behaviour the full force of her internal bad father.

This recurrent projective identification was one of the factors that had been pushing Eric into a bad and powerful male identification. It was also supported by the passivity of Eric's father, Lars, which stemmed from the same internal dread of powerful males. Lars was passive, sexually and characterologically, because he shared the internal assumption that an assertive male could only be destructive. Eric then took on the shared projection of the good and assertive male, which both his mother and father longed for him to do, but he also began to internalise their conviction that he could not be the assertive male they longed for without also becoming the angry selfish male they feared.

We were able to establish that Velia's fear of Eric's potential badness was a projective identification, and that it was her way of evacuating the badness of her internal father, which she then felt return through Eric's behaviour. This behaviour of Eric's began as ordinary childhood aggression, sibling bickering, or greed. But Velia habitually read it as confirmation that her father's self-centred abusiveness was reincarnated in her son. Angry at him for this incarnation, she then felt she became her father, harming herself in Eric. The cycle haunted her, and then she had trouble tolerating Eric because he was a persistent reminder of her struggle.

For Lars, Velia's depression and anger also represented a return of the repressed. He hoped to take care of his victim-self by refusing to be the aggressive man, only to have the aggression reappear in Velia. Further, his unconscious hope to grow a harmonious family and to do better by his son than his own father had done, also backfired. He, too, suffered the return of the repressed when he saw Eric and Velia in combat, and he was helpless, not knowing to whom he should offer solace.

In this session, Velia was able to express her anguish at finding her father in Eric and in herself. This allowed her to re-express her love and concern for Eric, while Lars could also find comfort through his helpful fathering activity. Relatively wordless and uninsightful, he nevertheless reached out to Eric at the same time as he gave solace to Velia. He tolerated her grief, and contributed considerably to the repair of an extremely painful moment. My therapeutic contribution let Lars supply the holding he had previously been unable to do, and so to build toward repairing the relationship between son and mother, which, for that moment, was the leading symptom of the flaw in the family's holding. That having been done, the family experienced a sense of repair, of forgiveness and love which could overcome hate.

Shortly after this session, Lars and Velia began couple sex and marital therapy with me while the family therapy continued. Over the next months, the family learned to work well in treatment, owning projective identifications, improving empathy, and supporting each other's growth. Gradually the sense of organisation of the family improved enormously. Well-constructed play and co-operation between the children replaced the sibling bickering and destruction in the play of early family sessions. Now the themes that remained difficult for the family could be seen and heard inside the play, in conversations between Velia and Lars, and between them and the children.

A year later in the sex and marital therapy, Lars and Velia had resumed a partial sexual life. She still did not experience orgasm but enjoyed sex. Their relationship had improved considerably. In a session just before the family session to be discussed, Velia reported recently remembering through conversation with her sister that her father had been physically abusive to her and her sister. This had prompted Lars to remember episodes of anal intercourse with his father and brother when he was twelve. The work in both couple and family therapy had been going along well. Then I was away for a scheduled two-week vacation. The following session, fourteen months after beginning family therapy, took place upon my return. It specifies the link between the adults' sexual difficulty and the children's issues, but this time not through producing such fundamental disruption as it did at the beginning of the treatment, but through a regression contained within the treatment. At the time of this session the children are two years older than they were at initial evaluation: Jeanette is five-and-a-half, Alex seven, and Eric nine-and-a-half.

The family met me as usual in the video studio—a fully equipped studio equivalent to a high-level television studio. They had come to know the crew and editors, who would play back portions of the session for the children when frequently requested to do so, giving the children delight.

Velia began the session, holding her head in her hands, saying, "I have a headache, and I don't feel like things are going well sexually between Lars and me. I feel helpless to change anything. And I have a terrible headache."

Jeanette, gesturing to her mother and demonstrating that she was building something to house a small paper airplane, called out, "Momma, look. I'm building his hiding place!"

I could not tell for some time, but later I thought Jeanette was introducing the theme of the destructive but treasured male who had gone away (the hidden airplane), and who must be captured and hidden. In my two week absence, I was being seen as destructive but longed for. I turned to Lars, and asked, "How do you feel about things?" Jeanette continued talking to her mother, rather loudly, "*No one* knows this is his hiding place."

Lars answered me, "I'm having problems with sex, too. Probably more than Velia." Alex was talking. I looked over, and said, "Are you worried that Jeanette will take all the blocks from that ship you're building, Alex?" Jeanette said, "I won't take all the blocks!" Turning back to the parents, I asked, "Are things worse since we haven't met in two weeks?" Velia said, "Yeah. They have been."

I noticed with dismay how depressed and disheveled Velia looked, and saw also that Jeanette was building onto her plane's hiding place. I asked Lars, "Were things worse for you in that period?" "Yes, they have been," he said. Velia, crying, continued, "We discussed it for forty-five minutes last night, and right now I feel it would be unproductive for him and me to do anything sexual 'til we've met with you next week. There isn't any progress, and then I get resentful. For the last several days, I've had the sensation that something was snowballing out of my control. I don't know what it is. I'm trying to put the brakes on, and I'm scared."

"Is it just in your sexual life, or are there other things?" I asked.

"Other things, too," she said. "I'm cutting back my individual therapy to two times a week. I feel it's the right time, but since I did it, I've felt terrible."

A few minutes later, the couple told me obliquely of two episodes in which the home sex therapy exercises did not go well. They referred to their sexual failures in non-explicit language appropriate to this family therapy context.

I asked, "Do you feel worse after the two of you had those failures?" Velia said, "I don't know if you could really call them failures. I feel worse after a period of stagnation."

Alex and Jeanette were playing with two dinosaurs that were climbing on top of each other. There was a sexual theme in the play, but it did not disrupt its thematic development. All three of the children were quietly engaged in organised play. Eric now took a space shuttle and bombed Jeanette's dinosaur.

"Oh, no!" squeaked Jeanette. The play continued with Alex asking, "What happens next, Jeanette?" Jeanette said, "Make mine be captured by yours." From the corner of my ear, it sounded as though their play represented an appropriately sublimated echo of adult sexual coupling with a theme of the woman capturing the man.

Velia continued, "I feel angry because I work so hard to learn to do something, and then he can't do his part, so nothing happens."

I said, "So you feel left high and dry?" I turned to Lars and said, "But you feel hopeless?" Lars nodded. "Yes!" I continued, "And you don't want to relate the difficulty to the time away from me, even though three weeks ago things were okay?" Lars said, "I'd say so." I said, "Something has fallen back." Lars said again, "I'd say so." I tried to lead him to make a connection, a link of the elements of his difficulty and my absence, something I now knew well was difficult for him as part of his learning difficulty. I asked, "Do you want to link those?" Lars laughed. Meanwhile, Eric was flying two toy fighter planes around in the air toward me. One plane was chasing another, making noises. I saw that the children's play on couple relationships was continuing, but, under Eric's influence, was getting more aggressive.

Now Lars responded to my question by saying, "Do you remember the problem I was having with my self-esteem? It seems cyclical, and it's coming around again."

I asked, "Does it affect just sex, or everything?" Lars said, "Well, that affects everything!"

A few minutes later, Jeanette and Alex were playing. Alex's helicopter flew away, and Jeanette's doll called, "Bye-bye-e-e-e!" She explained, "She's waving at the helicopter." "What are your two dolls doing in the bathtub?" I queried. Jeanette set me straight. "This isn't a bathtub. It's a boat! She's waving at the helicopter while she's driving her boat."

At this moment, Lars noticed that Jeanette's short dress was practically up at her waist, and said, "Pull your dress down, Jeanette!" Jeanette smiled. I noticed that this attention to a sexualised issue had occurred at a moment of anxiety about separation and sexuality.

Now Eric left off playing with the two planes in their dogfight, to intrude on Alex and Jeanette's game. Alex whined, "Eric! We're not playing with you!" Jeanette called, "Bye-bye! We'll see you tomorrow. We'll see you when we get home!"

At this moment, I felt drawn to the play. I asked, "Eric, what's happening? I see your guy is shooting down a lot of folk!" Eric nodded. "Yep!"

"Is he mad?" I asked. There was no answer. "What's happening with him?" No answer. He now crashed the plane that had been shot at.

"I see he crashed," I said. I had the distinct impression he did not like this moment of attention on his play, probably any more than his father liked my attention to him. I felt the play was going on in parallel to the adult conversation, so I turned back to Lars and said, "So your self-esteem is doing badly, but you don't want to link that to my absence?"

Lars said, "I don't feel like it is."

Eric picked up two planes again and repeated the chase. Seeing this, I felt I saw a metaphor for the danger in the parents' sexual life and for my pursuit of Lars in the session.

I said to Lars, "So you just feel empty? But I do want to link these things, Lars. It seems to me that we know that you can't make links, that's one of your troubles."

Lars nodded, "Yep!"

I continued the pursuit, feeling this was an appropriate time to confront his defence. "Since you have so much trouble making links, let's guess and see. You and Velia both feel hard-hit by my not being available the last two weeks, and you feel it by losing both your sense of self-worth and your sexual competence. I think that's linked to the sense of loss of your father as a man who supported your growth." I could see that Lars was nodding now, so I continued. "You didn't get help from him, and on the contrary, you said not long ago that when you asked him for help, you got something very painful instead." I was thinking about the sodomy his father committed on him, but did not want to say so directly with the children present.

Lars nodded. He seemed to be staying with me. Velia was looking down at the floor in continued distress.

Suddenly there was a dramatic snorting from the play table across the room. Eric was kneeling out of sight behind the table with a pink pig puppet perched on his hand.

"Snort, grunt, snort," he insisted.

"What's going on, Mister Pig?" I asked.

Jeanette joined in instantly. "We're going to do a puppet show." "All right then," I said. "Ask the pig what it's snorting about, will you?" Eric said, setting me straight, "He's a pig! That's why!" Jeanette and Alex went to the table, too. Eric's pig was devouring the magic markers on the table, chewing them greedily. I said, "He's sure eating those markers up. It looks like he's a hungry pig."

Eric said, in his best deep-voiced grunt, "That's because I am!" Velia laughed at Eric's puppet play. I continued to interview the pig. "What made you so hungry? Didn't you have anything to eat?" "That's right," said the pig. "I didn't have nothin' to eat." Eric was fully in role as the starving pig. "Are you mad about it?" I asked. "Yeah!" he exclaimed. Alex chimed in. "Here's another pig." Suddenly, Velia was no longer looking depressed. She said, "Eric's stomach ought to be pretty empty by now, because he emptied it on the way up here." I noticed Lars was smiling, too. The whole mood of the room had been transformed. "He was car sick again. The morning traffic on the beltway doesn't agree with his stomach," she continued.

Alex and Jeanette had now fully joined in the play. Jeanette, with the pink rabbit on her hand, said to Eric's pig, "Why are you eating my food?"

"Grrrrunt!" said the pig.

"He's eating my food!" said the rabbit. "Okay! I'll just eat his food!"

Alex, with a purple large-nosed monster puppet, asked, "Is there any hamburgers anywhere? Or not?"

The pig seemed to have devoured enough magic markers. "I'm going to take a nap. I'm tired from eating!"

"What have you been eating?" I asked.

Alex's monster answered, "Carrots! Where are the carrots?"

Jeanette's rabbit said, "I'll go in the house and see if I can find any carrots."

"Well, what do you think Lars and Velia?" I asked, turning to them. "Do you feel starved for attention for two weeks, from me?"

Velia said, "I can answer yes!"

"And you can't answer, Lars?" I asked.

Alex's puppet now attacked the nose on Jeanette's rabbit as he loudly said, "Honk, Honk!" I thought it was another comment on my "picking on" Lars.

"Stop 'honking' my nose!" said the rabbit.

Alex's monster said to Eric, "Don't eat her carrot!"

Lars now answered my question by saying, "My first impression was: 'You don't even want to think about it that much.'"

Noticing a kind of slip in what he said, that his idea really seemed to refer to me rather than to himself, I said, "You mean that I don't think about it much?"

Lars shook his head and pulled at his eyebrow.

Velia corrected me, "No, he means that *he* doesn't think about it."

"That's not what he said," I countered humorously. I was counting on their comfort with a teasing quality, which they used frequently themselves, both with each other and with me, to get this point across. It seemed to work.

Lars smiled at Velia, and said, "That's what I meant, though."

I repeated his words: "What you actually said was, 'You, meaning me, don't even want to think about it that much.'"

"Nyanh-nyanh, nyanh-nyanh, nyanh-nyanh!" teased Velia to Lars. "You got caught in a Freudian slip!!"

Lars grinned widely and hit her leg in a friendly retort. "I don't think about it that much!" he insisted for the record.

"That's true, too!" I countered.

Velia added, in therapeutic support, knowing how to get through to Lars, "But you don't think *he* thinks about it either."

Lars said, "I don't know about that. But I know *I* don't."

"But," I said, "You get down emotionally, and you stop functioning."

"That's true," acknowledged Lars. "I have more difficulty functioning."

"And you feel rotten, but you don't link it to the thoughts and feelings you have."

"That's right," he said.

At this moment Eric wandered off the set, over toward one of the TV cameras.

Alex called out, "Eric, where are you going?"

Eric said, "I just wanted to see what they are projecting on."

I was momentarily consumed with the pun on projective identification, but I kept silent.

Velia said sternly. "Would you get back over here!"

And Lars said with considerable insight for which I was grateful, "You just wanted to get us off the subject, huh?"

Now Jeanette joined in the diversionary activity. "Bumpity-bump-duh, a-bumpity-bump-bump," she sang to the tune of the *Star Wars* theme. And she took the pig Eric had previously used and marched off the carpet, and around the room, her heels loudly and rhythmically on the hard studio floor.

"So you think Eric is trying to distract us?" I said to Lars.

Lars answered, "He's been trying to all morning."

Eric whined, "I just want to see what they're projecting on."

Jeanette interrupted, saying to me, "Hey! I want you to have something."

As Jeanette and Alex brought some puppets over to me, I remained focused on Eric, asking him, "How have you felt during the weeks we haven't met?"

Eric rolled his big, appealing blue eyes under his blond hair, as if he had no idea.

"Stop imitating your father," said Velia. "You do too know."

As I put the purple monster puppet on my hand, I continued, "You know, Eric, I've been impressed that even though you get car sick on the awful, long ride here ... [here Eric nods his head vigorously] ... you keep on wanting to come."

"Uh-huh!" said Eric, nodding his head even more.

Jeanette now had the pig puppet, which suddenly giggled loudly, bidding for my attention.

"What's that pig laughing about?" I asked.

Jeanette said, "He's honking his nose." And she began to take the nose of the purple monster puppet they had put on my hand in her pig's mouth and squeeze it, saying, "Honk! Honk!"

Eric got another puppet and came in to join in honking the nose of my puppet with determination.

I looked at Lars and Velia, and said, "Maybe those two aren't the only two who want to beat me up?"

Velia laughed and rubbed her eyes. Jeanette was now using puppets on both her hands to tweak the nose of my puppet. It was a kind of orgy of tweaking.

Velia said, "I can laugh, thinking what if the kids tweaked *your* actual nose!" Lars said, "You love the idea!" I said, "That's right. And they wouldn't be the only ones wanting to do it, right?" Velia laughed, holding her head, reminding us of her headache. Lars gently taunted Velia, "Why don't you go over there and tweak his nose? Get it off your chest."

"No!" I said, instantaneously caught off guard, feeling for a moment she might actually do it. "Why don't you talk about it?" Immediately I felt foolish for acting as if she would join in the aggressive play. Later, watching the video, I understood it as a sign of the power of the projective identification in captivating me. Now, in the moment, recovering, I said, "If you could tweak my nose, maybe you wouldn't have such a bad headache."

Velia nodded slowly and laughed, "It's possible."

Jeanette interrupted, "Wheee! Ha, ha, ha!" And she and Eric squeezed my puppet's nose some more, as in a full-fledged torture. Then she took my puppet and marched victoriously around the room, singing, "Doopy, doopy, doopy!" as her footsteps rang again on the tile floor just off the set. Having completed her march of triumph, she came back to me and handed me a yellow dog hand puppet.

"Hi!" she said.

"What's up?" I asked, speaking for my new puppet.

She said, "I been honking someone's nose!"

"So I heard," I said. "Why would you do a thing like that?"

Jeanette answered, "Because he been mean to us, so we been mean to him!" I felt she had just made a marvellous transference interpretation!

Meanwhile, Eric was once again asking Velia if he could do something with the TV camera. I looked over at him and said, "Eric, you're having a lot of trouble seeing what we're projecting onto right here. What do you think about what is happening here? I think today you're upset. I can tell because your 'bad guys' started winning ..."

At this point, Lars grabbed Jeanette by the dress, partly to keep her from interrupting, and partly to tease her. "Hey! Let go my dress!" she insisted.

I continued, over the distraction. "And you know what else, Eric? I think the bad guys win when you're upset, and when your mom and dad are upset."

"No!" said Eric. "They didn't win. The good guys won."

"I saw that in the beginning," I said. "But later your two green planes chased Alex and Jeanette's planes, and they looked like they were giving them a heck of a bad time. I think that happens when people are upset in the family. And this time the upset began when your dad said he felt he couldn't function, and your mom felt she couldn't speak." I turned to Velia, "And you felt bad about Lars, and about decreasing the frequency of therapy with your individual therapist, and about not seeing me."

Velia said, "That sounds accurate."

I continued to Velia, "And also you're clear that you would be angry, too, if you weren't so low! And so you start laughing, feeling light-hearted, when the kids tweak my puppet's nose."

"Yes, it's true," she laughed.

"And Lars," I continued, "You do, too. But you can't make a connection or think about it. We just hear that when I'm not available you happen to fall apart for no apparent reason, without your even knowing you're angry or why you're upset."

Vella said, "I didn't recognise it initially, but it's easier for me to recognise it than it is for Lars."

"Is that true, Lars?" I asked.

"Of course!" he confirmed.

"Then in the family," I said, "as the two of you withdraw the kids start to react. Today we've seen the pattern in the play. The angry, bad characters start to dominate. That's what happens inside each of you. You feel taken over by the bad stuff. It used to happen with the kids getting disorganised and fighting. Things are better now, so we see it mostly in the stories of the play."

Alex was playing with a building made out of blocks with a helicopter inside. It reminded me of play with a fire truck in a firehouse in the first family session two years before. I had thought that play had symbolised the destructiveness of parental intercourse, because it had occurred as the parents were referring obliquely to their problem with "conjugal relations". Now in this session, Alex began to bomb the building with blocks as I spoke to the family. Then the helicopter emerged and flew off. Meanwhile, Eric was throwing the toy airplanes on the ground.

I said to Eric, "Boy, my planes are taking a beating. They're crashing all over the place. Eric, you do recognise those are *my* planes you're throwing on the ground, right!"

Eric smiled and said triumphantly, "Yep!"

"Do you think they deserve it?" I asked, knowing the answer. "Yep!"

"That's what I thought! So you're mad at me, too?"

"I don't know … it's just playing," he protested.

"I know you're playing, partly, But it tells us something. And that ambulance is taking a beating, too!" I added, seeing that now he had taken a slightly broken plastic ambulance and was slinging it around by its convertible top.

"No," he said. "It already was broken." Here Eric took the toy ambulance and rammed the block building that Alex and Jeanette were constructing together.

Alex protested, "Eric! Don't!"

"Sorry! I didn't mean it," said Eric perfunctorily.

"Eric, you did, too," said Lars.

"I did not!" said Eric.

"I wonder what it might mean," I mused, "since ambulances are associated with doctors?" Jeanette was saying to Alex, about their dolls, "They don't have a momma or a daddy."

I continued, "Any thoughts, Lars or Velia?"

Lars said, "I wouldn't know."

Velia said, "It's very clear, This ambulance-slash-doctor was crashing down this house that had been built up."

"You thought it was clear?" I asked.

"Yeah, when you make the connection between ambulances and doctors, it's perfectly clear," she said.

"I like the part about the 'ambulance-slash-doctor'," I said, laughing.

Velia blushed, and laughed heartily, holding her face. "I was seeing the typographical slash," she explained, as she sliced the air with her hand to demonstrate a backslash. "But, yeah, now that you point it out, it does have meaning: 'Slash the doctor!'" She laughed again.

Eric interrupted, "Dr. Scharff! Look!" He showed me his play.

I said, "That guy is dancing with a tiger, huh?" And looking at Velia, but speaking to the whole family, I added, "Well, if you're so angry, aren't there tiger-like feelings around just like that? But if you don't know you're upset or angry, then things just disintegrate in the family. And that costs everyone. This play and the session today let us see the repercussions, which ordinarily make you, Lars and Velia, feel worse because you feel like things are out of control. That's been the cycle."

They nodded. I saw it was the end of the hour, and said, "Well, we have to stop for today." Jeanette cried out, "No! No!" But Eric, for the first time ever, gave a gleeful, "*Yea!*"

"Yea?" I said.

"That's a new one!" said Velia.

"You've really had it with me, haven't you, Eric?" I said.

Eric giggled.

"I want to still play," said Jeanette, but she joined in cleaning up the toys and they all left cheerfully.

Discussion

This session demonstrates how a chain of influence develops, from the therapist to the couple, to their children, and to the whole family. Because the couple's difficulties were frequently organised around sexual issues, it was in their sexual functioning that they most acutely felt my loss. Clearly, there was a more generalised effect, however, which the children led the way in acknowledging. Their sexual setback, Velia's depression, and Lars' fall in self-esteem were echoed in the children's play, which resonated with the adults' themes more specifically as the session progressed, until the final play sequences when the children brought the play directly to bear on the transference loss of their therapist as the source in the here-and-now of their sense of loss and anger. Because this family was particularly adept at understanding play, they could use these events to further their growth of insight into the unconscious sources of their depression and anger, and to further their collective and individual growth.

The couple was able to complete their sex therapy treatment shortly after this session (conducted without the children present, of course). Each of the children had matured appropriately, and Lars had passed a promotional exam that had previously eluded him. They were able to terminate family and couple treatment with a sense of achievement. There is, of course, more to the story, but repeated follow-up over many years, instituted by Velia (in the studio at their request), allowed me to see the lasting effects of this family treatment.

Discussion of "Treating the family ramifications of sexual difficulty" by David E. Scharff

Julio Moreno (Buenos Aires, Argentina)

Generally speaking, family sessions with children are full of technical and practical specificities associated with the situations that arise. For instance, at least two ways of perceiving and understanding data will overlap. Adults (including an adult aspect of the analyst) tend to favour the ability to "understand" what is going on in the session by listening to participants' words, and to offer causal interpretations. For example, we may state as follows: "What is happening here has been caused by this or that historical precedent", or, "We are witnessing the repetition of this or that childhood trauma". Alternatively, we easily link what is happening to the transference situation.

Children, instead, are likely to resort quite clearly to a different mechanism based on what we could call grasping. They *grasp* the gist of what is taking place through an operation that I have designated as "connectivity". This operation is like a photograph that by-passes the meanings conveyed by verbal communication and resulting from association and thought. Still, connection can also encompass, bring together events that have taken place in the session and are part of the transference process or stem either from family history or from patients' relationship with the analyst.

There are two types of understanding: associative—mediated by alleged comprehension; and connective—mediated by grasping. The two types may overlap, and an inevitable, seemingly chaotic, succession of disparate productions may unfold that family analysts try to address as best we can. One way of doing so, which is sometimes deceptive, is thinking that we need to understand the cause of what is taking place in the session. Instead, we should patiently provide a holding environment without hastily intervening, and wait for the meanings generated by the links to emerge.

In this vignette David Scharff makes openly clear that his main key to understand the family dynamics is Lars and Velia's sexual life, marked by their individual histories of child abuse, resulting in sexual difficulties riddled with inhibitions. At the beginning of the session, for example, Velia states that she has a strong headache, and adds that she does not feel that things are going well sexually between Lars and her. Jeanette, who is five-and-a-half, shows her mother a kind of hangar where a plane can be stored. "I'm building a hiding place," she says. David remarks that later he thought that this statement could refer to a transference matter. Since he had been absent for a long time, Jeanette was alluding to her wish to capture him because he had been destructive (by going away) but also longed for. Still, David acts cautiously and does not offer an interpretation focused on these ideas.

Jeanette insists with her hiding place, and now claims that nobody listens, while David turns to Lars, who continues to talk about his problems with sex. We actually do not know the meaning of this hiding place that Jeanette insistently mentions. What has the girl captured? Could David's surmise be right? Perhaps this would be the appropriate time to say, "You were angry because I left you alone". Or maybe Jeanette was trying to help her complaining mother? Then, the interpretation could have been, "Did you want to help mommy?" Or, why not a reference to the fact that the daughter (and her brothers) require a certain degree of privacy, that hearing Lars, Velia, and David talk about sexual problems is disturbing and they want a hiding place? The interpretation, in this case, could have been, following Jeanette, "I want you to stop talking about sex", or something of the sort.

There is a third mode of intervention that David aptly uses: remaining silent and waiting (while providing a holding environment) until the meaning becomes clear. This is important, because the other interpretive lines could set the course for what unfolds in the session and/or inhibit link production. As David does well in this instance, though not in others, family analysts must tolerate uncertainty and not clog the session with hasty explanations in order to provide meaning.

Later on in this vibrant, turbulent session, so full of interventions and where different fronts coexist that are hard to address, something happens that is crucial, in my opinion. David was interpreting Lars's difficulties to make links between what is happening in the present and what happened in the past, or between his father and the analyst. In his account of the session, David also admits that at that time he was thinking of the sodomy Lars's father had committed on the patient (that is, he was thinking of the introduction of adult fantasies into the childhood world, a veritable confusion of tongues, in Ferenczi's terms, with real acting out episodes).

Suddenly there was a dramatic snorting from the play table across the room. Nine-and-a-half-year-old Eric was kneeling out of sight behind the table with a pink pig puppet perched on his hand. "Snort, grunt, snort!" Eric insists. David wants to know what the pig is snorting about. To David's question, Eric answers, "He is a pig! That's why." Jeanette and Alex join Eric at the table:

> Eric's pig was devouring the magic markers on the table, chewing them greedily. I said, "He's sure eating those markers up. It looks like he's a hungry pig."
>
> Eric said, in his best deep-voiced grunt, "That's because I am!" Velia laughed at Eric's puppet play. I continued to interview the pig. "What made you so hungry? Didn't you have anything to eat?" "That's right," said the pig. "I didn't have nothin' to eat." Eric was fully in role as the starving pig. "Are you mad about it?" I asked. "Yeah!" he exclaimed. Alex chimed in. "Here's another pig." Velia was no longer looking depressed. She said, "Eric's stomach ought to be pretty empty by now, because he emptied it on the way up here." I noticed Lars was smiling, too. The whole mood of the room had been transformed.

Velia remarks that Eric's stomach is empty because he threw up on the way to the session, and now he can be hungry. She laughs, and Lars smiles. David penetratingly notes that the family mood has shifted. It is as though the pigs and the snorting brought by the children had acted as an interpretation. And a very good one! These allusions to pigs, this disturbing confusion, are perhaps reinforced by the fact that everybody takes turns (in the game) to say what food he or she will eat, along with the comment about Eric's vomiting as a cause of hunger. What cannot be digested must be eliminated so that eating becomes possible—what is contaminated must be expelled in order to ingest. It is not an interpretation where causes are made explicit but a game introduced by the children in order to talk about the confusion that overwhelms them.

This sequence shows the emergence of something unexpected in a family session, an emergence that is always welcome. The children (or the parents) contribute an "unscheduled" interpretation that clarifies what is going on in a connective sense, that is, without pointing to the causes that tend to prevail in our analyst minds. (We think that everything that is happening can be entirely or largely explained by finding the cause.) Such an unexpected intervention can illuminate a crucial moment in the analysis. Perhaps the children are stating that this combination of sex therapy, family therapy, and private therapy is a matter for pigs. This development, as David's sensitive gaze clearly notes, has obvious effects on the mood of the session, which constitutes indisputable evidence of a good interpretation. Eric made it! Anyone else could have made it, but the analyst must have provided the adequate holding environment for this true analytic act to happen, and this is no trivial matter.

Bion's Grid and the selected fact: a commentary on David E. Scharff's mid-phase session of family psychoanalysis

Timothy Keogh

Introduction

The mid-phase session material with the Simpson family demonstrates the impact of the absence of their family psychoanalyst (occasioned by his break) on their psychic functioning. In particular, mother (who had contemporaneously reduced her analysis by one session per week) had become notably depressed and there had also been a breakdown of intimacy in the marital relationship. During the session the children provide rich play material, which demonstrates hostile/attacking feelings which the family has towards the analyst that appear to have been evoked by his absence. Technically, what we observe in the session is the analyst interpreting the family's transference to him and delineating its differential layers of meaning.

The analyst appears to operate on a theoretical assumption of the presence of an internal (unconscious) world of self-object relationships in the family, which are activated by their attachment to him and in particular by his absence. The therapeutic action is achieved by bringing into awareness (by interpretation) these relationships and taking the opportunity to restructure them in their new (transference) relationship with him. The session vividly demonstrates the value of the children's play as a developmentally specific and group variant of the free-associative process, which allows the therapist to have access to the family's internal world and moreover its unconscious dynamics.

The analyst takes an inductive (scientific) approach to the session material, which is informed by his countertransference. Each foray into making meaning of their seemingly inchoate presentation, with which the analyst is first faced, becomes the basis for progressing or discarding his implicit assumptions or allowing a "selected fact" to emerge (Bion, 1962a). This is essentially the same approach that I, as an Australian analyst, would take with such material, perhaps with a particular theoretical compass, which I will now describe and illustrate.

A theoretical compass for the session topography

Following Freud, both Klein and Fairbairn (the latter whilst eschewing instinct theory) described a psychic world structured in terms of internalised self and object relationships, which operate as unconscious templates for the experience of current, external ones. Bion (1962a) added to these understandings and articulated a model of mind and brought an understanding of how a mental apparatus, which facilitates the production of thoughts and thinking, is built up through a relationship with another mind. His model, which also highlights the importance of unconscious processes, suggests there is a level of raw emotional experience, which he calls "beta-elements", which, when not transformed by thought, build up and need to be "evacuated" or expressed somatically.

To transform these "beta elements" into thoughts, or what he called "alpha elements", requires a functioning mind. Such a mind, he argued, is one capable of linking thoughts together into thinking, which can help turn often-unbearable raw experience into tolerable thought. From this vertex, the psychoanalytic process can be seen to assist the development of a mind, which has a capacity to reflect on, and think about emotional experience, enabling it to be transformed and tolerated. Bion's Grid (Bion, 1963) summarises the processes whereby another mind can help develop these processes of alphabetisation and thinking.

The Grid consists of rows and columns (see Figure 1). The columns describe activities of the analyst (many of which are activities carried on in his mind) and the analysand's (or, in this case, family's) reactions, which can hinder or promote the transformation of beta into alpha elements and ultimately alpha functioning. The rows describe the development of thought to the level of concept and beyond. Pickering (2011) has previously demonstrated the value of Bion's concepts to couple work. Here I make a case for their value with family work. In particular, I am proposing to examine the Simpson family session material, retrospectively applying Bion's Grid to the analyst's interventions, in order to examine them in terms of movement within the Grid and to also see how a "selected fact" emerges through these interventions and the related underpinning implicit assumptions. I also indicate how my approach might have been different with such a presentation.

Applying the grid to the session material

Following a two-week break, the family present as flooded with beta elements, which are dealt with by evacuation (a Column 2 response on the Grid). The family is unable to think or reflect on their experience and is overwhelmed with these beta elements, in part expressed somatically (e.g., mother's headache and Eric's vomiting on the way to the session).

In the first sequence of the session, Dr. Scharff enquires if mother feels that the sexual difficulties she describes having with her husband have worsened since they had not been meeting with him. As an intervention, I see his question to mother as a Column D5 activity, given that it involves language but is still short of a conception. Mother describes her overwhelmed state as like things "snow-balling out of control" (describing a state where alpha functioning is absent). This leads to more inquiries by Dr. Scharff about whether other things have been affected in her life (D3). Dr. Scharff notes with father that things have been worse since the break and invites a link between the break and these difficulties. As an internal activity of the analyst, this constitutes a D3 activity; as an action with the family, it constitutes a D6 activity.

THE GRID

	Definitory Hypotheses 1	ψ 2	Notation 3	Attention 4	Inquiry 5	Action 6	...n.
A β-elements	A1	A2				A6	
B α-elements	B1	B2	B3	B4	B5	B6	...Bn
C Dream Thoughts Dreams, Myths	C1	C2	C3	C4	C5	C6	...Cn
D Pre-conception	D1	D2	D3	D4	D5	D6	...Dn
E Conception	E1	E2	E3	E4	E5	E6	...En
F Concept	F1	F2	F3	F4	F5	F6	...Fn
G Scientific Deductive System		G2					
H Algebraic Calculus							

Figure 1: Bion's Grid (1962b) reprinted with permission, Karnac Books.

Next, Jeanette in her play notes that there is a woman in a boat waving to the helicopter (revealing that someone—perhaps the family—needs to be rescued?). She exposes herself and is told to pull her dress down. Dr. Scharff then enquires about Eric's play, which involves someone shooting. Attempting to elicit unconscious affects in the family, Dr. Scharff asks, "Is he mad?" (another D6 activity). Dr. Scharff next suggests (to father) that he thinks there is a link to how he (father) is feeling and his (Dr. Scharff's) absence. Father says it doesn't feel like it is linked, from his point of view. This could be seen as what Bion (1959) has described as an attack on linking and in terms of the Grid, the response represents a Column 2-type reaction (evacuation). In such a situation I might interpret with father more tentatively and wonder about his reluctance to make a connection as perhaps an aspect of the family's resistance to a painful truth. However, I am also mindful that, depending on how such interpretations are heard, they can reinforce a sense of omnipotence and inadvertently lead to a greater resistance.

Following this sequence the toy pig is made to snort and Dr. Scharff turns his attention to this (internally a D4 activity and, in commenting on it, a D6 activity). He suggests that the pig is angry, and that this might be linked to his being hungry. Dr. Scharff thus tries to bring some meaning to the free-associative play of the children, initially by his internal mental work involving his noting (D3), paying attention to (D4), and enquiring (D5) what their play might mean. Following this Dr. Scharff uses the play of the children to make an interpretation to the parents: that they (like the puppets) may have felt starved for attention during the break (D5–E5). Mother agrees, but father, once again, perhaps representing the part of the family that wishes to attack linkages, says he is not sure. At this point I think I may have wanted to comment on the different responses of mother and father and explore this as perhaps expressing different aspects of the family's transference.

Following this, father uses a personal pronoun that reveals an unconscious thought when he says, "*You* don't even think about it that much." Dr. Scharff again notes that father will not make a link between his (Dr. Scharff's) absence and feeling starved of attention and again puts to him that there is a link between his absence and father feeling down. Following this, Jeanette starts singing the *Star Wars* theme, perhaps suggesting a battle of empires. My approach here might also have been not to insist on the connection but to keep wondering about the "constant conjunction of facts". Symington has noted that this important precursor to a selected fact refers to the phenomenon "when a number of facts or events are seen regularly to occur together ... [and that] the named constant conjunction is one of the facts that may come together and be given meaning with the emergence of the selected fact" (Symington & Symington, 1996, p. 99).

Next Dr. Scharff helpfully attempts to uncover the ambivalence in the family by commenting that, despite vomiting on the way, Eric still seemed keen to come to the session (internally D3 and in his action, D6). Eric confirms this. Dr. Scharff then makes a further significant interpretation about the family's anger towards him for being absent and their somatising responses. He suggests, in responding to the children's play in which the puppets continue to attack, that mother's headache might go away if she were able to tweak his nose (as the children have done with the puppets). I identified with this intervention, as it gave mother (and moreover the family) a connection to consider. As a consequence, mother accepted the invitation with a significant lightening of her behaviour (with a concomitant emergence of the selected fact). I thought the interpretation that was made by Dr. Scharff about the headache was located somewhere between D6 and E6.

Interestingly, when Dr. Scharff made this suggestion, father became very actively involved as a type of therapeutic confederate, encouraging his wife to tweak Dr. Scharff's nose. This led me to believe that father's anger may have been easier to talk about from the distance of the third person. I feel I might have also commented on father's behaviour here as a means of exploring his (and, moreover, the family's) resistance to accepting the connection. Meanwhile Jeanette, who launched further attacks through the puppets, adds weight to the emerging selected fact, when she justifies the puppets attack: "He's been mean to us, so we being mean to him."

Dr. Scharff, targeting the anger and aggression towards him, also notes to Eric that the bad guys seem to win when the family is upset (D4—analyst/D6—to the family). He also suggests that mother would not feel so low if she could be angry (building on the prior interpretation and attempting to increase the level of conceptualisation). He further notes that father will not allow these events to be linked, suggesting that he (father) cannot stand to be angry and that, moreover, when mother starts to withdraw in this depressed state, their children start to react (adversely) and that "bad stuff starts to take over" (D6–E6 actions). The intent of this interpretation seems to be to consolidate the mentalizing about (making conscious) the fact that angry feelings about absence are key to the deterioration in the family's functioning (D6).

Dr. Scharff once again uses the play of the children and notes the attack by Eric on Alex and Jeanette's play and on his (Dr. Scharff's) toys, and then notes that his toy ambulance, in particular, is taking "a hell of a beating." He then tries again to see if father will allow these ideas to be linked into a thought that could be transformative, but again it is mother who responds. She notes that it is meaningful when she realises she has referred to "the ambulance-slash-doctor". This slip allows Dr. Scharff to make a final and more definitive interpretation, again building on his previous one, and as the session comes to an end, he comments that when anger (about feeling abandoned) cannot be acknowledged in the family, it can lead to the type of deterioration with which the family presented. This last interpretation can thus be seen as a further D6 to E6 action on the Grid, which has had the impact of moving the family to being able to conceptualise and transform (digest) their experience. The naming of this, as we see, has an impact on the movement from a paranoid-schizoid to a more depressive mode of psychic functioning (represented as Ps<->D) (Bion, 1962a).

As the session progressed there was a constant conjunction of facts concerning the break and the consequent deterioration in the functioning of the family, even though initially it was not possible to be sure how mother's headache, Eric's nausea and vomiting on the way to the session, the play of the children involving the hungry pig, and that involving the attacks on the ambulance, all fit together. To arrive at the selected fact involved being able to tolerate uncertainty and not knowing, to swim in the pool of the inchoate until meaning emerged.

A selected fact thus ultimately proves itself to be such, if it has a catalytic and transformative effect on a family's emotional functioning, as it did in this session. If, however, the analyst imposes a theory or logic that is not felt by the family, it is unlikely that we could refer to a selected fact, but will rather find an imposed theory that is unlikely to be transformative.

Conclusion

The use of the Grid in combination with the notion of the selected fact is a helpful post-hoc tool that can be employed to analyse movement and therapeutic action in a family psychoanalytic session. In applying it to the session material with the Simpson family, it demonstrates the scientific and inductive quality of the psychoanalytic process in this instance, and allows a forensic examination of the session material, which helps to identify how the analyst allowed the selected fact of the session to emerge and how this transformed the emotional experience in the family. Bion's concepts originally designed for use with individual analysands can therefore be seen in this example to have an important applicability to our understanding of moment-to-moment psychoanalytic processes with families. I would suggest that the transformations extend beyond the paranoid/schizoid-depressive axis (Ps<->D) and include primitive (somatically expressed) anxieties. As such, I feel it is helpful to extend the continuum of anxieties to be able to incorporate the autistic-contiguous mode of experience and to be notated as Ac<->Ps<->D (Keogh & Enfield, 2013).

Acknowledgement

I wish to thank Neville Symington for his assistance in reviewing and clarifying my application of Bion's Grid to the session material reviewed in this commentary.

References

Bion, W. R. (1959). Attacks on linking. *International Journal of Psychoanalysis*, *40*: 308–315.

Bion, W. R. (1962a). The psycho-analytic theory of thinking. *International Journal of Psychoanalysis*, *43*: 306–310.

Bion, W. R. (1962b). *Learning from Experience*, London: William Heinemann (Reprinted London: Karnac, 1984).

Bion, W. R. (1963). *Elements of Psycho-Analysis.*, London: William Heinemann.

Keogh, T., & Enfield, S. (2013). From regression to recovery: Tracking developmental anxieties in couple therapy. *Couple and Family Psychoanalysis*, *3*: 28–46.

Pickering, J. (2011). Bion and the couple. *Couple and Family Psychoanalysis*, *1*: 49–69.

Symington, J., & Symington, N. (1996). *The Clinical Thinking of Wilfred Bion.* Routledge: London.

CHAPTER ELEVEN

A journey from blame to empathy in a family assessment of a mother and her sons

John Zinner, M.D. (Washington, DC, USA) with discussion by Jill Savege Scharff (Washington, DC, USA) and Yolanda Varela (Panama)

A salutary therapeutic process in family therapy is frequently characterised by a particular sequence of events. This progression begins with a state of conflict, blaming, and negative attributions among family members, each one feeling like the aggrieved party while the source of the problem is seen as residing within the others.

This blaming activity may be interrupted by moments where family members acknowledge their own contributions to the interpersonal difficulties. This is a period of great vulnerability because that admission may be perceived as a weakness and subject a family member to intensified attack by the others. Now under assault, the once vulnerable member becomes defensive and retreats again to the familiar stance of blaming. The therapist's task in this situation is to facilitate the acknowledgment of all members of the part they play in generating the problem while maintaining the safety of the therapeutic situation, so that the ensuing vulnerability is not exploited.

As the shift from blaming others to reflecting upon the self evolves, the level of conflict within the family diminishes. Poignant affects take the place of anger, and there is a sharing of underlying fears, hurts, and feelings of loss.

Excerpts from a conjoint family interview, the first session of a four-session consultation, will illustrate this sequence. The Smith family consists of mother, Sue, a thirty-five-year-old college student, and her sons Adam, age eleven, and John, age four. The family is African-American, and was referred for consultation by Adam's individual therapist in order to assess the potential value of family therapy.

When Mrs. Smith was pregnant with John, Mr. Smith was killed suddenly in a tragic accident. Adam was seven at that time and quite close to his father. John, of course, never knew his father, but, supported by Mrs. Smith, maintained an image of Mr. Smith and constantly carried a photograph of his father in his pocket.

One year previously, Adam revealed to his mother that he had been sexually and physically abused for several years in a day care setting. Adam experienced the ensuing medical and police procedures as intrusive and as a punishment, as if he, himself, had been responsible for the abuse. Mrs. Smith had difficulty empathising with him and was exasperated with Adam's post-traumatic irritability and somatic complaints. He became profoundly depressed and suicidal, prompting hospitalisation.

Following discharge, Adam was seen in twice-weekly exploratory psychotherapy. Two attempts to initiate conjoint family treatment were unsuccessful. Adam's individual therapist sought this family consultation out of her concern that she and mother had not established a rapport, and that mother's consequent feelings of exclusion might jeopardise Adam's therapy.

Discussion of the introduction—Jill Savege Scharff

John Zinner's case consultation to Sue Smith (thirty-five) and her two children Adam (eleven) and John (four) brings forth many family issues—the single-working-mother family, the post-traumatic depression and suicidality following childhood sexual abuse, the loss of a father, the shock of a tragic accident causing the loss of a father substitute, and sibling rivalry among half-brothers, one in late latency, the other in the oedipal stage. The younger boy is now the age at which Adam's father left (and close to the age at which the mother's father left, as we will later learn). Dr. Zinner sees the prominent defence as one of blaming and defensiveness in the face of conflict, and he tries to move beyond that to the selected theme of love beneath rivalry and self-hatred beneath hatred of the other's lack of success and lack of control.

The consultant's stated task was to arrange interviews for teaching purposes and to assess the potential value of family therapy for a mother and her two sons. The family was referred by a woman therapist who while treating the elder son, had been unable to establish rapport with the patient's mother, and felt that the boy's individual therapy was threatened by the mother's feeling of exclusion from it. Thus the family therapist also had the task of shoring up the individual therapy. A pressure on the consultation is that if the family therapist should do too well, he might actually jeopardise the individual therapy. A hidden assumption is that as a man Dr. Zinner will be able to establish rapport with the woman and help her deal with her sons in the absence of a man at home. A question arises as to how Dr. Zinner negotiates the racial and cultural differences among family members and himself as a white male therapist.

Discussion of the introduction—Yolanda Varela

Dr. Zinner's case depicts the moving drama of the consequences of unmourned losses both intergenerational and transgenerational. We are told that Adam's individual therapist is having trouble relating to his mother because she feels excluded by her. We see that Dr. Zinner makes every effort to include the mother. He shows the patience and respect needed when treating these situations, and demonstrates how to introduce the themes without retraumatising the family. It seems that the individual therapist cannot work effectively with the mother because mother cannot separate from Adam. I wonder what it is that she is living through him.

We meet a widowed mother and her two sons. Dr. Zinner's introduction is centred on Adam's difficulties and relationship with his mother. Then I have my first glimpse of John. I am curious about the way he talks as if he were the oldest son, the father, or his mother's partner, which leaves Adam in the position of the younger child. Will we find a dynamic of sibling rivalry? Are there doubts about who will be the heir of the father?

In the introduction, Dr. Zinner informed us that during the first seven years of his life, Adam experienced abandonment, death, the birth of a rival sibling, and chronic sexual abuse. Adam's sexual abuse is a secret he kept for almost eight years. What prompted Adam to disclose it after all that time? Why now and not before? Did he know it would be too hard for his mother? The mother, as the analyst explained, had difficulty in empathising with her son, and he became more depressed and attempted suicide. I am thinking that the mother cannot deal with her son's distress and I am wondering if she is feeling guilty. There is the probability that Adam's attempts at projective identification are being rejected by the mother, leading to the projections being given back to him without processing or metabolising, putting Adam in the position of receiving by return more toxic content than he had projected. All the badness stays in him. He experiences his internal world as so intolerable that he thinks of getting rid of himself.

Dr. Zinner reports that Adam's father left the family when Adam was four years old. This must have happened around the time of Adam's abuse. Is there something Adam is not saying? What is the role of this absent father in the life of Adam and the rest of the family? Can Adam not afford to feel entitled as the firstborn of a living father? Does he have to be the fatherless and powerless one?

The following excerpts illustrate interactions characterised by conflict, blaming, and defensiveness between mother and Adam.

Clinical segment one

DOCTOR: But you were talking, Adam, about why we were meeting here and you said the first reason was because we're wanting to help other psychiatrists and therapists learn about ways to help families. So that's one reason. And you said you don't care so much about that part, helping them one way or the other. But the other reason is to be helpful to you and your family to see if there's some way for everyone to get along and improve things.

JOHN: My brother loves me, but sometimes he doesn't like me, but he's a good brother.

MOTHER: Sometimes he's a little rough. We're not beating up on you [to Adam].

JOHN: It's not that.

ADAM: You always gang up on me. They always gang up on me.

MOTHER: We're not ganging up.

DOCTOR: Let's hear about it, the ganging up.

ADAM: Those two just verbally bash me together. It's not really fair.

JOHN: No, we don't team up on him.

ADAM: And they just team up on me like I'm lower than both of them. And you know you do that.

JOHN: Every time Mom does something, he starts fighting her. And then every time he says he's the best. And that's teaming up on us.

DOCTOR: "Us" is who?

JOHN: Me and Mommy.

DOCTOR: But that's what Adam is saying in that you and Mom are a team.

JOHN: But we don't team up on him.

ADAM: And she loves him better, trust me. And we've had numerous times where she's gone in his favour.

JOHN: The problem is that like when he goes to school and doesn't finish his homework and I finish my spelling test and Mom hugs and kisses me, and he gets all mad.

MOTHER: Did you understand what he said?

DOCTOR: Sure. What did you hear?

MOTHER: He said I hug and kiss him and Adam makes, well …

ADAM: That's it? I understand him more than … see, see, look at that! [Mother has put her arm around John, who cuddles up to her.]

DOCTOR: What is it that you see?

ADAM: [Sarcastically] Oh, honey dear. Oh, John!

MOTHER: He did that probably because I have my arm around him.

JOHN: It don't matter who Mommy loves the best because she's a grown-up.

MOTHER: He said it does not matter.

DOCTOR: And why doesn't it matter?

JOHN: Because she can do whatever she could to make us be good.

DOCTOR: But Adam, you said it hurts your feelings.

MOTHER: Adam, do I love you? You know I love you.

ADAM: And she will scream at me for no reason.

DOCTOR: I have a suggestion. Instead of talking to me, talk to each other. Tell your mother directly, "You will scream at me".

ADAM: [To his mother] You'll scream at me for no reason at all. Then an hour later you'll say you're sorry and I know you don't mean it because you'll do it over and over again. And that's where I get "I'm sorry" from. Because I say I'm sorry a lot when I make a mistake. And then you just scream at me for that, too. And then you say, "I'm sorry", and it just makes this big thing. And it's all your fault.

JOHN: Because sometimes she does scream at him because he makes me cry and stuff.

ADAM: How?

JOHN: Like tricking me and laughing at me.

ADAM: That's what brothers are for.

JOHN: No. Brothers are for to love each other.

ADAM: Whatever.

DOCTOR: Brothers are for to love each other. Now, you've said that you love Adam, right? And you've said he's a good brother.

JOHN: Yes.

DOCTOR: But sometimes he beats up on you.

ADAM: No, I don't.

JOHN: No, sometimes he just tricks me and laughs at me.

DOCTOR: I see.

ADAM: Oh, right, well yesterday he scratched me with a chip.

JOHN: But today he threw a ball at me.

ADAM: A potato chip, a Dorito chip here; he scratched me

MOTHER: Now what did he do to you?

ADAM: I probably have natural cheese in my blood now.

DOCTOR: What do you think about what John said, that brothers are to love?

ADAM: I feel sorry for him.

JOHN: He threw a big ball right here.

ADAM: No, I didn't. I bounced it off your head.

JOHN: No, no. You did.

DOCTOR: I want to hear from Mom about her reactions to what you're hearing.

ADAM: You're just sitting here.

MOTHER: This goes on all the time.

DOCTOR: A lot has to do with love. I'm hearing the word love used a lot.

MOTHER: Adam is hard love. He knows it's hard. I love him. He knows I love him. I tell him I love him. And a lot of times I do tell him I'm sorry because I'm stressed out.

ADAM: And you take it out on me.

MOTHER: I have seven classes, an eleven-year-old and a four-year-old. And I expect my eleven-year old to participate in a lot of things in the household.

ADAM: And I do.

MOTHER: And I don't make him do anything other than take out the trash. We have a dog.

ADAM: I feed the dog. I love the dog.

MOTHER: I'm talking. Let me talk because when you talk, I let you talk.

ADAM: Okay, I'll let you talk

DOCTOR: We have lots of time. Everybody will have their say.

MOTHER: I put him in a role as being almost an equal in the sense that I talk to him a lot. And I never talk to him like a baby. I always tell him exactly what the situation is and what I need or want from him. And so he looks at me like that. So now that's why he won't give me the respect that he should give me and let me speak because I'm an adult. And that's the things John hears me saying to him, and so that's why he might have said that he's an adult. And that's the kind of thing I say to Adam, that I am the adult and he has to listen. And I do holler at Adam because I'm stressed out; it's a stress thing and he stresses me out. But I love Adam. I don't treat him any differently as far as the things I do for him. We do family things as a group. I may do a little more for Adam. And actually I am around Adam more because I pick him up earlier than John. We may go to the library. We may do a little bit more and I spend a little bit more time with him. I try to talk with him and reason with him. We have our good times. But sometimes when he's not listening and I want to get his attention, he tells me he's too old for timeout, which I had learned from Children's Hospital. John goes in timeout. Adam acts like he's too old for timeout, so I put him on punishment. So I holler at Adam much more than I holler at John. And because of that, it appears to Adam that I don't like him as much. But I do.

Discussion of segment one by Jill Savege Scharff

The first segment begins with Dr. Zinner dealing with the family's possible resistance to meeting the family in the studio for teaching purposes. He acknowledges that this family does not care about that. He then establishes a helpful, enquiring attitude, clarifying perceptions and misperceptions, making space for everyone to have a say, encouraging them to speak to each other directly, not through him, and asking about their reactions to one another.

Adam complains that his mother and John gang up on him to complain about his work, put him down, and exclude him from their affectionate relationship, which leads to an assumption that she loves her little boy more. John protests that Adam taunts him to put him and their mother down. Behind all the complaints, fights, and teasing, Dr. Zinner detects a longing for love among the brothers instead of the fighting relationship they have. "Brothers are for to love," John says. But Sue, the mother, says that Adam is hard to love. She says that he does not respect her as an adult. He says she takes her stress out on him.

At this point in the session, I see Adam picks up his pad and crayons (not noted in the transcript). I am eager to see what he draws to help us understand more about how hard he is, or how hard Sue is on him, and how he feels about her and about himself. Sue picks up the theme to insist on her love, which, however, she expresses in hollering at Adam for being negative, not finishing his jobs, unfairly accusing her and John of teaming up against him and for his not being all he could be. While Adam claims that Sue loves John more than him, she denies it, at the same time cuddling with John. Adam is too young to be the man of the house, and too old to accept limits like the younger child, and so she is at a loss how to deal with him and he makes it hard for her.

Dr. Zinner creates a safe space for discussion, builds a therapeutic alliance, and begins the conversation as I have just reported. But none of the work addresses the most striking feature of the family, revealed on the video but not in the transcript. My immediate response was to the image of the family in terms of skin colour—a dark four-year-old, a cream-skinned eleven-year-old with dark blond hair and wearing dark glasses, and a mother with medium skin tones, possibly of mixed race, African-American, Latin, or Arabic. It is possible that Sue's late husband, John's father, was dark or that her abandoning first husband, Adam's father, was white, but more likely Adam has albinism. As an albino, Adam would likely face a number of challenges due to misunderstanding and cultural attitudes. For instance, the mother may be ostracised for marrying a man presumed to be white, or accused of cheating on her black husband with a white man, or having sinned in general for which God sent her an albino child as a punishment. On the other hand, the albino child might be regarded as a golden child, but not in this family. Adam says that he is "the one lower than both of them", and yet claims he is the best (according to John). Adam feels less special, less loved than John, and defends himself by boasting. I guess that the difference in skin colour has played a part at the family level, as well as at school where an African-American albino may be teased or set apart, possibly identifying as white in desperation. John is quickly and confidently expressive in a typically black accent, while Adam in a much less pronounced accent, is mocking of John's "motormouth".

Dr. Zinner does not address the impact of skin colour. Perhaps he edited out that part of the interview or felt it was too sensitive an issue, but I do see here a difference between our approaches in that I would have wanted to explore the social, cultural, and unconscious meaning to Adam, John, and Sue of Adam's looking different, having different skin, and a different father than John and the impact of me as a white woman (as Dr. Zinner is a white man). And I would have wanted to know how John felt about Adam having known John's father for longer than Adam knew him, and therefore remembering him and having a more secure image of their relationship.

Discussion of segment one by Yolanda Varela

The dynamic between the three family members is highly conflicted. Oedipal issues seem impossible to resolve, as the family dynamic tends to idealise dyadic relationships instead of a more mature dynamic that takes into account the perspective of a third. Adam's perception of the mother-son couple seems sexualised, as when he mimics his mother's way of talking to John: "*Oh, honey dear. Oh, John.*" Adam sounds as if he is witnessing a primal scene. John responds as if he is the father protecting a defenceless woman.

We could think that Adam's pain at being excluded from this loving but aggressive interchange stirs a sadistic part of Adam's internal world to which he has a valency to act out because of his traumas. It is my experience that sado-masochistic dynamics are put in place in order to avoid painful but also fearful states of mind. What are the fantasies around the absent father? Is a man more loved in his absence than when present? Are we dealing with transgenerational issues as well?

As the segment continues I notice another quality in John's speech, conveying highly idealised feelings towards his mother, projecting omnipotent power. He said, "*She can do whatever she could to make us be good.*"

Now Dr. Zinner appears as a father figure who establishes the limits in relationships, when he directs the manner of speaking. He says, *"Instead of talking to me, talk to each other."* The analyst structures the interchange and puts an end to the way they talk to each other through a third. This important manoeuvre will help family members focus more on external objects and talk less to internalised ones.

Now Adam feels empowered to talk directly to his mother, telling her directly, *"You screamed at me."* An important shift occurs. So far, Adam, in a passive primary identification with the mother, prefers to believe that there is something wrong with him rather than accept that there might be something wrong with his mother. Contemporary psychoanalysis has shown us that, while subjects project their badness into external objects, it is also true that bad external objects really exist. The task then is to help subjects to assume responsibility for their actions but at the same time, to place responsibility on external objects for actions that provoke the projections. If the subject is unable to do this, psychic guilt is established, and provokes both masochistic and sadistic ways of relating to self and others. Thanks to Dr. Zinner's intervention, Adam is able to confront his mother with her manic reparatory defences.

In a full display of the sado-masochistic way of relating, now John assumes the victimized masochistic state, saying, *"Sometimes he screams at me and makes me cry and stuff."*

The session continues and then Adam offers this comment in response to John's scratching him with a Dorito: *"I probably have natural cheese in my blood now"*, as if contaminated by John. Then, following Dr. Zinner's recognition of John's expression "brothers are to love", Adam says, *"I feel sorry for him."* This is an important moment. Adam might be expressing sadness for John because he did not have the opportunity to know his father, and feeling guilty because he, Adam, did. But these feelings cannot be shared by the family.

So far, I have shared my thoughts about the dialogue from the transcript. However, when the video arrived, I was shocked by Adam's physical appearance, his whiteness. I thought of a ghost. I was reminded of how, in the unconscious, "all of the essentials are preserved; even things that seem completely forgotten are present somehow and somewhere; and have merely been buried and made inaccessible to the subject" (Freud, 1937d, p. 260).

A second impact came from hearing the family talk. While reading the transcript, I imagined the words being expressed in a serious, direct way. On video, I saw smiles and laughs leavening and facilitating serious discussion without falling into denial. Dr. Zinner and the family were enjoying being together. I felt even more appreciative of Dr. Zinner's work. At the centre of such intense bombardment of projective identifications, it is difficult for analysts to stay in tune with affect and maintain their capacity to think, as Dr. Zinner did.

John was another surprise. Whereas Adam looks like a ghost, John looks like a puppet whose strings are pulled by the mother. Sometimes while the mother was talking to Adam, John was looking at his brother as if the mother's words were his, spoken through a ventriloquist.

I became aware that my ability to think around the video was less prolific than with the transcript. This is what happens to us in sessions, where our reactions are intense and complete because we participate in the visual components of unconscious emotional communication.

Clinical segment two

DOCTOR: Let me ask you what you're hearing from your kids now. Because we're getting caught up in the facts of what happened. But in terms of the feelings you're hearing, especially from Adam, what are you hearing?

JOHN: Mommy loves Adam because …

ADAM: Who was she asking?

JOHN: … that means love.

MOTHER: I hear Adam. I look at it this way. I hear what he's saying. I know he has some inner problems, some other problems. And they make our whole family …

ADAM: Oh, so you mean it's all my fault?

MOTHER: No, no that would be a percentage of it. The other percentage of it is that I know. I try to make Adam reach his potential. I don't know if it's a potential I didn't reach or what, but I try to make him reach out. I do understand that because of some certain situations that he is in a time in his life where he's laid back or where things are not as they should be and he's not happy all the time. Because of certain things that have happened and I tell him that. I tell him he's not happy.

ADAM: How can you tell me how my feelings are?

MOTHER: Because I look at you and I hear what you're saying.

JOHN: He's not happy because how …

MOTHER: Don't holler, honey.

JOHN: ... how Adam treats Mommy. Mommy treats Adam how Adam treats Mommy because Mommy gets her feelings hurt except for when Adam is bad to her when her feelings get hurt. And then when her back was hurting is when Mr. Jackson broke his tape, his record that he loved, and ...

ADAM: John should be a talk show host. He's just like a motormouth here. The guy has a worst reputation than Geraldo.

JOHN: ... and we didn't want nothing to happen to Adam. And he knows he's a good boy but he know he's got to be better than that.

DOCTOR: Were you worried, John?

JOHN: Yes. I love him. I didn't want him to be hurt before.

DOCTOR: Has Adam been hurt?

JOHN: Yes, he broke his leg before and he was in a wheelchair.

ADAM: No. Yes, I was in a wheelchair.

DOCTOR: What was it about?

JOHN: It was about this boy who could throw real hard and he tried to catch it and he slid and fell on his knees.

ADAM: No, you see, I was playing kickball and I was second base so a guy threw it to me until a girl knocked it out of my hand and so I ran for it, then my knee twisted and I landed on my knee. Then I fractured my knee. I don't think I fractured my knee though but it was twisted.

DOCTOR: This was recently?

MOTHER: A week ago.

ADAM: No.

MOTHER: It was last week.

ADAM: It was like two weeks or a couple.

MOTHER: It was last week.

DOCTOR: So this was recently. You have some hard times, your mother was talking about lately. Is that right?

ADAM: [Whispers something to Mom]

MOTHER: I didn't tell him. I don't think ...

JOHN: Don't listen to him because he's got the wrong question to say. And Mommy don't just scream at him.

MOTHER: I scream at him, though John.

JOHN: Yeah, you scream at him but he don't try to say sorry. He's lying about that.

DOCTOR: Let's hear about that. What were you whispering to your
              mom about?

ADAM: Nothing.

DOCTOR: Are there other things you don't want to talk about?

ADAM: Yeah.

DOCTOR: Because it would be helpful to help me understand what has
              been going on.

ADAM: Some things are better kept secret. Right, Mom?

Discussion of segment two by Yolanda Varela

Now Dr. Zinner intervenes again. Adam joins with him complaining about his mother's lack of reaction. It seems as if the mother's
passivity turns Adam on. Is he blaming her for his abuse when she
wasn't present and active? Dr. Zinner empowers the mother to react
to her sons. He continues his efforts at taking them back to their loving feelings, as a way of re-establishing a positive link among them.
This effort could lead them to their own avoided feelings of loss and
sadness.

Mother then explains how she talks to Adam as an equal. We can see
again how she is looking for a partner in each of her sons. Adam rebels,
but seems guilty and sorry when he does. He seems clear that he is the
scapegoat of the family when he asks, "*Do you mean is all my fault?*"

John complies in total passivity, but feels empowered by his
mother's preference of him over Adam. At one point he even tries
to interpret Adam's behaviour, taking on the role of Dr. Zinner. At
this moment I feel more worried about John's prognosis than Adam's.
The way the mother talks to Dr. Zinner about Adam seems as if she
is an adolescent girl complaining to her father about her brother's
behaviour.

Discussion of segment two by Jill Savege Scharff

We hear more from Sue about how she tries to make Adam reach his
potential. She understands (but tends to dismiss her understanding)
that trauma has affected him and that she is trying to get him to do better because *she* hasn't reached *her* potential. John symbolises Adam's
hurt in terms of an actual hard fall on the playground, and Dr. Zinner
brings the discussion back to hard times in the family. Adam whispers

to his mother, and they keep a secret of some sort. Dr. Zinner enquires gently but without success. The segment fades out before we hear more.

Clinical segment three

DOCTOR: And there was one thing I wanted to ask you about was that you said you are trying to get Adam to reach his potential.

ADAM: I've already done that.

DOCTOR: And that you were saying that you felt maybe that has to do with your feeling that you didn't reach yours. Now I was wondering what that was about?

MOTHER: Well … where you going, son?

ADAM: He wanted to go sit. Can I put my feet up?

MOTHER: How are you going to sit on his chair when he's already sitting in his chair?

ADAM: Can I put my feet up here?

MOTHER: Are you actually going to sit on him? Explain to me where you are? Don't do that, honey. You know you don't want to do that. You're just doing that because Adam is doing that. Now tell me how you're going to sit on his chair if he's sitting in it.

JOHN: He can sit right here.

MOTHER: Now you're going to make everybody …

DOCTOR: Did you want to sit on my lap?

JOHN: No, I want to sit in your chair.

DOCTOR: You want to sit in my chair? But not on my lap?

MOTHER: Okay, partially I think I'm harder on Adam because … I know why I'm harder.

DOCTOR: Okay, let's hear that.

MOTHER: Because I've already thought about it. It goes back to my childhood. I was in control of the house. My mother worked. I was always in control. I was told at a young age that I had full responsibility of the house as far as cooking, cleaning, washing, and telling my older brother what needed to be done, by my mother always leaving instructions with me. And he would do whatever he felt to do. But there was a lot of things he didn't do. He had to take out the trash or something and I would remind him that the trash needed to go out. And depending on how he felt, he might not take the trash out because she couldn't make him take the trash out either. So he would just not do it. And there was a lot of things he didn't do. And because of that I had no control over him.

ADAM: Me or uncle?

MOTHER: I'm talking; now if you want to listen you can listen. But don't interrupt.

ADAM: I know, but which person?

MOTHER: Well, if you listen and continue listening, you'll know who I'm talking about. So, because I couldn't tell him what to do, I could just relay the message to him. And now I'm in my own household and I have that control; I try to make Adam to make more than how he was.

DOCTOR: More than what your brother was?

MOTHER: Yes. Because of what Adam has been through, he may be in a state, a depressive state, where he doesn't want to carry out a lot of functions as far as responsibilities. So, I try to lessen his stress as much as possible. The dog that we had, we gave it up. Because no one really wanted to take care of the dog.

ADAM: I took care ...

MOTHER: He has a love-hate relationship for the dog. He wants the dog in a sense, but he doesn't want to do anything for the dog. The dog is a responsibility. When we got the dog, I told him exactly what he had to do for it.

ADAM: I used to take care of the dog so well.

MOTHER: "Used to" is not the point. The dog requires walking; he requires cleaning up after him if he makes a mess; he has to be fed and he has to be loved.

ADAM: I do love ...

MOTHER: Adam has a love-hate relationship with him and he's using therapy on the dog. The dog has a cage.

ADAM: Oh, come on, Mom. Don't say it.

MOTHER: Well, you may do certain things, without saying. And it lets out the tension in you. And it gives the dog this type of complex where he doesn't know what's going on and he's kind of afraid. And I don't think the dog should be used anymore like that. But above that, John has an allergy of the dog. So we're going to rid of the dog.

DOCTOR: Is that upsetting to the family?

MOTHER: It wasn't when I presented it to them. Then, nobody cared.

ADAM: No, I care now.

MOTHER: Oh, Adam, that's such a story.

ADAM: No, no.

MOTHER: What did Adam say when I said I was going to give the dog up?

JOHN: He said he loved him, but …

ADAM: See, see!

MOTHER: No, he said "good".

JOHN: He loved him, and he don't [John repeats this phrase often with accompanying hand motions, quite evocatively].

ADAM: You've got a big mouth. He just goes on.

DOCTOR: You guys are just great talkers actually.

MOTHER: And I know where they got it from.

ADAM
AND
JOHN: Hey, hey!

MOTHER: That's a compliment.

DOCTOR: That's not a negative thing.

ADAM: I know you don't get it from me.

MOTHER: They get it from me. I mean I'm not as good a talker in that we talk a lot. I don't mean that we're good talkers, but that we talk a lot. I come from a family that talks and they don't hold any feelings in and anything is an open book.

DOCTOR: Continue talking about you and your brother. You were explaining why it is that you are harder on Adam. And then it seemed, I thought you were saying, that you see Adam like you see your brother. Is that right?

MOTHER: I do.

DOCTOR: Talk about that. Your brother's name is …

ADAM: Roger.

MOTHER: Roger. Yes. Uncle Roger. He's a veteran, a disabled veteran now. He's had some problems. But growing up, he was going through some of the problems that eventually grew larger. I did see that in a way. I knew something was wrong. And I think he was depressed a lot of times and that's why he couldn't do certain things. And by us women, my mother and myself, in the household with him and because my mom was working hard and long hours and stressed, we probably kind of ganged up on him more or less because he was that male. He was probably not the male, the head of the household, but although she kept saying that he was the man of the house, she couldn't really have him do anything.

ADAM: I do more things.

MOTHER: I'm not talking to you. He could not carry out the functions of the man of the household, because of his age and who he is. But she looked at him like that and used words like "You're the man of the house". She expected him to do certain things. He fell short and couldn't. It was, maybe, too much pressure on him that we both put on him. As a result, as we were growing up, I just carried that on. What she did, I did. And I just did it in a more tougher form. My mother never put us down. That's the only way that I can see that I do kind of hurt Adam sometimes. Adam knows that I know that I hurt him because I do go back and talk to him and I tell him that I don't mean to hurt him. It's just that I want him to hear me.

ADAM: I hear you.

MOTHER: Some parts of me just can't understand why sometimes he can't follow out a complete task. He'll fall short on it. I can say, "Can you go get the tissue box for me downstairs?" Minutes later, I'll hear him playing in his room. And I ask him, "Where's the tissue box?"

ADAM: What?

MOTHER: Now, that's just an example.

DOCTOR: Is this like Uncle Roger and what you were saying.

MOTHER: I couldn't really tell him to get anything. I would tell him just what he was asked of him to do. If I said you're supposed to get your clothes together so I can wash clothes today, I might tell him, he would just sit there. I'm not talking about you [toward Adam]. And it's funny that you're getting yourself mixed up with him. Maybe it's the way that I'm saying it. I would say, "Roger, you need to get your clothes together because I have to wash clothes." I would have to go and find his dirty clothes under the bed, in the closet, sticking out of here, and sticking out of there. Whereas I would put mine all in a hamper so I wouldn't have to go through that and my mother would do the same thing. So I'm doing more work to compensate for his job. So I couldn't tell him to do anything like what I could tell Adam to do. What I tell Adam to do is what I know he can do. I never give Adam a job that I know he can't do.

DOCTOR: Who was at home then? Your mother, Roger, and you, the three of you. And your dad?

MOTHER: No, he remarried.

DOCTOR: Your dad left when?

MOTHER: When I was young.

DOCTOR: How old?

MOTHER: About five.

DOCTOR: So, you knew your dad.

MOTHER: Oh, yeah, I've known him all my life. I know his other family.

DOCTOR: Is that a very sad thing for you?

MOTHER: No, I never felt sad behind it. My mother never said anything negative, so I never thought anything negative of it. I just knew that he had another family. And I accepted that. I would go to their gatherings as well as my own. I didn't feel like I was really a part of their family, but they accepted me and we do things together.

JOHN: I just want to know when we're going to cut off the lights [in the studio]?

ADAM: Yeah, how much time do we have left?

Discussion of segment three by Yolanda Varela

It seems to me that Adam is fighting against both his mother's and John's manic defences. He compares John with Geraldo as a way of denouncing his lack of empathy. John doesn't want anything to happen to Adam, but at some level John knows something already happened and fears bad things happening to him if he gets closer to Adam. It is sad to witness this family dynamic stirred up by their terror, sadness, and impotence.

Meanwhile Dr. Zinner is trying hard to reach the mother, helping her to explore what Adam's behaviour has to do with her own feelings. Then we see how both boys mobilise to distract both Mother and Dr. Zinner. John wants to sit on Dr. Zinner's chair. Is this his way of showing that there is something beyond their mother's feelings, probably related to a male figure? Is he showing acceptance of Dr. Zinner's intervention? Is he communicating that one is sitting on top of another, and that this issue is being ignored?

Although there is a strong resistance to take in what Dr. Zinner is saying, at the same time there is a longing for what he might provide. The analyst calls to the unconscious wish. John responds with an omnipotent defence of being the analyst, a derivative of his unconscious wish to be the father.

The session continues with the mother talking about her relationship with her brother and how Adam's behaviour reminds her of him. Adam is conscious of how his mother's confusion creates confusion inside him. He finds it difficult to follow her narrative, uncertain if she is talking about him or about his uncle.

Dr. Zinner's efforts penetrate the resistance, enabling Mother to talk about males and females in her family. A transgenerational theme opens, that of male figure being devalued, disabled, or absent. As the mother talks, she confuses her feelings and Adam's.

Following the affective path, Dr. Zinner asks Mother about her sadness at being left by her father. There is a strong denial of sadness and loss in her reaction. Like John, Mother has a passive identification with her own mother who never said anything negative about grandfather's leaving, so she says nothing about it either. Her repressed wishes to rebel are projected into Adam because she is avoiding the guilt of letting grandmother down. As she starts to get in touch with her own history of losses, John again interrupts as though on his mother's behalf, saying: "*I just want to know when we're going to cut off the lights?*" It seems overwhelming to face Mother's sadness.

Discussion of segment three by Jill Savege Scharff

Dr. Zinner pursues Sue's comment about reaching potential. Before she can answer, the boys get in a fight about who sits in which chair, including possibly the therapist's chair—a vivid enactment of the issue of being the older or younger boy, taking or evading responsibility as the child or the man of the house. John wants to sit in Dr. Zinner's chair, and wants Dr. Zinner to sit in John's seat, not to sit in his lap, as Dr. Zinner thinks, but to have Dr. Zinner "sit right here" that is to say, squeezed on the sofa close to Sue. I think there was a fantasy of Dr. Zinner replacing the missing fathers and pairing more graphically with Sue to manage the boys' needs. As Sue continues to speak we learn that her focus on Adam's need to "man up" derives from her childhood irritation at her brother who was unhelpful to her growing up as the hard-working child-housekeeper in her family, and who is now depressed and disabled. Sue tries to save Adam from turning out like her irresponsible brother. The discussion continues in the displacement to the love and hate of the dependency needs of a dog (and a hint about Adam's abusing the dog in some way). Activity heightens as Sue talks of getting rid of the dog.

Dr. Zinner brings the discussion back to how Sue sees Adam as her brother. We learn of another repetition in that Sue and her mother ganged up on her lazy brother who failed to meet their expectations as the man of the house (her father having left when she was five). Sue continues to speak until it is not clear if she is talking about her brother's failures or Adam's. She denies loss over her father leaving—although her firm "No" is preceded by a wistful "Mmmm!" that suggests otherwise. She appears to accept her role as an occasional visitor to his second family—an amazing mixture of acceptance, resignation, and denial of longing. The boys want to know how much time is left, as if they have tuned in to each other's hidden pain and seek their escape, and at the same time prepare to re-experience loss as Dr. Zinner ends the session.

Clinical segment four

ADAM: Yes, I like her better than Mommy. Not because she lets us do everything, but because she is more caring. I don't want to be treated like a baby, but she will care for you, she will care. But Mom ... [mumbles something] Like for dinner, she says ... [mumbles something]. But Grandma, she will fix you a feast every day. She will make sure you are happy. You, you leave. You will give us something and don't even ask us if it's okay.

MOTHER: Why should I ask you if the dinner is okay?

ADAM: Don't you care?

MOTHER: It makes you full. You eat it.

ADAM: Yes, so?

MOTHER: I don't need to know if it's okay.

DOCTOR: Did you know Adam has these feelings?

MOTHER: Yeah, he complains constantly.

ADAM: And she doesn't do anything about it.

DOCTOR: Somehow the feeling that you're not caring, are you aware of that?

MOTHER: Sort of. Like I said, Adam has some problems. And he's trying to put everybody else as the enemy.

ADAM: I am not.

MOTHER: So I don't take it all so personal. I take it to the point where I try to spend time with him and do things with him. Adam is introverted. He's captured ...

ADAM: Introverted? That's a word?

MOTHER: ... it's between him and the TV. That's all, just him and the TV.

ADAM: That's all I have because you always leave me home. It's not that I have a problem being left at home. But you say this yourself that you don't spend enough time with us and that's the only thing that I have. I know John, but ...

MOTHER: I admit school puts a strain on you [meaning herself]. It's not like an eight-hour job.

DOCTOR: What is it like for you? Because I remember trying to reach you. It was hard for us to get connected.

ADAM: Gosh, I don't want to talk about it.

JOHN: Excuse me, my brother just likes Grandma because she lets him eat bubble gum and "vitamin Cs".

DOCTOR: What vitamin Cs?

MOTHER: Vitamin Cs. They're like little cough drops.

ADAM: They're not cough drops. They're throat lozenges.

MOTHER: Well, whatever. They say vitamin C on it. They're orange.

DOCTOR: Well, what about your hard life that's hard to talk about?

MOTHER: What hard life? Hard life ...?

DOCTOR: You were talking about your school. You got no help?

MOTHER: I don't want to talk about school. I could talk about school in January, probably.

JOHN: Mommy didn't get any help except for Adam who was before the day ...

MOTHER: John, that's not what I'm talking about.

JOHN: ... when she didn't get much help and she had nobody and she was a little girl.

MOTHER: How do you know about that?

JOHN: Because you told me.

MOTHER: When did I tell you?

ADAM: I'm the one who said she didn't have …

JOHN: You told me that when you were little, your nose was all turned up. And every time when she was little and her nose was turned up, everybody said "Ha, ha, your nose is big". And Grandma didn't say anything.

MOTHER: I think I was telling him … let me clear that up.

DOCTOR: Let's find out some of these things about you and your life.

MOTHER: No, I was telling him something about not to tease people. And I was telling him about how I was teased.

ADAM: My drawing.

DOCTOR: Let me hear what your mom has to say and then I'll hear about your drawing. What is it about the teasing and that you didn't have any help.

MOTHER: I don't know where they got that from.

ADAM: Mom, you know you did.

MOTHER: I didn't have any help doing what? Cleaning the house when I was little?

ADAM: No, but you had problems, too.

MOTHER: We're talking about … what are we talking about?

ADAM: Don't look at me. Look at him. He's the one.

MOTHER: But you brought it up.

ADAM: No, I didn't. He brought it up and John brought it up.

MOTHER: I'm talking about having a hard time and all that stuff. I was talking about school; that's what I was talking about.

ADAM: Other things lead to another.

MOTHER: What did I tell you about touching?

ADAM: Well, he talks too much.

MOTHER: Well, then, you can't touch. He can't touch you and you can't touch him.

DOCTOR: What is it about touching?

MOTHER: They can get physical. Little as he is, he will defend himself from him.

ADAM: Did I tell you that he scratched me with a …

DOCTOR: … a Dorito?

ADAM: Right, with a Dorito. He scratched me with a Dorito.

MOTHER: It will only take one person to hit another. I don't want anybody … I know you're restless; draw me a picture [to John].

DOCTOR: I know people are getting agitated when we're talking about your life.

ADAM: About me?

DOCTOR: No, Mom's life and some of the hardships and everything like that. That's when people …

ADAM: Yeah, I can talk about my hardships, but she can't.

MOTHER: No, I didn't hear you talk about your hardships.

DOCTOR: [To Mother] And both you and John are getting kind of excited or nervous when we start hearing about your mom. Are you feeling sad?

ADAM: Me?

DOCTOR: No, Mom.

ADAM: No, she's feeling very embarrassed and enclosed.

JOHN: No, she's feeling sad every time Adam teams up.

DOCTOR: What is it that you're feeling?

MOTHER: Oh, nothing.

DOCTOR: Let's say it.

MOTHER: Nothing.

ADAM: Mom, Mom you need …

MOTHER: I was just saying we all need some help.

DOCTOR: It started with school. You didn't want to talk about school.

MOTHER: Yeah, I didn't want to talk. I didn't do very good this year, this semester.

DOCTOR: Go ahead. You're feeling sad about school.

MOTHER: Yes, school is not a good subject right now. In January, I know I'll be over it.

DOCTOR: But you know we have to.

MOTHER: I don't want to talk about school at all.

ADAM: Because she's bad in it.

DOCTOR: Are you're disappointed in yourself?

MOTHER: Uh-huh.

ADAM: And so that causes a stress for her. And then she'll take it out on …

DOCTOR: Well, let's stay with your mom.

MOTHER: School is not a good issue.

ADAM: She's crying.

MOTHER: I'm not crying.

ADAM: I can tell.

DOCTOR: You have a lot banking on this. What is it that you're planning? You're getting your degree, right? And this is a dream of yours?

MOTHER: Yes, it's okay. I may have not gotten the grades that I wanted to get, but I'm still graduating.

DOCTOR: So, this was a big disappointment. Was it this semester that was a big disappointment?

MOTHER: [Nods, wiping tears from her eyes.]

DOCTOR: You're comforting your mom, right?

ADAM: Yes, see, I care for her, but no she can't …

MOTHER: The only reason I'm doing this is because I just had finals and I know that I didn't do what I could've done.

Discussion of segment four by Yolanda Varela

Now we see Adam's defences lower as he talks about his longings for his mother's attention, something that he gets from grandmother. When Dr. Zinner tries to explore the mother's reaction about being perceived by Adam as not caring, she retreats again into seeing Adam as the problem. She argues with Adam about his constant use of television. Adam says: "*That's all I have because you leave me home.*" This moving statement is both plea and complaint. He is searching for something missing, looking to television when his mother is not inside. Out there, maybe there is something. For the first time Adam talks directly about his feelings.

Dr. Zinner tries again to rescue Mother from her detachment. Recalling the difficulty he had in arranging the appointment, he reminds her: "*It was hard for us to get connected.*" Again John tries to abort the feeling state, and talks about bubble gum. This time Dr. Zinner blocks his escape. Finally John points to his mother's history: "*She didn't get much help and she had nobody and she was a little girl.*" Mother asks how he knows that. He answers directly: "*Because you told me.*"

The analyst's has uncovered the anxiety behind John's defences. Mother has burdened John by sharing her emotional issues with him, so he worries about her. At the same time she has weighed Adam down with her own internal battles. Apparently unconcerned, he now adds to her distress.

When Dr. Zinner asks a direct question to Mother—"*Let's find out some of these things about you and your life*"—Adam interrupts, trying to get the attention onto his drawing. It is Adam's turn to jump to his mother's rescue. We become clearer about the repetitive cycle. Every time Dr. Zinner gets near to a painful emotion or a difficult piece of history, they gang up on him trying to distract him.

Following Dr. Zinner's advice, Adam returns to the problem and confronts his mother with her denial. Something interesting happens in the following sequence:

> MOTHER: I'm talking about having a hard time and all that stuff. I was talking about school; that's what I was talking about.
> ADAM: One thing led to another.
> MOTHER: [Suddenly harsh] What did I tell you about touching?

Mother was referring to Adam's roughing up John. I was curious about the possibility of an unconscious meaning behind the sequence. What else happened as a result of school's difficulties? Is she really talking about school now, or is it loaded with past history? Was it something to do with the uncle? Or, with touching each other? Is this Adam's history of abuse or hers? Are failing and getting physically punished connected to abuse in more than one generation? We can only wonder.

Following the affect of the moment, and confronting the boys' agitation when he is trying to talk about Mom, Dr. Zinner asks about the meaning behind touching. He presents Mother with a direct question—"*Are you feeling sad?*"—which Adam thinks is directed at him:

> ADAM: Me?
> DOCTOR: No, Mom.
> ADAM: No, she's feeling very embarrassed and enclosed.
> JOHN: No, she's feeling sad every time Adam teams up.
> DOCTOR: What is it that you're feeling?
> MOTHER: Oh, nothing.

This excerpt of dialogue exemplifies the family's dynamic, the children expressing feelings for the mother while she feels nothing.

From the family's perspective, going back to a female therapist is not appealing. I wonder if their defences against mourning the loss of, and the longing for males is projected into the female therapist in such a way as to make it difficult for her to provide her own internal identifications with male figures as support for this family. Relying on a woman is both disappointing and dangerous, as she cannot guarantee safety or gratify the need for a man.

Dr. Zinner's generosity at sharing his experience with this family with us allows us to examine the multiple subtleties in the way families express conflict and difficulty. His work lets us see how the drama of loss, separation, and abuse had this family locked in a closed system of hopelessness, anger, and fear. His analytic stance allowed him to offer containment and support from a strong, empathic male figure—a new experience for all of them. Saying goodbye at the end of the session was difficult.

This family lives with many ghosts. It is difficult to call them back from paranoid-schizoid ways of relating towards the depressive position, to leaving lost objects and embracing new ones. But I saw movement as the family began to work. This gives hope for a good prognosis.

Discussion of segment four by Jill Savege Scharff

Adam compares his depriving mother to his nurturing grandmother. This seems to be retaliation against Sue for preferring his half-brother and for being too busy with work and school for him. Sue defends against accusations of her "not caring" by saying that Adam's complaints come from his being introverted because of his difficulties, and so she does not take it personally. Adam says plaintively, *"You don't spend enough time with us and that's the only thing I have."* Adam may think he is referring to his attachment to the television being the only thing he has, but I think that here there is a reference to the fact that he has lost two fathers and has only his mother to rely on. When Dr. Zinner connects Adam's impression of her not being there to her having difficulty in returning his phone-call because of being in school, Sue says she will not talk about it, and John then repaints the picture of the grandmother as indulgent.

Dr. Zinner sidesteps this topic to get back to the hard life of being a single mother who is struggling at school. Again Sue refuses to talk about it, but John stands up to tell the story of her getting no help as a little girl and being teased for having a big turned-up nose. Adam yells into the microphone and wants to pick his nose, Sue blows her nose, and Adam blows his nose. Adam tries to call attention to his drawing, and Dr. Zinner says he wants to hear about the drawing, but first he will ask Sue to take ownership of her narrative. She is reluctant to engage and the boys offer a couple of distractions as Adam tries to block John's mouth, and shows the scratch John gave him from a fight over a Dorito chip, and moves his microphone. Dr. Zinner interprets the agitation occurring to avoid talking about her hardships. Sue leans right around Adam to fix the microphone (which he has previously done for himself) and it seems an excuse to embrace him in order to comfort herself as she tries to hide her tears. Sue demurs until Dr. Zinner says directly that she is avoiding the topic of school.

Sue refuses again to talk about it, or to be heard on the tape, because she has not done as well as she wanted to. She pretends that she feels nothing, but Adam says she is embarrassed and John says she is sad. Dr. Zinner says that she is disappointed in herself and she agrees, wiping her eyes. Now we are shown that the projection into Adam is not only that from the lazy brother, but even more so of Sue's feelings of inadequacy and shame over having had trouble at school as a child and now as an adult in college. She begins to cry, and thus takes back pain that she has projected into Adam. She will still graduate, but not with the grades she wanted. Adam asks quickly if his drawing would look better with two eyes or three, and concludes that two is better. Identifying with her disappointment, and probably relieved that she is acknowledging her own failings instead of his, Adam is the one to comfort her.

By the end of the session, we have seen the struggle for love and support. We have seen the family members talk a lot and behave much as I guess they do at home, showing themselves as they are to the therapist. Dr. Zinner, relating as an interested, benevolent figure, establishes an easy rapport with them, making space for each one to have a say. He has a wonderful clinical presence. We have seen him develop a working alliance and establish a process towards ownership of a projection and the mention of a secret. Dr. Zinner does not pursue the content of the secret or its function in the session. Did he feel that was premature? Or did he miss an opportunity because he already knew the secret from the referring doctor? Much remains to be accomplished. We have seen no discussion of the family's trauma at losing two fathers and no work on Adam's sex abuse trauma.

The segments chosen privilege verbal narrative over observation of non-verbal communication and children's play. At two places Adam drew attention to his drawing but was put off, his art ultimately ignored. Was he drawing a monster? Why were three eyes considered? And why were two better? Is a pair better than a triangle? Is moving from three to two a reference to loss of a father? We do not have the advantage of Adam's art work to help us reach the unconscious life of the family. As yet, there has been no dream.

We have seen the therapist work with close attention to the experience of all three participants but we see him drawn towards the mother as a central part of the problem, or perhaps he is consciously trying to engage her and develop a level of rapport that eluded the individual therapist. We have seen no explicit transference interpretation, and we do not have access to the therapist's countertransference. Not all psychoanalytic approaches to couple and family therapy include transference interpretation. This is an example of working *in* the transference but not *with* the transference. Perhaps Dr. Zinner has deemed it too early in the process to relate dynamics of the session to perceptions of his person, his professional authority and helpfulness, and his role as a white male physician meeting with an African-American widow and her family.

Dr. Zinner's approach is one that creates a good holding environment so that family members feel free to express themselves. Indeed they are all good talkers. In future sessions, I think the work would be given added dimension by his including the art work as a link to the family dynamic unconscious, interpreting the transference to him as a missing father and grandmother, and by addressing the social unconscious in discussion of cultural and religious values. In the meantime Dr. Zinner will use his clinical presence to create a safe, emotionally responsive, reflective space in which a mother and her sons can deal with shared loss, hurt, fear, and guilt to rebuild their family.

Reference

Freud, S. (1937d). Constructions in analysis. *S. E.*, 23: 255–270. London: Hogarth.

CHAPTER TWELVE

To fulfil from within what was built from around

Hanni Mann-Shalvi (Tel Aviv, Israel)

Theoretical background

My psychoanalytic understanding of unconscious couple dynamics is based on a weaving of psychoanalytic attitudes that relate to unconscious dimensions of the intersubjective and intrasubjective spheres dialectically.

Jill and David E. Scharff (2011) termed the unconscious dimension of the couple relationship: "the interpersonal unconscious" and elaborate that "[I]t forms an interpersonal matrix, it is constructed as a dynamic system internal relationships, and it is expressed in personal choices, behaviours and relationships … . Even though my unconscious is unique to me, paradoxically it is also shared with intimate partners, work groups and social groups as I engage with them in reciprocal interactions. In this state of mutual influence, their unconscious minds and mine are constantly under construction across the life cycle. The unconscious mind develops in dynamic interaction with the unconscious field in which it is delivered. The field consists of the shared unconscious assumptions in the family and the society—repressed or ignored aspects of social life, culture, history, values and family relationships" (Scharff & Scharff, 2011, p. 1).

Other theorists have focused on the intersubjective component and thus allowed me to try to identify the unique characteristics of the identity of the couple relationship.

Such is Ogden's understanding (1994) that can be applied to couple relationships, that the dialectical movement of subjectivity and intersubjectivity is a central clinical fact of psychoanalysis, as is his description of "the intersubjective analytic third (Green's [1975] 'analytic object'), [that] is a product of a unique dialectic generated by/between the separate subjectivities of analyst and analysand within the analytic setting" (Ogden, 1994, p. 64).

Pichon Rivière's definition of the "link" highlights the understanding that the "individual's psyche is built on two pillars of the constitution of the internal world and the influence of the social" (Scharff & Scharff, 2011, p. 25). René Kaës's (Kaës, Faimberg, Enriquez, & Baranes, 1993, 1994, in Kirshner, 2006) conception of shared psychic space that is constituted from the interplay between the two psychic spaces of the intrapsychic and the intersubjective, adds another dimension.

The integration of these contributions allowed me to understand the "link" as a third that takes on attributes of an independent entity as it is created by the intricate interaction between the entangled unconscious emotional dynamics of both spouses. The three—the spouses and their link—are subsystems that work together to form the couple as a single unit. Because each of the three has its own identity and emotional structure, in order to allow growth within the couple's realm, all must undergo significant therapeutic emotional processes, in a way that needs to be done simultaneously and moderately. In order to allow continued expression of each spouse's changing unconscious emotional structure, a bridge between internal reality and its expression in external reality needs to be built through the entire therapeutic process (Mann-Shalvi, 2010). Another important theoretical component of my understanding of couples is the transmission of intergenerational content in general, and of trauma in particular, as important constituents of the unconscious (Gampel, 2005; Kogan, 1995; Mann-Shalvi, 2006). This legacy can announce itself through the couple relationship in succeeding generations, a phenomenon I named intergenerational transmission of couple encapsulation (ITCE). Couple psychoanalysis enables working through of the traumatic encapsulated material, builds obstacles to transmitting potentials of trauma to the next generation, and allows couples to experience new satisfying personal and couple emotional equilibrium (Mann-Shalvi, 2016). When transformation in couple relationships occurs, we need to be aware that it touches all spheres of life so that we can intervene where and when needed.

Case presentation: Ruth and Rami

The couple's history and emotional dynamics

Ruth and Rami are in their late sixties, with two boys aged twenty-five and thirty-three. Both beautiful successful people, they lead separate social and cultural lives. Unlike the atmosphere of satisfaction that characterised their separate lives, there is constant tension between them, accompanied by constant accusations and endless quarrels. They have been in couple psychoanalysis for the last year, coming twice a week for a double session, which means four hours a week, which adds up to, approximately 350 hours at the time of this report.

Rami initiated several high-tech projects, which were sold for a large profit. Today he is in the midst of developing his next project. Ruth worked in high tech as well, and left a successful job to join Rami in the current project.

Ruth and Rami's parents were sent to concentration camps as children during the Holocaust. Most of their families perished there. The few that survived emigrated to Israel. Ruth and Rami said that their mothers never hugged them, and that there were no other displays of affection in the family. Both parents divorced when Ruth and Rami were children.

When Rami was seven years old, his father discovered that his mother was cheating on him. He threatened to take his two children and disappear. Since Rami's younger brother was under the age of six, the father knew that the law would not allow him to do so. One day his father took him to live in another town, explaining that from that day he would live with him while his brother would stay with his mother. Rami recalled that he was frightened and thought that because of his behaviour his mother did not want him anymore. From that day on he felt guilty and believed that there must be something very wrong with him, that he was a monster.

Rami's life looked like a chapter from *Les Misérables*. Living with an uncle who was mentally ill, he wandered the streets. In the early years he was trying to please everybody, but when his uncle became abusive towards him he became wild and aggressive. One day his father called him and said that if he continued to behave like that, the father would send him away. "From this moment," he said, "I realised that I'm alone in the world. I cut myself off from everyone and just lived on the streets." Joining the youth movement saved his life because he received a role there and benefitted from its hierarchy and order. The youth movement became his first home. He came home only to sleep.

Ruth grew up in a small, closed religious community, a place where everybody knew everybody. Everyone had to live up to the same Spartan standards, according to which one should not indulge oneself with nice clothes or crave for special foods. Parents that spent too much time with their children were considered to be spoiling them. Ruth is the youngest of four siblings. One day, her mother came to take her from kindergarten but instead of going home, she took her to another house, where she met her father's best friend. Her mother told her that from now on they were all going to live there. From that day on she remembers walking alone at night between the two houses, frightened of moving shadows of what looked like monsters, afraid of Arab terrorists who used to sneak over the border to carry out attacks. She became a frightened, lonely, angry girl, socially rejected and isolated.

They came to therapy after Ruth experienced an emotional breakdown; she became physically ill and suffered from a severe depression. They said that they had not been having sex since the first year of their marriage, and that they were at a crossroads.

The analytic process

The early sessions were characterised by angry accusations from Ruth towards Rami, while he apologised, trying to please her and never succeeding. They said that when they moved in together, she made them a "home". He felt things that he had not experienced since he was young. Then he knew that she was the one for him. She was attracted by his confidence, and she felt protected by him.

The first year of their marriage was characterised by friendship, optimism, and satisfying sexuality for both. After the first year, although they stayed good partners in founding big projects, their intimate relationship deteriorated. Ruth shrank into herself, giving up genuine expression of her identity and experiencing Rami's sexual behaviour towards her as violent.

The notion that nothing is certain, and that the loved one can suddenly become distant and alien, was one of the unconscious cornerstones of their relationship. When the history of the parents in the Holocaust unfolded, we understood that these emotional dynamics had been transferred from their parents through intergenerational transmission of trauma, and had then been re-enacted in their life history. We began to identify how they had re-enacted these traumas in their marriage and in parenthood. It seemed that they had created a split structure in their relationship that unconsciously allowed each to continue living with the emotional defences that had been built during childhood.

Early in therapy we understood that since Rami thought that because he was a bad boy his mother had sent him away, he refrained from any expression of dissatisfaction, anger, or negative feelings. That was complimentary to Ruth's emotional dynamic, in which anger was the only emotion she allowed herself. So in mutual projective identification, Rami's anger was projected into Ruth, while her guilt and rage were projected into him. Ruth was constantly angry as her only way to give voice to distress without feeling vulnerable, and as a defence against her depression. All this meant that she could be constantly angry at Rami.

Carrying constant guilt, Rami accepted Ruth's accusations and resentment. For both of them, it was easier to experience their individual intersubjective conflict as intrasubjective, as a problem between them as a couple. Only when the child Ruth was had entered the therapy room, could we recognise her for the child she was, the one who did not understand why all of a sudden she had moved to live with her mother and her friend's father, who could not be in touch with her fears, helplessness, who was confounded by her new reality, not to mention her needs for love, tenderness, hugging, and soothing. She was left with only aggression as an emotional outlet.

For the first few months, treatment felt harmonious, with a sense of intensity. The couple described their childhoods, and I found myself adding words of recognition to their distress. The room filled with empathy for the children they had been. But still it was clear to me that the unconscious dynamic of splitting was still active. However, for the moment, instead of feeling guilty or angry, both connected to their pain, fears, and distress.

We began to understand the complex structure of the projective identifications that had begun in their survivor parents. Now the splitting began to crack, and the resulting storms came into the therapy as well.

When the therapeutic prism includes four generations—grandparents, parents, and spouses and children—it is difficult to convey the full picture, so I will move to a clinical vignette.

Clinical vignette one

This session comes after a year of couple analysis, when some new feelings of intimacy and trust had been created. They felt new hope for a new kind of relationship.

Ruth began, saying that a week ago they had bought a new house and that for her it means that this is a commitment to stay together. "It's like remarrying, for better, for worse." She said that it allowed her to be much more relaxed. Rami said that it gave him confidence to counter his terror that she would leave him.

RUTH: Lately I feel that I have more space within me, when things are not done according to what I wish, I no longer find myself flooded with such difficult emotions and becoming so aggressive.

RAMI: I am also not projecting my feelings onto Ruth as before. Now I know that when she is angry or wishes to be on her own, it does not mean that she is leaving me. But in spite of that, something happened that I wish to discuss.

RUTH: Yes, go ahead.

RAMI: After a calm and nice weekend, Ruth had a complicated project to prepare for her work. She tackled a problem in an area of my expertise that she could not solve. She was very disturbed. When I asked her if she needed anything, or if I could help her, she said, 'No', and I felt rejected because she did not wish me to help her. I felt that you [he turned to Ruth] pushed me away. It made me feel lousy. In spite the fact that I had three other options for interesting plans for the evening, I found myself in bed, in a bad mood. At the end I went to sleep.

ANALYST: Can you elaborate on your feelings of being rejected and in a bad mood?

RAMI: If I were in Ruth's situation I would turn to her for help. So when you Ruth push me away, I felt that you rejected me.

(It seemed clear to me that Rami could not differentiate between what was good for him and what was good for her.)

ANALYST: [To Ruth] How was it for you?

RUTH: When I am stuck, I like to concentrate by myself and slowly, slowly to figure things out. It is important for me to be able to take care of myself.

ANALYST: Can you say more?

RUTH: When I was a child, my mother would leave me by myself at night, even when I was sick or frightened. She told me to call her if I needed anything. I knew that I would not call her, and I lay down alone and imagined things, or made myself something to eat. It was important for me to know that I could take care of myself.

ANALYST: How old were you?

RUTH: I was five, six, seven … always. When I grew up, even if she asked if I need anything from her, I said, "No!"

ANALYST: I can imagine you in bed sometimes with temperature, a headache or a stomach ache, maybe just frightened and wishing so much that Mommy would not go to work, because it was frightening to stay alone.

RUTH: You know, I remember now: once, I think I was five years old, I was sick, alone as always, lying in bed. I needed to go to the toilet, but when I tried to stand up I felt as if the whole room was circling around me. I was so afraid. I stayed in bed holding myself, trying not to pee in bed, feeling so humiliated to find out that I fell asleep and woke up in a wet bed. My mother was so irritated I could feel it in her eyes.

(In order to give recognition that was not given at the time, I now gave more voice to the unjust distress of the little girl she was, and illustrated the coping mechanisms that she developed: how she found that she could withdraw into herself, and discovering that she could calm and soothe herself.)

RUTH: You are right. Ever since then I'm better off on my own when I have a problem.

[Rami looked deep in thought.]

ANALYST: [To Rami] Where are you?

RAMI: I was thinking that when I went to bed, I heard Ruth in the kitchen preparing something to eat for herself, and not asking me if I wanted something to eat as well. It took me back to the time I lived at my uncle's house. His wife would prepare dinner for the whole family and would not ask me to join them.

(I thought that maybe since his feelings were not acknowledged he was not available to listen to her. Ruth who did not feel empathy retreated into a compliant response.)

RUTH: You told me that you did not feel well and were going upstairs. That is why I did not offer you something, and I apologised for that. If you ask that every time I make myself something to eat, I should wake you up, I will do that willingly.

(But he was in another place and I thought that it was too soon.)

ANALYST: [To Rami] Maybe we need first to listen to the world that was opened in you. It sounds so cruel to see the whole family sitting at the table to eat and you are not invited, and sit looking at them from the side. It's abusive.

RAMI: [Tears running down his cheeks as he described this scene he had not thought of previously.] I did not understand why I was not called to be with them. Why was I not invited to sit down with them to the table? I was so hungry. The smells of the food served to the table made me even hungrier. I understood that I must be so bad that no one wanted me near. I felt so rejected. When they would finish eating, I would go to the kitchen and take some bread and what was left in the fridge.

(I was shocked at the brutal description.)

ANALYST: It seems that Ruth's response to you opened a festering, bleeding place inside—the cruelty and abuse of your uncle's family towards you. Not to let a child to eat with his family when he has no other place in the world is an abuse.

(Ruth now offered words to the child that he had been, the same words she had trouble giving the girl that she portrayed before.)

RUTH: It is really unforgivable. I always hated this uncle and his wife, and now I know why. How could they behave like that? And you did so much for them in the last years.

ANALYST: [After feeling that sufficient working-through had been done for today.] You described your feelings yesterday in saying "I was despairing … I felt alone … everything is worthless … I do not feel anything." Maybe these words belong to the time, when no one had heard your distress. But that part of you has not given up hope. It was waiting for the right opportunity to speak and be heard.

RAMI: I disconnected myself then, and built worlds of my own where everything was good.

RUTH: Well it seems that we are alike after all.

(Ruth now spoke with warmth in her voice, repeating what she had said before.)

RUTH: I understood that you were going upstairs because you didn't feel well. I apologised for that. If you wish that every time when I make myself something to eat I will wake you up. I will do that willingly!

(I thought that Rami was moved by her words, but I heard his voice hardening with what he said next.)

RAMI: I learned how to be on my own, not to consult anyone and always to gallop ahead."

RUTH: I can see this pattern in all spheres of your life including in work.

(I felt that Ruth was now taking the role of the therapist, and I figured it derived first from jealousy at the intimacy that had been aroused between me and Rami in the moments when I related warmly to his distress. It also stemmed from projective identification. When he described his distress, she took care of her own distress that was hard for her to recognise.

I was aware of my countertransferential feeling that I was not needed as before, like a mother that sees her children become able to continue their life without her. I wondered if it was a sign of their development, or did I hold something else of which I was unaware. I realised that I needed to continue to contain and reflect within myself. While writing this report, as an après coup, I came to understand that perhaps I was experiencing their feelings of being pushed aside, being unimportant, and needing to cope on their own in congruence with the mirroring process that was taking place before.)

RUTH: It is always painful for me to see you in these situations, racing ahead alone, and blaming me for your feelings without awareness that they are yours. What happened here today might allow you to be less harsh and more tender.

(It was one minute before the end of the session. I saw her defence of putting things on him, but did not think that she would be able to understand me if I spoke of it, certainly not without enough time to process, so I stayed quiet, realising that now she was in the role of the understanding mother, which was a change from her previous position of shutting herself in.)

RAMI: [Like a small child] It is not fun!
ANALYST: It is true, but only when one can feel the pain can one can feel the fun.
RAMI: So that is why I could not bring myself to go out that night, and that is why I felt so disappointed with myself.
ANALYST: When you are disappointed with yourself, you treat yourself with the same lack of compassion that others gave you. You probably repeat the trauma in order to try to overcome it. Probably that is true for both of you.

(They remained quiet for some minutes, then looked at each other and at me, smiled small smiles, stood up, and left.)

Clinical vignette two

Ruth started off by saying that they had a pleasant weekend when they hosted good friends. While Ruth felt they had a pleasant and intimate time, Rami again split in a manner that always felt unsettling to me, but I could not figure out why.

Rami said with indifference, "Well, that's our social function, but nothing is getting better in our intimacy, and I am not prepared to accept that at my age, I do not I have sex. Ruth, you withdraw every time. I'm troubled and don't know what to do."

Ruth looked hurt and said, "Well, if you feel so …"

Feeling her dissatisfaction, Rami said, "Actually we've made progress in intimacy, because as we sat in the living room in front of the TV, you gave me leave to stroke your hand as far as your elbow. And I hugged you."

(I was aware of the technical, cold manner, in which he measured caresses and hugs, calculating to what height, how many times, as if that was the measure of success or failure, despair or hope).

I said, "You each experienced this weekend differently. You, Ruth, described the whole weekend as being intimate, while you, Rami, distinguished between having company, parenting and intimacy."

Ruth said, "In preparing for the guests together, there were many intimate moments, even when you were standing on a chair replacing a lightbulb. When you gave me the burnt-out bulb and I give you the new light, our hands touched. For me that was intimacy. For me, when we were preparing for the guests together, there were many intimate moments."

(I looked at Ruth surprised, aware of her use of the word 'light' vs. the 'burnt out bulb'. For the first time, I could sense the young sexually free "flower girl" she described herself being in her youth, but who died in her after the first year of marriage).

Rami said, in a way I felt was compliant, "It's true this weekend was fun. I liked it when we did things together."

(I noticed that he neutralised the element of intimacy, talking once again in terms of fun, friendship, and doing things together).

Ruth said, "Rami, she is right. You always segregate things, and then I feel like an object, feeling that you negate me."

(I remembered Ruth describing "feeling like an object" when she was relating to their sexual lives. This made me realise that maybe throughout this Saturday, Ruth was feeling close and intimate towards Rami, feelings that might lead to a possible sexual encounter. Therefore when Rami divided parenting, friendship, and intimacy, she felt blocked, as if she were a child, rejected and frozen when trying to come closer to her parents. Only when she was withdrawn could he come to her, now angry that she did not want sex. I thought that maybe he is the one who is intimidated by sexual intimacy, projecting this fear into her and attacking it in her. Meanwhile she gets support once again for her childhood conclusions that it is dangerous to long for closeness).

I summarised this, noticing that Ruth was nodding in agreement. She said, "It is just so, Rami. I approach you warmly, and you reject me, not allowing me to be near. Then as I back away, you come to me with demands."

(I felt Rami looked exposed, as if hearing something difficult to contain. He seemed to realise that it was important for him, but at the same time difficult to face).

I asked, "Where are you Rami?"
He replied, "Really, do you think so?"
I said, "It's hard for you, Rami?" He nodded.
I said, "It seems, Rami, that being sexually intimate brings you fears of being dependent and too close to someone you need so much. Now we know what that this topic holds for you. But it was too difficult for you to recognise it, and so when Ruth came closer you stopped the action, and then were angry at her instead of knowing that you are angry at yourself."
Rami looked very sad. I said: "Rami you look so, so sad."
He said, "I'm really sad about what I do to myself. I can see that I have a big problem."
Ruth said, "We did this work together. This is the world I knew."

(I thought of the intergenerational aspect of the trauma that was playing a role here as well, but I knew that this was enough for now and anyhow it was the end of the session. I felt that it was difficult for them to leave).

I said, "We will continue next time."
Together, they said, "Yes!" And again, they slowly stood and left.

Discussion of "To fulfil from within what was built from around" by Hanni Mann-Shalvi

Karen Proner (New York, New York, USA)

Dr. Mann-Shalvi is interested in the transmission of intergenerational content, and specifically in terms of trauma. What is transmitted constitutes the deepest layers of the unconscious and is particularly poignant in this couple. It challenges us to think about how one can work with primitive unconscious phantasy and its effect on relationships.

The couple's individual traumatic experience is understood as an intergenerational expression of something un-metabolised or unprocessed. In a recent paper on Bion's concept of "fear of dying", I wrote that at the time of trauma, the infant's ego is overwhelmed and stays encapsulated and unprocessed because no one is there to express it to. The infant feels alone with this terror of falling apart. The rage of abandonment becomes combined with ongoing internal agony. With this discussion, I would like to stimulate thoughts about how we work with these early anxieties with couples.

Despite knowing that Ruth and Rami are pseudonyms, my first thought was of the mythical twins Romulus and Remus, the archetypically famous abandoned twins. We are told by Dr. Mann-Shalvi that their life as a couple is marked by "separateness "and "endlessness", expressed by complaining, accusatory aggression. Dr. Shalvi's unconscious processing of the material to make a "story" for us is illuminating. They are twinned in many ways: both "hi-tech", both Holocaust children's children, both parents immigrated to same place, both mothers did not hug, both parents divorced. Both suffered sudden shocks in childhood denoted by the author's phrases such as "from that day", "one day", "from this moment", expressing overwhelming, unexpected change as marks of psychic trauma. Psychic trauma adheres to the most primitive unconscious, in which the time-space of the infantile relationships to objects is marked by potential overwhelming unpredictability.

This compromised psychic space constructs interlocking enactments that make it seem as if one is not alone while not touching dreaded aspects of early infantile psychic phenomena, leading to overwhelming feelings, with no container to put them in.

Ruth and Rami are aware that monsters and monstrous terrorist aggression accompanied their childhood experiences. Rami became aware of his own monstrous rage towards parental objects (displaced onto the uncle), but his father told him that his rage could kill his father. His father's response re-projected the fearsome feelings. So Rami and Ruth both walked around, alone with their rage, magnified by abandonment by their parents' internal worlds which became magnified "no space" and no container worlds. They were alone as monstrous sounds bombarded them like multiple ripples, ever further from the original tragedies. The anxiety became what Bion calls "nameless dread". Both Rami and Ruth described object worlds of sudden loss, with inaccessible, dead objects such as a dying/damaged father. Spartan (no-time) parents convey that emotional needs kill parents and leave an inner world where there is no one to turn to. These parents "know" and "cannot know" about their child's turmoil lest it bring them closer to their own pain—what Bion calls "–K" (minus K) mentality. So the story goes that in the beginning of their marriage the couple had warmth, friendship, sex, and hope. Did they find this by leaving their historical identifications and defence systems in the wish for idealised optimism (the in-love stage of relationships) that they could only sustain for a year? Then they reverted to the "shrunken state" (Ruth) of projective identification with these unprocessed early anxieties, and their parent's anxieties. Such unprocessed anxieties are often expressed in somatic terms, and indeed, Ruth and Rami enter treatment when Ruth's body is "breaking down".

The therapist talks of the first treatment stage of harmoniously building a container that recognises conscious and unconscious distress. But, she notes, the couple is still "split" in action. Rage has turned to pain, fear, and distress. You could say that neither partner wants to contain the other. It is like having two babies both screaming in pain without any containing objects. This is exactly what happens when an infant with annihilation anxiety has a mother with unprocessed, uncontained anxieties herself: the potential container does not hold the projections. It becomes "flattened" and propels them back into the baby, now not only with the baby's own "beta" (unsymbolised) elements, but with the mother's unprocessed beta elements made more malignant by being combined with bits of harsh superego. It returns unprocessed experiences to the baby, both of baby and mother, augmented by hatred that there was no one there for baby or mother when they needed someone. In the subsequent session, Ruth has a screen memory of her mother's face expressing the hated vulnerability of the child.

The first session starts with a new house, perhaps to house the relationship. It comes with a commitment of a couple that "stays, for better or for worse!" Is this a new idealised phase or an expression of ambivalence or, perhaps, true development? In Rami's words, it brings his confidence back, but also the terror of dependency. Was the previous house built with defences of separateness, withdrawal, and endlessness in which aggression was kept at bay? Ruth agrees that she has regained a space for managing overwhelming emotions without having to employ her old obsessional defence system. Is this a container? As they tell their therapist that they have found a new container/house for their relationship, Rami says he is able to contain Ruth's states in a different way. But in spite of having the new container, he needed to go back to the usual hurt. I hear him say: "I did not have a container, so why should I contain Ruth." Or "I didn't have one when I was a child, and so I will not allow myself to have one now!" Klein makes us aware that spite and envy can be expressed as intolerance of gain in treatment. This impacts the therapist's countertransference of feeling pushed away, not needed, rather than feeling acknowledged as successful in helping them build this new house. As Rami returns to the difficulty containing Ruth's bad objects, Ruth tells her story of two painkillers: her omnipotent self-care, and her vengeful punishing of the cruel mother when she arrived with tea. Rami, the butt of her vengeance, does not know why! He suddenly remembers his own moment with cruel parents. Probably Ruth found it too difficult to hold bad object projections in mind. Dr. Mann-Shalvi senses that Ruth's placation hides her pain. As the therapist provides a container, Rami, crying, expresses shocking emotional details of how it felt and how he thought about it. I agree with Dr. Mann-Shalvi that Ruth's inability tolerate pain and Dr. Mann-Shalvi's acknowledgement of the need to listen to Rami, brought the tears and relief. Ruth now can see, if only for a moment, that Rami found the words that she could not find them. Then the therapist can put into words the despair of being alone, when no one hears your distress.

Now Rami and Ruth, in warmer contact, discuss the similarity of their defences. But this cannot be sustained. Ruth moves away from the moment, to identify with a re-projecting partner/mother/therapist, who perhaps stares in irritation at the helpless child. The therapist who is pushed aside is linked to the therapist who understood them as helpless children. Ruth also pushes aside the terrified child in herself, while picking up on feelings focused on Rami instead. The therapist, identified with Ruth's vulnerability, sees her attempting to understand in a much better way than her usual schizoid tactics. Rami is left poignantly containing Ruth's little child. The therapist reassures overloaded Rami, but also follows Ruth's projective identification with a therapist-mother who projects into her patient. The session now focuses on Rami's ways of dealing with trauma. He speaks about the way he cannot get out of this "claustrum" (closed circuit of projective identification) that he and Ruth have formed. His blame binds him. They are alone again as each copes in their individual retreat. The analyst says that projection is better than withdrawal, and joins in Ruth's analysis of Rami's ways of dealing with trauma. But she then tries to bring it back to both of them when she says, "It is probably true for both of you." They seem more thoughtful again.

The "proof is in the pudding" of the second session. Ruth is relieved because she has "hosted the children and spouses". Ruth has played mother. But Rami feels un-helped: "Nothing is better". What follows this "truth of the moment" is another collusion between therapist and Ruth, acting to pressure Rami to act as the container. He remains both child and inaccessible spouse. He wants to have sex with Ruth—wants to put things in Ruth, but she withdraws. He says she just gives a bit of herself, only "up to the elbow".

However, there are meaningful intimate moments, as when "one gives the burnt bulb and the other gets the light". Ruth says that for a moment there is contact: "hands touch".

I think Ruth did feel relieved by this brush of contact, but actually Rami had to carry the containment of infantile pain. Still, he is in trouble and despairing. His underlying helplessness and resentful rage make him placate Ruth, frightened of her dissatisfaction. The therapist notes his defensive distancing. The therapist perhaps does not understand that Ruth prefers this limited contact with Rami, and therefore projects the infantile part of herself into him. The sexual flower girl is really detached from her own needs! The therapist, taken by Ruth's beauty and apparent invitation, pressures Rami to comply, and Ruth joins with Dr. Mann-Shalvi to push for Rami to contain Ruth's defensive withdrawal.

As focus is once again on Rami's problems with closeness, Ruth and the therapist are in agreement that Ruth's and Rami's problems are his problems. He says, "I do it to myself. I have a big problem." I believe that Dr. Mann-Shalvi understands the problem is both that of the couple and that of the individual members, but in this moment, she frames it as Rami's problem. Finally, Ruth helps leaven the situation, when she admits that they did it together, because it is also the world she knew too.

I propose that under the influence of this interlocking enactment, the therapist unconsciously chose the stronger of the two as a container for the other partner, because of her unconscious identification with Ruth's fragile schizoid defences. Rami appears superficially sturdier, more thoughtful, more masochistically inclined to take responsibility for their anxieties. I find this a common problem in my own work with couples. How easy it is to become identified with one member of the couple, especially when they use splitting to deal alone with intolerable anxieties. We are talking about the realm of a kind of psychotic anxiety that pushes therapy into this area, with primitive annihilation anxiety of being left to the agonies of falling apart at the heart of what these two have endured in their traumatic childhoods. The sharing of anxieties breaks down into blaming one spouse, breaks down the basic therapeutic commitment to building a container for the couple.

Dr. Mann-Shalvi says that in the beginning of this treatment Ruth and Rami shared feelings and felt relieved. Dr. Mann-Shalvi acted as a thinking container for their pain. The treatment now seems to be in a new phase of helping them find containment in each other. However, progress appears complicated by the therapeutic emergence of relationships with their internal objects. Why did Ruth move back to projective identification of the critical superego of her mother when opportunity for growth emerged? Similarly, Rami moves to a masochistic identification with a damaged object derived from his own rage projected into his father. Is this invocation of childhood still the only choice for these two hurt children? By repeating the painful relationships, they hold on to some measure of relationship to the old painful objects. Is this what drives us to repeat these familiar responses? In *Plea for a Measure of Abnormality*, Joyce McDougall (1988) wrote that in these relationships, people use unconscious phantasy to repeat hurt to internal objects as solutions from an early time in life when the ego was overwhelmed. There seems to be no alternative to what later contributes to impasse in therapy. It is left for us to discover how to speak to unspeakable anxieties, to the state of each person's persecutory and damaged internal objects that prevents them from building containers for their partner's pain and terror.

References

Gampel, Y. (2005). *Ces parents qui vivent à travers moi: Les enfants des guerres.* Paris: Fayard.

Kirshner, L. A. (2006). The work of René Kaës: Intersubjective transmission in families, groups and culture. *Journal of American Psychoanalytic Association, 54:* 1005–1013.

Kogan, I. (1995). Love and the heritage of the past. *International Journal of Psycho-Analysis, 76:* 805–824.

Mann-Shalvi, H. (2006). German and Israeli Jews: Hidden emotional dynamics. In: H. Parens, A. Mahfouz, S. W. Twemlow & D. E. Scharff (Eds.), *The Future of Prejudice: Psychoanalysis and the Prevention of Prejudice* (pp. 255–268). Lanham, MD: Jason Aronson.

Mann-Shalvi, H. (2010). Three Minds—One Space: a combined emotional development of the couple and the *link.* Presented at the 4th conference of the International Association of Couple and Family Psychoanalysis, 28–30 July 2010, Buenos Aires.

Mann-Shalvi, H. (2016). *From Ultrasound to Army.* London: Karnac.

McDougall, J. (1988). *Plea for a Measure of Abnormality.* Madison, CT: International Universities Press.

Ogden, T. H. (1994). *Subjects of Analysis.* Northvale, NJ: Jason Aronson.

Scharff, D. E., & Scharff, J. S. (2011). *The Interpersonal Unconscious.* Lanham, MD: Jason Aronson.

CHAPTER THIRTEEN

Dora and Carlo

Diana Norsa (Rome, Italy)

A nalysts increasingly acknowledge the need for couple therapy, even when one or both partners are undergoing individual psychoanalysis. Analysts who are knowledgeable about relational dynamics see that parts of the analysand's personality are entangled in a couple link and remain unavailable to analysis, kept outside the transference relationship by resistance of both the patient and partner, blocking adequate interpretation and leading to possible impasse.

The couple I will describe sought help for violent arguments that erupted suddenly and without apparent reason. It is common to observe wrath in a couple, even though individually each partner is usually controlled and self-reflective. The impulsive reaction of one partner is triggered by the other's behaviour, reactivating a traumatic core previously split off and therefore psychically inaccessible. The couple's acting out, accompanied by mutual blame, is a defensive behaviour that limits each partner's self-awareness and activates defensive repetition compulsion. This triggers regression to superficial levels of couple behaviour, where adequate defence mechanisms are lacking.

In presenting this case, I will illustrate some specific aspects of work with couples: moments when explicit unconscious elements that need containment appear simultaneously in both partners, such as

239

helplessness and distress. Casual circumstances can affect both people unconsciously, with neither partner able to recognise what is transpiring with the other. Immediately refusal and deeply rooted defences arise to keep pervious traumatic events out of consciousness. Additionally, the conflict activated within the couple conceals inner unconscious reality that they share deeply.

My second point concerns how couples communicate. As we know, the process of symbolising enables us to use words with commonly shared meaning. In particular circumstances, words lose meaning because used to expel rage and pain concretely.

On this primitive level, couples function defensively: painful affects are driven out and each partner seeks to avoid becoming the container, succumbing to stiff, fixed roles. Such connections cause partners significant unease because they are incapable of psychic elaboration in being individually endowed with self-reflection. Despair ensues, indicating the need for couple therapy. Frequently, their uncontainable and impulsive explosions pose specific technical therapeutic problems (Norsa and Zavattini, 1997).

Dora and Carlo

Dora requests psychoanalytic psychotherapy for herself and Carlo because they are in "a state of intolerable discomfort". They are in their early fifties, both professionals, with one child, and each with a failed marriage behind them. In the past, Dora was in analysis and Carlo was briefly in psychotherapy. Although they had known each other for a long time, only later on did they notice a reciprocal attraction during their previous marriages. They started a passionate relationship that led Dora to separate (consensually) from her husband, while Carlo kept the affair secret for much longer. For many years, sexual attraction kept the couple connected, but arguments became more frequent, triggering their unease. They have been partners for over twenty years but have never married because, as we learned subsequently, Carlo never divorced his first wife due to the religious convictions of his mother.

Carlo and Dora agree that the main problem is Carlo's sudden outbursts of rage often followed by physical violence. The therapist they contacted is an experienced psychoanalyst working both in individual and couple therapy (I thank her for permission to discuss her material).

The therapeutic couple process started two years ago and continues once weekly. The analyst asked me to supervise her because in the first six months she found it hard to communicate when the couple's narratives had an impulsive, violent, unrestrained character. Communication was dense, heavy, and tended to fill her psychic space, making it almost impossible, to think, as in Bion's concept of "attacks on linking" (1959) or in Rosenfeld's (1971) considerations when he noticed that some patients use words like stones to hit the other or to intrude in the other's private space.

So how can we intervene clinically when our main tool for change, the function of elaboration, is constantly thwarted? I believe a classical analytic setting in which the couple is treated instead of the individual, is the best answer to their request for help. By this I mean a setting with clear rules concerning times, frequency, and duration of sessions. The words supplied by each partner are seen as free associations, because their flow is considered as single continuous material. Interpretations are addressed to the link and not to individual patients. The couple is the patient.

These are the basic elements which may contain the couple's overflowing anxiety. Gradually, we try to build the type of therapeutic alliance suggested by Bollas, which he defines as the patient experiencing the feeling of full participation in the analytical process with an analyst who listens and interprets.

> Indeed a part of any therapeutic alliance is the mutual recognition and use by patient and analyst of a procedure which precedes, holds, and will outlive any specific analytical couple, and which is implicitly present as a third object: the patient, the analyst, and the analytical process … . If people are unconsciously familiar with the structure of the analytical encounter, they bring their prior intersubjective experiences of such division to the clinical place. Further, the setting is often likened to the dream space which calls forth insider knowledge of the therapeutic alliance. (Bollas, 1998, p. 26)

The therapeutic alliance does not focus on the therapist but on the therapeutic process. This concept should be extended to psychoanalytical couple therapy.

The following clinical material highlights events to facilitate understanding of this case.

First year

Initially, the sequence of the sessions is regular. Dora takes most of the space, telling of episodes in which she accuses Carlo of being careless, off-putting, or even violent without cause. Carlo lets her speak. He is defensive but he cannot justify his behaviour, although he says that Dora gets on his nerves with constant requests for attention. Dora seems uninterested in listening to him and is prone to emotional outbursts that leave Carlo drained and unable to react.

The analyst feels a sense of helplessness. During supervision, we start identifying a pattern: Each time they start doing something together, an element breaks the harmony, Dora threatens to leave; Carlo cannot bear this and becomes violent. The analyst starts making interpretations about this collusive mode. The patients seem not to hear.

Dora brings a dream to the session that offers better understanding:

> The couple is in a beautiful, green valley about to have sexual intercourse when hostile people appear and threaten to rape or kill her. Carlo, impassive, doesn't move a finger; she wakes up distressed and treats Carlo as if he were the man in the dream.

As Fairbairn (1952) writes, each object in dreams (in this case the desired Carlo and the impassive Carlo) represents a sequence of objects in the dreamer's life (Dora's father, her brother, her first husband). It is also a split-off part of the dreamer. From the associations of both patients, it becomes clear the dream represents how impulsivity covers up fear of passivity. Material from later sessions allows connection to intrapsychic defensive structure emerging from Dora's dream (impulsivity covering up the fear of passivity) and to Carlo's intrapsychic functions, making a shared unconscious construct.

Considering the couple as the patient, we utilise the dream independently of the dreamer as associative material of the couple as a whole. We encourage participation of the partner to freely associate to the dream, building interpretations that refer to both. The dream function in couple psychotherapy is the "work of the co-construction of sense", which makes sense for both partners if the analyst is used, in the transference, as a third party (Nicolò, Norsa, & Carratelli, 2003). Dora dreams most in the couple, so in a sense Carlo leaves her the task of that function, which he tends to avoid. In such cases, the active dreamer contributes to psychic couple work by dreaming the couple's problems.

We can also trace reference to transference in Dora's dream. The third, the analyst, is seen as an intruder into the couple's private space, becoming the keeper of the partners' fractured aspects, considered abusive and violent. Therefore she is rejected. The prevailing feeling in the dream is anxiety deriving from the experience that the relationship provides no protection for the fragile, female parts of the couple. In this way, the analyst is also the "environment", the intermediate world.

In summary:

1. Impulsivity covers up the fear of passivity;
2. This defence is present in both partners;
3. This defence appears when the need for being taken care of becomes urgent;
4. Impulsivity risks overwhelming the fragile parts of the couple.

The dream is also about a couple trying to have sex, but interrupted by a violent intruder. The dream represents a sexual impulse with power to unite individuals who feel reciprocal desire. Simultaneously, the sexual impulse is seen as negative and capable of separating, committing rape, or even killing. The prevailing sentiments are fear, and then anger directed at the male figure who appears weak and unable to react or be protective.

In the dream, Carlo takes on the affective and psychic state of passive weakness. On awakening, Dora continues to accuse the real Carlo, maintaining that this is exactly the way he really behaves in not protecting her. Here we have a "symbolic equation" (Segal, 1957) that uses the language of reality to represent emotive states when internal part-object relations are confused with external ones. This is possible because Carlo unconsciously identifies with this representation. Indeed, in the dream Carlo is both the object of desire, capable of seeking out passionate encounter, and conversely, impotent and passive, reflecting a hidden part of Carlo's personality. Thus it is impossible for Carlo to dissociate himself from this projection.

Yet, it is more than a projection. In Dora's dream there is an unconscious unveiling of two contrasting aspects of Carlo: one capable of desire and affection, the other destructive and insensitive. These two aspects do not enter into direct conflict in the individual because they are split. Therefore, revealing these aspects through Dora's dream becomes dangerous not only for Carlo, who would have to deal with his double personality, but also for Dora, who in turn would have to deal with her double personality represented by her feminine and masculine components. We may add that the Carlo—the part-object of the dream—represents a failure in fundamental function: protecting the fragile feminine components. The failure of the primary environment for both of them, as confirmed by stories of the traumatic events in childhood, emerges during sessions immediately after the dream.

For a long time the equation that led Freud to identify femininity with passivity and submissiveness, and masculinity with activity, was rejected, since this associated a negative meaning to femininity/passivity and a positive one to masculinity/activity. However, Winnicott's (1971) recognition of passivity as receptiveness makes it easier to understand the process enacted here. We assume that a basic defect in the relationship came about during the developmental stage for both Carlo and Dora, referring to early experiences of passivity. Following Winnicott (1966, 1986), we conclude that passivity/receptivity taken on by the subjective self relates to the primary environment, and is not limited to the mother in her couple function of caring for the child. The term "environment" in its wider meaning indicates the affective atmosphere surrounding the arrival of a child in a family, and the ability of the environment to accept all its gloomy or sunny nuances (Norsa, 2014). In this sense, family or couple psychoanalytic therapy goes beyond the analyst/patient dyad, and is the best context for the emergence of the original environment.

When a couple relationship is preserved over time, a link is built that creatively amalgamates past and present, individuality and groupality. The couple has the task of elaborating past traumas that tend to repeat, in order to open the door to new possibilities. The procreative function of the couple (and family) is not only a biological imperative but is also a way of revitalising the subject mentally (Erikson, 1978) concerning themes of life and death—an indispensable component for the development of individuality. Dora's dream is "good" in representing the conflictual situation, but to be good, it needs a welcoming environment similar to the caring environment where a newborn child is cared for in three-dimensional space and movement. Therefore, the combination of the setting and the receptiveness with which the analyst listens to the implications of this dream regarding the couple's problems has created that transformative function essential for restarting their processing of the traumatic areas indicated by Carlo's impulsive reactions.

After this session, Dora and Carlo are more capable of listening to interpretations and reflecting on emotions, giving rise to a new phase in the therapy. In the next session Carlo, usually the silent one, is more willing to discuss feelings. He recounts that they were going shopping; while he is waiting for some information, Dora browses around the shop. This bothers him. He shouts violently, yanks her arm, and tells her to stay still. Dora was surprised by his reaction. "I cannot live with a man like this," she says convincingly. This time Carlo is not overpowered by the rage and fear that Dora's words usually trigger. His effort at self-control is evident. He describes how at the beginning he was enthusiastic about Dora's shopping for new lights for the house. However, when he noticed she was examining them and perhaps even choosing the lights on her own, he felt abandoned. The sense of co-operation was destroyed. He felt scorned and rejected. The analyst acknowledges the change represented by Carlo's admission of feeling abandoned and by Dora's dominance over him. They are both more explicit in expressing their wish to have the other by their side. But what does this wish mean? And why does it need to be countered every time it is expressed?

The family secret

In this period, the couple seems more willing to talk and to let the other talk about him/herself. They tell the analyst, now seen as non-judgemental and close to the couple, important events of their story. In order to respect the patients' privacy, I will not divulge personal details of the families. Some episodes of unknown violence came about in the family of Carlo's father before he was born. It was hushed up, never mentioned in the family. Dora refers to a break-up between her mother and mother's parents. No motive was ever given; no one in the family ever dared ask.

They also talk about Dora's job as a fashion designer, which she began as a young girl. This opens discussion on an atelier for Dora in their home. The flat they live in is large, with an extra room designated as Carlo's office, which he rarely uses. Dora uses the living room for her dresses and fashion models, requiring a lot of work to clear it every evening. They reflect on why they never managed to empty the extra room, which they agreed would be good as Dora's atelier. Each time they tried to clear the room of the years of accumulations, a fierce argument blocked the plan, much to their chagrin.

In supervision we reflect on the hypothesis that this room represents a common space that cannot be used because it is full of ghostlike aspects that cannot be elaborated: the unbreakable secret in Carlo's family before his birth, the family secret that prevents Dora from fulfilling her desire to be accepted. We decide it best not to interpret this unconscious level, but rather try and see if the couple can continue to elaborate these aspects that block them. On another level, the full room could represent Winnicott's potential space for imagination, necessary for building a good dream (Bion, 1992; Khan, 1974). In such a space, the "me" and "not me"—the other's alterity—could be accepted as less foreign.

In a very emotionally intense session where the partners are again involved in the usual fight that leaves them helpless and dejected, Carlo owns up that he cannot control himself when Dora threatens to leave him, while he would never leave her: a moment after having attacked her violently, he repents. He confesses that at that point he has a doubt that makes him feel terrible: did his forebears suffer from this same reactivity; was his impulsivity inherited?

In therapy, Carlo now asks Dora to admit that her relationship with her father, whom she had always considered an example of love and understanding, was strewn with fights. Dora admits she wanted to negate the frequent fights with her father, who died years ago, because she wanted only to remember good things about him. This allows her to accept interpretations that highlight her provocative role in the fights with Carlo, interpretations that had been made in the past, but that she had always rejected. The climate becomes more relaxed as they are able discuss their families. Carlo's mother emerges as strong-willed. Dora expresses her admiration for her. Her own mother was weak and ill, always in need of care and support. Dora had little respect for her, and consequently had little respect for those parts of herself identified with her mother. The analyst interprets the couple's transference to the analyst as the strong mother who survives their fights and facilitates their link. Dora weeps on remembering her deceased parents and her feelings of being alone. Carlo reassures her that he never will leave her alone.

In the following session, they are delighted to relate that they have managed to empty the extra room at last. Carlo woke up on Sunday morning saying he was going ahead with it, and managed to find someone to take the cumbersome couch away. Dora was incredibly happy when she saw the empty room. Carlo was surprised to see how quickly Dora brought the new atelier to life with tools and materials.

At this point Dora wants to talk about her childhood with her mother. For as long as she can remember, Dora understood that her mother needed to be protected and cared for. Something happened during her pregnancy with Dora, which Dora thinks caused the break-up between mother and grandmother. Probably her gynaecologist, who was her mother's brother, did not deliver the baby properly, risking the lives of mother and daughter. Grandmother always protected her son against insinuations of malpractice from Dora's mother, thus fracturing their relationship. Similarly, Dora remembers that she was always afraid of losing her mother.

The sense of emptiness and the creation of a potential space

In the following session, when the analyst opened the door, she was surprised to find nobody there. Then Carlo and Dora suddenly appeared together. They began by saying there had been no fights, so they were having difficulty saying anything. Dora saw a movie and was moved at the story of the illness and death of a mother. She realises she has an underlying feeling of death. Deaths of loved ones furtively embed themselves under her skin.

Carlo says he took his mother to a ceremony at church in memory of his father (he shows an almost imperceptible sign of emotion), but her observance and habits bother him. He finds it hard to be on close terms with her, yet he knows he must see her. The mother complains that her caretaker is unkind, but Carlo sides with the caretaker, trying to mediate.

The analyst notices that Carlo moves his chair closer to Dora, who moves further away. The analyst thinks Carlo wants to be physically close to Dora when he talks about death, but she rejects this contact as too much to take. The analyst tries to contact Carlo's emotion regarding his father's memorial, but he withdraws. Dora continues, saying that Carlo stifled his emotions when his father died. Carlo takes this as an accusation.

The analyst says that they have a sort of rubber band reaction to these issues: when communication on painful emotions is stretched to the maximum, they withdraw for fear the rubber band will break, so it goes slack. They are unable to discuss emotions, so feelings simmer in the background.

During an unusually long silence, the analyst feels the concentration and tension of all three of them as they sit. Then Dora remembers the smile of Carlo's father. It was a remarkable smile: "He would look at you and it felt like a caress, a sweet, caressing gaze. Carlo used to be like that too, but he no longer is."

Carlo recalls his father's death: he died silently without drama, consistent with the cultural traditions of country people where death is seen as a natural event. The only thing he wanted of his father's was his keychain. When tears start to flow, he compares his emotions to a flooding river. He evokes the road trips with his father, a privilege awarded only to him and not his siblings. He recalls the phrase engraved on the medallion of the key chain: "When you speed, remember us at home!"—a popular phrase in those days. Dora listens in earnest silence.

In supervision, we discuss how the session started with the analyst fantasising on emptiness. The themes of emptiness, death, and pain were expressed in metaphors: the analyst uses the rubber band metaphor, for example, and Carlo, the flooding river.

In the following session, Carlo brings a dream for the first time. He has always been sceptical about dreams. He hardly dreams, but when he does, his dreams are dreary and refer mostly to simple past events. "There's nothing much to interpret there," he usually says. Now he too is surprised that he is telling a "real" dream.

> Carlo is in a sun-baked, desolate prairie unknown to him. He has difficulty walking but he has to hurry because a truck is coming and he needs to reach the petrol station to hitch a ride. If he doesn't get there, the truck won't stop. The ground is sandy and he sinks into it with each step. When he reaches the station he has to hold up signs so that the truck sees him. When he hears the truck arriving, he also hears horsemen galloping behind. He's afraid and wakes up sweating from fear, but doesn't know why.

The interpretation of the dream is limited to what concerns the couple, so the analyst works on the associations of both partners. Dora connects the dream to Carlo's father and the trips they used to take together. In supervision, we wonder if the horsemen, a clear symbol of sexual potency, are there to protect, or are potential outlaws ready to assault.

It is useful to remember that in psychoanalytically oriented couple therapy, some intrapsychic levels cannot be reached and therefore are not analysed. At times we must wonder what depths can be reached in couple therapy.

One year later

They come in smiling. Carlo says things are going well now. They co-operate and feel hopeful. Carlo says they made love and both felt better after it. It had not happened for a while, because he had some sexual failures, but not this time!

Dora shrugs this off and says she has never been so upset and worried. After the last session, she reflected on weighty issues that put her in contact with unconscious questions. She had the same dream she had previously during her individual analysis, of an aborted, stillborn baby. I think it refers to myself, she says pensively.

Silence. Then she adds that she had another dream that made her feel better.

> She was pregnant and wanted an ultrasound. She goes to the laboratory, but it is totally dark and she can't see anything. She is worried, then somebody takes her by the hand and makes her lie down. There is now a little light and she sees the back of the foetus, it is a formless mass, like clay when one sculpts. It is an ugly monster, but then it turns around and it's a girl with features that are much clearer than she expected. She is surprised and happy when she sees the girl looks like herself and Carlo.

As usual, she fills the session with her own problems: her anxiety as a child when her mother was pregnant, and the thought that she would die, her experiences of being confined to bed when she was pregnant losing their second baby, and not being able to have children afterwards.

In a quiet moment, the analyst asks Carlo what he was thinking while Dora spoke. He says he is sorry and knows how painful the miscarriage was for her. Carlo reflects on how they would have had a twenty-year-old daughter now. Dora goes back to her own thoughts without taking into account the suffering Carlo felt regarding her dream. The analyst, thinking they are two "sweepers", is exasperated and sees the previous progress diminishing.

Carlo turns to the analyst: "See what we're like? When I say things are getting better, she talks of her despair." Dora says that if she feels something, she has to say it. She also adds the importance of the fact that they like doing things together.

The analyst says, "I wonder if we can pin our hopes on a child who will grow up to have its own life. It seems that each of you has a need to state your autonomy, after which you are sorry if the other does not acknowledge it. Maybe, as Carlo said, only this constant struggle makes you feel alive, strong and fierce."

Dora is struck. "It's true," she says. "Whenever something beautiful happens, I am afraid that it can die, as if I can't accept that things can go well because they could disappear."

The analyst tells them that in opposing each other they challenge their link. They want to check that, despite all the anxiety and misunderstanding, their relationship is still strong, their sexual attraction still alive, that they have a future.

Carlo admits that he needs to learn to communicate emotions without waiting to come here. If only he could tell her what he feels, their dialogue would be more useful to them. The analyst confirms that when Carlo does not communicate what he feels, he is asking Dora to do it for both of them. On the other hand, Dora waits for Carlo to solve all the practical questions, so she is frustrated when this does not happen. This causes Carlo to feel offended, and think there is no longer co-operation between them, and he shuts down.

The analyst continues: through her dream, Dora says she appreciates when someone takes her hand and leads her with a light in the dark. She is discovering that something is growing inside of her despite the fear and anger. It's a girl like her, and it looks like both of them.

In supervision, we reflect on other important aspects concerning emerging male and female elements in the session. They had sexual intercourse, proving they still feel attraction for each other. But Carlo also mentions his guilt for his failures towards Dora. We wonder if his sexual failures refer to failures in his identification with his father, if he needs to acknowledge this in his male identity. Dora identifies with her mother. Her fear of death conceals her desire to be a woman who could bear a child, but also have a couple relationship with a life of its own.

It is interesting to note that the dream that upset Dora in her former analysis contained an aborted, stillborn boy. In my opinion, its reappearance indicates her depressive core. It could be that such a deep, depressive core can never be modified and will remain fixed and split from other parts of the personality that are more capable of relating to the outside world. The couple relationship stimulates each partner's regressive levels (and certainly their link is deeply rooted in their intrapsychic core), but it can also communicate with the original traumatic core and produce a new internal construction, a less traumatic image of the original self, as the girl in Dora's dream. It can help with healing. In this dream, we see the baby's back, representing an autistic closure, as all sense organs are in the front. Turning one's back is a primitive way of rejecting contact with objects. This corresponds to the countertransference impression the analyst has of Dora's behaviour, and in particular her prevailing attitude towards Carlo during this session.

Dora associates amorphous clay that can be transformed in an omnipotent and masturbatory play, with a lost child. Only when she is willing to risk communicating with the other (she turns the baby and exposes the side with sensory organs primarily open to the outside) can she become aware of a possible integration: it's a girl, in better shape than she thought, that looks like both parents. In this phase, all potential elements of communication with the other are present, along with recognition of the primal scene and individual identity.

The same intrapsychic level is moving in Carlo, too, when he recounts his dream with the truck and horsemen: self-recognition in his identification with his father opens the possibility of space for aggression and ambivalence. But just when Carlo can contact and communicate his emotions, Dora has to reject them because she can no longer use him to represent her idealised internal object. Now she also must face her own ambivalence.

I still believe the couple is moving in fear and doubt regarding their ability to face oedipal conflict. Male and female are still identified with primitive partial objects. Each is convinced of their omnipotence and strong sexual identification—Carlo with male elements nearer to a phallus than a penis, and Dora with a sexually seductive woman who expects to be served by a male—as if each were the stronger sex, with expectation that the other will fill them out. I am referring to stratified sexual identity levels in each, and the way in which the couple's sexuality is based on their emotional connection to masculinity and femininity.

Conclusion

In a world where the family has undergone so many changes, and social boundaries are no longer able to contain distress and unhappiness, the individual is more intent on seeking well-being, unable to support unelaborated inner conflicts. In the past, the processes of splitting and integration were left behind developmentally. A mature person could respond to the responsibilities assigned by society. Today, these roles are less rigidly defined.

The couple relationship has become a psychic space where unelaborated aspects of personality can emerge through acting out, often with violence. These mental spaces are complex and diversely articulated. Their diversity can be found in intrapsychic, intra-personal, and intersubjective space—all areas of unconscious expression.

I present this case is to illustrate how the psychoanalytic couple setting provides the analyst a way of working on the parts of the self that are outside of awareness. In a nutshell, obstruction in the development of identity provoked widespread uneasiness without manifesting individual symptomatology. Both partners had profound problems concerning identification due to traumatic elements of their same-sex parents, highlighted and addressed during the therapeutic treatment. Behind a reactive impulsivity there was almost always a traumatic scenario. When that event was brought to light within the couple, we witnessed "enactments" in the relationship.

In couple psychoanalytic psychotherapy the analyst has the opportunity to be involved as a witness, just as in classical psychoanalysis. In the session, the analyst becomes part of the internal dynamic and the real-life scene, but at the same time is the analyst in the real-life role. For the couple, this experience is important because the "me" and the "not me" can be registered in the same time and space as a different level of psychic reality, which can however be registered simultaneously. The process of psychotherapeutic work goes on, stimulating differentiation and dissolving the feelings of confusion and distress.

Discussion of "Dora and Carlo" by Diana Norsa

Lia Rachel Colussi Cypel and Susana Muszkat (Brazil)

Diana Norsa presents rich clinical material with thoroughly developed theoretical constructions concerning intrapsychic and intersubjective levels of this relationship. Commenting on someone else's clinical material is always difficult. Our point of view will lack the lived experience of the analyst in session. The countertransferential aspects can be communicated, but not experienced. Another difficulty is that it would be exhausting or impossible to elaborate on the innumerable points and situations brought up by Dr Norsa. She, too, had to select from what her supervisee had presented, as did the supervisee when bringing material to supervision. Hence, ours will be the selection of the selection of the selection.

For the sake of organisation, we enumerate the points for discussion:

1. The couple described by Norsa appears to have a link based on primitive psychic functioning. The anxieties and defences seem predominantly those of earlier stages of mental development. They report repetition of "violent arguments erupting suddenly for irrelevant reasons", indicative of minds unable to contain that impulsively expel threats to inner stability. Furthermore, the analyst describes them as incapable of being together or apart, relying on precarious resources to deal with intolerable feelings.

2. When close together, do they feel the threat of being lost in the other in a primitive fusional state? Whereas, when apart, they feel in terrible need of the containing aspect they lack, expecting the other to provide it, therefore unable to resort to each other for reverie and/or containment. This state of psychic precariousness is often felt as a violent purposeful rebuff of the needed other, as if the other were refusing to give what he or she actually has. Consequently, feelings of rejection, abandonment, and, ultimately, lack of love prevail, triggering angered-filled, violent responses. This repeated dynamic generates a particular link that reinforces their aggressive fantasies about each other, producing a specific co-constructed pattern that, in turn, effects their subjectivity. In other words, subjects (individuals) produce links, and links produce subjectivities (Berenstein & Puget, 1997).

3. The couple seeks analysis because of "a state of intolerable discomfort" due to "violent arguments erupting suddenly for irrelevant reasons." In *Civilization and its Discontents*, Freud (1930a) coins the expression "narcissism of small differences" to describe a violence directed against the other based on the wrongful idea that there exist meaningful differences between people. The differences in these cases are minor; the antagonism is a reaction stemming from fear of losing one's narcissistically idealised sense of self. In this way, individuals violently and expulsively project unwanted aspects of self onto the other.

4. Intolerable discomfort and impulsive violence also indicate lack of an adequate container (psyche), lack of inner space to take in and

transform sensations into symbolisable elements and communicate them in productive ways. The lack of alpha function (Bion) impedes the transformation of beta elements into dreamable alpha elements. It is worth noting that when the wife later presents her first dream, new metaphorical possibilities—alpha function—are opened for both of them. This development helps them put into words feelings that hitherto could only be evacuated by way of impulsive actions.

5. That they have been together for many years speaks of the strength of their link. However, links are mostly based on unconscious rather than conscious motivations. Therefore, a long-term relationship may also be indicative of a no-way-out pathological repetition, of infantile object relations seeking resolution through the relationship where neither can provide containment because they share a lack of psychic resources and are hence trapped in "intolerable discomfort", fear of abandonment, helplessness, and despair.

6. Miguel Spivacow (2015) lists three essential elements that constitute the backbone of structure and quality to couple links: unconscious alliances, unconscious bi-directionality, and intersubjective aspects. The couple analyst tries to assess its intersubjective dynamics or common discourse. What each member says influences and interferes with what and how the other replies. This ongoing interplay unconsciously determines their shared dynamic. How are we able to understand the interrelation of these three aspects? Spivacow says, "What constitutes the underpinning of the intersubjective dynamic, its core, is the way each one receives (takes in, absorbs) whatever comes from the other and the complexity of their bond. I am referring, for example, to their ways of disagreeing, containing, welcoming, refusing, rejecting, interpreting, validating, being in tune with or not, reflecting, manipulating, reaching consensus, or being able to see different aspects of the other" (2015, p. 67). Thus, the co-constructed link affects each of them at the intrapsychic level; it operates on their subjectivities. The analyst takes active part in this field and dynamic system.

7. As analysts, we participate in the analytic field with our entire being. Like each partner, the analyst is a presence. Our mind is our main resource. Beyond intellectual ability, we offer a state of reverie, a mind capable of taking in and transforming experience into productive elements.

In link theory (Berenstein & Puget, 1997) we work with the concept of the other as an interfering presence. Unlike the individual setting, where we only have access to a third person via patients' reports, in link analysis we take into account *presentations* rather than *representations*. Furthermore, the analyst is not a neutral but an interfering presence. Bodily posture, tone of voice, silence, receptiveness, the possibility of containing patients through their explosions, the true wish to understand and find meaning as well as tolerance of lack of knowledge and understanding (negative capacity), the ability to hold things inside instead of using words for evacuation or to fill the unknown space, are all aspects of vital transformative significance.

The element of presence requires that we deal with a real present and responsive other, a radically different other who bears singular, unreachable, and unknown aspects. We refer here to the other's foreignness (*ajenidad*), his non-representable and alien aspect (Berenstein & Puget, 1997). Presence as an element of couple and family analysis (and not of individual analysis) necessarily imposes a tension, a confrontation, a power struggle or imbalance. It is, nevertheless, an invaluable resource.

8. Another feature of this material is the couple's motivation. The way they communicate makes us think of them as continuously on guard so as to prevent a deadly blow (Dora speaks of a constant underlying sense of death; Carlo of unspeakable family violence). We understand violence as failure of psychic representation, pointing to poor working-through of necessary symbolic castration/cut, failure leading to a lack of boundaries necessary to self-differentiation.

Representation and symbolisation are products of bound psychic energy. Unbound psychic energy is unable to find a productive form of discharge (e.g., dreams, conversation, artistic manifestations). Consequently, it becomes traumatic in itself as it overpowers the mental apparatus, destructively projected outside into the partner's mind. This couple's violent projective identifications give rise to Dora's repeated threats to leave Carlo, which, in turn, trigger Carlo's physical violence. When threatening to leave, does Dora feel she will leave all her troubles behind without realising that she is part of the constitutive troubled element of their link and that the link would not be what it is if both of them were not who and how they are together?

On a different note, we speculate that in fantasy, Dora's threat acts in a powerful, protective manner toward herself. Or it could derive from a wish for emotional reassurance of keeping Carlo near despite her threats. Could this be an awkward expression of her wish to act powerfully?

Dora admires Carlo's mother's strength and feels threatened when unprotected by the powerful qualities she wishes her own mother and Carlo had. Consequently, in another confusion, she sees threats to leave as indicative of her own protective potency.

9. The analyst tells her supervisor of feelings of confusion, paralysis, and emptiness. She has trouble communicating "with an area of psychic elaboration in the couple". The couple's communications paralyse her creative thinking because her mind is constantly filled with "junk". We are reminded of the unproductive extra room in the couple's home, so chaotically cluttered that it serves no purpose. In the attack on linking and thinking, saturated elements (the junk) impede creative processes (Bion), suggesting Dorian Gray's portrait, hidden away in a room in a narcissistic attempt to hide rejected, split-off elements—violence as a counterpart to neglected, non-integrated aspects of personality.

An asymmetry marks a difference between analyst and couple. Her mind can act as a container for what circulates in the room without unproductively throwing it back at the patients, as they do with each other. The impact of their interaction on the analyst and her sense of helplessness are related to theirs. The analyst undergoes this real emotional experience in person rather than apprehending it as a representation. It is under the effect of this emotion that she seeks supervision. The supervisor, in turn, is a containing other who helps her clean up her mental room. In this way, she recovers creative potency and helps the couple do the same.

10. The cluttered unused room is also a shared split-off space that has been transmitted transgenerationally. Transgenerational elements are like "unknown secrets" passed on by previous generations and kept "out of circulation". Transgenerationality implies transmission that respects no boundaries, limits, or subjective spaces, not acknowledging the difference of the other as an autonomous individual. Thus, it is not transformative. The transmitted elements remain unrepresented, moving across generations as crypts— alien, non-integrated unconscious elements that only appear as symptoms. This transmission alienates individuals, impeding transformation and singularity. Individuals cannot appropriate what they inherited with their own, unique mark. Rather, they

are "stuck" to what was transmitted to them in a non-signifiable, useless manner.

Intergenerational aspects, in contrast, are conscious or unconscious foundations, values, codes, and binding elements whereby individuals experience belonging to a hereditary chain. They contribute to the link, unlike transgenerational aspects, which are disruptive and pathological.

We learn that Carlo is unable to divorce his previous wife and marry Dora because he is subjected to his mother's injunctions. He cannot transform what was received from previous generations into something novel, constructive, and pertinent. Dora is unable to think of them as a creative couple, remaining linked to a fantasised, idealised, and potent father figure, which she expects to find in Carlo.

Nevertheless, we follow the analyst's success in helping the couple construct new space for themselves, more aware of their implications for the relationship, learning more about their personal needs, their expectations of each other, and their reactions to frustration. Their newly gained capacity for dreaming is a rich result of their analytic process, helping create common discourse and develop a more supportive containing space.

We thank Dr. Norsa for the opportunity to discuss this rich case. Such exchanges always give an opportunity to expand our own space for creative production and reflection as analysts, to open ourselves to new theoretical and clinical perspectives.

References

Berenstein, I., & Puget, J. (1997). *Lo vincular. Teoría y clínica psicoanalítica* (The Link: Psychoanalytic Theory and Clinical Practice). Buenos Aires: Paidós.

Bion, W. R. (1959). Attacks on linking. *International Journal of Psycho-Analysis, 40*: 308–315.

Bion, W. R. (1992). *Cogitations*. London: Karnac.

Bollas, C. (1998). Origins of the therapeutic alliance. *Scandinavian Psycho-analytic Review, 21*: 24–36.

Erikson, E. H. (1978). *Adulthood*. New York: Norton.

Fairbairn, W. R. D. (1952). *Psychoanalytic Studies of the Personality*. London: Routledge.

Freud, S. (1930a). *Civilization and its Discontents. S. E., 21*. London: Hogarth.

Khan, M. R. (1974). *The Privacy of the Self.* London: Hogarth.

Nicolò, A. M., Norsa, D., & Carratelli, T. (2003). Playing with dreams: The introduction of the third person into the transference dynamic of the couple. *Journal of Applied Psychoanalytic Studies, 5:* 283–296.

Norsa, D. (2014). Transformations through repetitions of female and male representations in reconstructed families. In: A. M. Nicolò, P. Benghozi & D. Lucarelli (Eds.), *Families in Transformation* (pp. 109–195). London: Karnac.

Norsa, D., & Zavattini, G. C. (1997). *Intimità e Collusione.* Raffaello Cortina: Milan Italy.

Rosenfeld, H. (1971). A clinical approach to the psychoanalytic theory of the life and death instincts. *International Journal of Psycho-Analysis, 52:* 169–178.

Segal, H. (1957). Notes on symbol formation. *International Journal of Psychoanalysis, 38:* 391–405.

Winnicott, D. W. (1966). Split-off male and female elements. In: *Psycho-Analytic Explorations* (pp. 169–183). London: Karnac, 1989.

Winnicott, D. W. (1971). Creativity and its origins. In: *Playing and Reality* (pp. 65–85). London: Tavistock.

Winnicott, D. W. (1986). *Home Is Where We Start From.* London: Penguin.

CHAPTER FOURTEEN

Now you see us, now you don't: dealing with resistance in episodic couple treatment

Janine Wanlass, PhD

One of the common challenges in beginning a course of couple treatment is securing the couple's shared commitment to the treatment process. Resistance surfaces in many forms. Often one partner brings the other to be fixed, locating the difficulty in the other and bristling at any suggestion of a shared difficulty or problematic unconscious fit. Alternately, attacks on the frame revealed in missed or cancelled sessions sometimes surface as the couple dynamics unfold, creating a challenge in couple containment and threatening to end the treatment before it begins. Ambivalence about treatment appears in the couple's conflicting requests for help accompanied by their verbal insistence that therapy is futile. Such challenges are captured in the episodic couple treatment of Roger and Cathy, who insistently request help yet only remain for two to five sessions. They drop out of treatment and reappear some six or ten months later, again requesting help, and again demonstrating reluctance to stay engaged in the process. For the therapist, questions arise about securing a treatment agreement, understanding the couple's ambivalence, providing adequate containment for exploration, and managing countertransference feelings of frustration and failure. I feel entangled in acting out an aspect of the couple's dynamic, rather than finding a way to place it between us for reflection and understanding.

Roger and Cathy: session one

Roger (forty) and Cathy (thirty-six) were referred for treatment by a mutual friend of the couple. Cathy made the initial phone contact, offering little information other than "my marriage is in trouble". Both on the phone and at the beginning of the in-person consultation, I set up the frame for treatment, outlining the plan to meet for two to four sessions for us to assess whether or not working together could be helpful. When they arrived for the first consultation session, Cathy seemed anxious, speaking quickly and continuously in that first clinical hour. Although Roger stated that he wanted to work on his marriage, I was not convinced, guessing that he had complied with Cathy's insistence that they seek help. Initially, I had trouble understanding what brought them to treatment, as Cathy described their "communication difficulties" in vague terms. She mentioned that the couple struggled after the birth of their youngest child who was now four. When I asked Roger and Cathy to describe this "struggle", Cathy noted, "Oh, you know, the usual problems of having a new baby—no sleep, little sex, jealous older siblings, demanding work schedules." Thinking that their "baby" was now four, I wondered what had occurred in the interim. Noting Roger's near silence, I asked if he agreed with Cathy's assessment. He responded, "Yes, but the reason we're here is I had an affair." His curt, direct statement in the midst of her sea of jumbled words startled me. Cathy commented that she avoided bringing it up right away, worried he would feel hurt or embarrassed, "like I'm blaming him for all our problems". Roger continued, "I never meant for it to happen. I certainly wasn't looking for someone to cheat with, but Jenna was just there, someone to talk to."

As the session continued, I learned that Cathy felt overwhelmed balancing work stressors and the demands of caring for three children. Feeling her own mother had been neglectful, Cathy focused almost entirely on the children's needs to the exclusion of their couple relationship and her own needs. Although not stated directly, I sensed Cathy was angry with Roger for his limited involvement in scheduling the children's daily activities and weekend family events. Roger denied having a drinking problem, but Cathy felt his "one to two drinks a night" interfered with his family involvement. Frustrated, Roger again interrupted Cathy's flood of words, an edge of anger in his voice. "I'm not an alcoholic. My mother drank all the time, so I know the difference. I'm a cheater like my mother yes, but an alcoholic, no." Feeling the sting of his reprimand, Cathy looked at me, "I know I'm part of the problem. I don't really know how to be close. I worry about the kids all the time, and I know it drives him crazy, but I can't stop." As the session ended, Roger noted that his parents have a "good relationship", while Cathy's parents divorced when she was seven. I felt immersed in a competition, as though each partner were trying to pass the dysfunction award to the other. Roger made the last comment: "I don't know how my dad put up with her all those years, drinking herself into oblivion."

Discussion

How can the core concepts of object relations theory help us understand this couple interaction and their underlying couple dynamics, even in this first meeting? Drawing from Fairbairn and Dicks, there is a predominance of bad object relationships in this pairing, both in the individuals themselves and in the joint marital personality. Cathy takes up a great deal of space without much emotional presence, and her longing for approval is palpable in her words and in my countertransference. Her fragmented self-structure and eclipsed central ego is reflected in her verbal communication, which lacks cohesion and direction. Like the neglected child, the way she both pulls for relating and negates herself is evident in her lack of overt complaint about Roger's affair, her over-investment in the needs of others at her own expense, and in her self-critical demeanour. Although she must be angry with both her mother and Roger, she has difficulty directly expressing any negative feeling. Given her report of childhood neglect and her way of interacting within the session, I thought she was unlikely to have experienced a good-enough mother who could contain her overwhelming anxiety and impart a thinking function. In this session, Cathy displays a preoccupied attachment style that disorganises under stress.

In contrast, Roger demonstrates a dismissive attachment style, offering little elaboration of his emotional experience, minimising his dependency needs, and mostly remaining out of emotional contact with me as I struggle to read his emotional states. This avoidance is peppered with episodic announcements, defining his experience in the black/white terms of the paranoid-schizoid position. He splits his parents into good/bad, wondering why his father put up with his mother, but showing no curiosity about why his mother drank excessively or had affairs. His views of his parents' relationship seem contradictory, telling me that they had a "good relationship" while describing conflict and acting-out. He moves into the depressive position briefly, when he expresses guilt and regret about his affair. I feel his anguish over actions that align him with the mother he detests. This is an example of how a bad maternal object becomes fused with a part of the self, repressed to manage the painful affects, yet acted out in his sexual behaviour.

I experience this couple more like a pair of young siblings than lovers or parents. This suggests something about the couple's developmental functioning, speaking to unmet childhood needs for nurturance and feeding. They seem to have little sense of themselves as a couple, lacking a "couple state of mind" (Morgan, 2005) and its creative potential. This is apparent in my difficulty fantasising about the ways they parent or intimately relate. In the session, they rarely look at each other when speaking, directing their words more to me than to each other. There is a sense of profound loneliness and sadness in both partners. Cathy diverts her needs for intimacy to her children, using them for comfort that sidesteps adult sexuality. Roger projects his dependency needs into Cathy and alcohol, splitting off his sexual desire outside the marriage, perhaps protecting his sense of vulnerability. The couple seems caught in a closed system lacking creative space, and bad feelings predominate in a repetitive cycle. They either blame the other or themselves, exhibiting anxiety that gets channeled into non-productive rumination in Cathy or edgy aggression in Roger. He holds her anger; she holds his neediness.

From the standpoint of chaos and link theories, we just see hints of possible organising patterns that may help explain the couple's unconscious fit and current difficulties. We hear that Roger's mother had affairs and a drinking problem, which would represent a potential vertical link, but we know nothing of his grandparents' generation. In Roger's startling, blunt entrance into the session, I wonder about his conception—was it planned, a surprise? This idea gains additional footing given Cathy's explanation that their problems began at the birth of their third child. Cathy made no mention of her father, leaving me thinking about absence and emotional withdrawal. What is the nature of their internal couple representations? Roger told us that Cathy's parents divorced when she was seven, and I wondered about the ages of this couple's children. Is the eldest child seven? Despite Cathy's insistence about her devotion to their children, there is no mention of the children by name in this first session. At times, I find myself forgetting that the couple has children, leaving me to question if the children are attended to physically but not seen as developing individuals in this family. And what of the couple's social, economic, and cultural standing? They did not enquire about my fee before coming in, nor did they baulk at the amount. Roger is Caucasian; Cathy is Latina. What does this ethnic difference mean to them and how does it play out in their families of origin and, in the current horizontal link with their extended families now?

At this point, I can only hypothesise and conjecture, formulating ideas yet remaining open to revision and change as the treatment progresses.

Session two

Roger and Cathy enter the office. He chooses a place in the corner of the couch, up against the armrest and furthest from me. Cathy sits down, first placing herself on the opposite end of the couch, then moving closer to Roger. They exchange a glance.

R: [Looking at Cathy] I know I always sit here, which leaves you kind of relegated to a distance or just in the middle, but I feel I need the support.

(Roger's use of the word "always" strikes me, as the couple has only been here one time. He seems to grasp the edges of the couch to define him, almost like an autistic object. He is aware that he's leaving her "unsupported" but is unable to move toward her or find another way to couple. She seems to be flailing, with no edges without Roger. Her identity appears fluid to me, defined in her role as "wife", yet I cannot place the two as a couple. My mind puts them in a class of prepubescent fifth graders, and I expect him to slug her on the arm as a form of affection.)

[The couple exchanges a smile, and Cathy reaches for Roger's hand. She turns to me.]

c: I think we're doing better. [To Roger] Do you agree?

r: I do. I wouldn't say things are great, but it's better than last week.

c: I'm almost afraid to say we're doing better, because usually when I do this, you contradict me.

r: No, I agree.

(I notice that they are talking to each other, much different than last time, when they barely glanced at each other and mainly engaged with me. Feels too quick for "better".)

j: And what is "better"?

c: Ummm. Closer. We're not so far away. We spent time together last night, when we would usually be apart. We tend to gravitate to our own quarters. He stays in his office, and I go into the bedroom. He does stuff on his computer, and I do work stuff on mine. That is, once the kids are in bed. I think we're pretty collaborative and involved with that. [She stops abruptly] Hmmm. Maybe that's not right. We pass the baby back and forth, so maybe it's not so together after all.

(Again, that word "baby". The child is four. What is it about a baby place? The neediness and dependence? And what of the passing the baby back and forth? Is this the way they pass their baby feelings to each other, like a hot potato?)

r: [To me] I don't know that the separate quarters means anything really. I mean, she could come into my office to do her work if she wanted. I'm there because my computer is there, and I'm usually doing stuff like bills. It's just easier to sit in there. I can get work done.

c: Or surf the net. [They both laugh. A bit of playfulness between them.] I don't really like it in there, because there's no soft place to sit. I just feel more comfortable in the bedroom. Besides, I'm really trying not to bring work home.

r: Have I complained about that lately?

c: No, but I'm trying to make an effort. I know I don't act like it sometimes, because I'm always caught up in the kids, and I tense up when you try to be affectionate.

r: I don't try much anymore.

c: I am working on it.

r: But that's just the thing. You've been working on this for years. You keep telling me that you're talking about it with your individual therapist. I'm trying to be understanding, but nothing really changes. I don't know why, I don't understand about the sex [He looks at me] She's always so distant.

(I feel drawn towards C in this moment as he locates everything problematic in her.)

c: I know it's my problem. I create the distance.

(I'm struck by this comment, as Roger has his own way of distancing in the session, body closed in, inaccessible. Also, I think of his drinking in the evenings as a way of distancing. I feel sad as I listen to the two of them.)

r: I used to try, but I really don't any more. I figure this is just something I need to accept about the marriage ... there will always be distance. I used to want something more, but marriage is about compromise, right? [He sounds angry, looks up at me]

j: Compromise? Feels a bit more like a frustrated surrender or a defeat.

r: Hmmm. Yeah, I think so. A hopeless defeat. I've given up, I mean not on the marriage, but on any closeness or connection. [To her] And not just sexual.

c: [To me, anxiously] I mean when I said things were better earlier, it is true. We are getting along better, we're talking more. We're watching a movie together at night. We haven't done that in a long time.

r: I didn't mean that nothing's better, but our basic problems haven't changed.

c: I don't know what's wrong with me, why I can't be close. I try to let him in, but I don't seem to get anywhere. I've tried to think about my past, whether or not there's some kind of abuse. I mean, I know my mother is a hard person to live with.

r: We agree on that. Sometimes when I have to deal with her mother, I think, "No wonder she is that way." Her mother is critical, chaotic, drives me crazy to be in the same room with her for two seconds. Good thing she lives in another country [I think of the separate quarters] I also know her parents hated each other [I notice that Roger is talking for Cathy]

J: Do you agree with Roger's description?

C: Umhmm. I remember wanting to be close to my mother, but she would just push me away. You know, like when you are a little kid, and you just want to stand next to her, feel her body next to yours. But she couldn't tolerate any of that "childish foolishness". She was too wrapped up in her own world to deal with me. I think that's why I connected through sex when I was younger. I don't mean really young—as a late teenager.

(I have this flash of seeing her with another woman. Where is this coming from? I notice she doesn't say the gender of her adolescent partner.)

J: You got involved with someone?

C: Yeah, a guy friend of mine. That's why this is so confusing. It's not like I'm not attracted to Roger. I think he's very attractive physical-ly, but I can't move into the physical connection. Something stops me. Keeps me at a distance. I don't know what it is, but I know I'm distant. And it's not just physical. I create the distance between us.

J: [To Roger] Is it just Cathy or is there some sort of distancing in you too?

R: Why do you ask?

J: I'm just trying to understand how you relate as a couple. You want closeness, and yet you married someone who has trouble with it.

R: But that's just it. We, she, didn't have trouble at the beginning. [He looks at his wife] You remember, we were always sneaking around, having sex downstairs while your mom was upstairs. It was a little awkward at first, because she had more sexual experience, and I was nervous. But we actually had no trouble, and not just being sexually close. I think we were emotionally close too.

J: And what happened?

R: I don't know. We had kids, the baby was sleeping between us.

C: But it happened before that I think … I know you probably don't want me to say this, but I think the drinking was very hard for me. I know you do it to relax, but it made you so distant, like you were just checked out. I didn't feel like having sex then, because it was like I wasn't having sex with you.

R: I wasn't drinking that much then. I don't even drink that much now. I mean, I probably would drink more, but she hates it.

J: Drink more?

R: Yeah, because I have to do something. I always feel anxious every second of the day. The psychiatrist diagnosed me with a generalised anxiety disorder. I tried therapy for it, I tried medication, but nothing really helps. Sometimes, it just feels paralysing. Drinking takes away the pressure, from work, from her. I don't feel it so acutely, and I'm less irritable with her, less impatient. But then we often start fighting about it.

J: Maybe the drinking serves multiple purposes. It's a way of quieting the constant anxiety and a way of signaling the unhappiness between you. It also starts a fight, burying any feelings of wanting to be close.

R: So, I am distancing after all. Is that what you mean?

(There is tension, and I feel he is angry with me. Perhaps I moved toward interpreting too quickly.)

C: I know I create the distance. It isn't Roger.

J: So what just happened here?

C: What do you mean?

J: Roger, I think, you felt criticised by my comment about your drinking, almost as though I was proving you wrong about your statement that you don't think you are distant.

R: [Interrupting] No. Well maybe. I just felt really irritated with you all the sudden. I guess it was sort of like "Hah! I caught you at it."

J: Like I wanted to be right.

R: Yeah, and probably tell me it's my fault.

J: And then, Cathy when you felt the tension between us, you jumped in to say it was your fault.

R: [Looks at wife] We are quite a pair, aren't we? I say, it's not me. You say, no it's me, at the same time you're saying, but it's really you. [To me] See, this is where we always go in therapy. "Whose fault is this?" And that gets us exactly nowhere.

C: See, I don't really blame Roger for having the affair. I can see how it happened. Jenna was there for him in a way I was not. I can even understand him missing her. We talked about it after you saw her last week.

(He saw Jenna? I thought the affair was over. Where did this come from?)

R: She came by my office, sobbing. My secretary said, there is some-one named Jenna here for you. What was I supposed to do? Her husband is so furious with her. Living with him is just torture. They don't see us at all any more. I just tried to calm her down, like I would any friend. And I told Cathy about it. I mean not right away, but that evening. I mean, I want to be married to Cathy. I do. That's the decision we've made, but we don't have that kind of closeness. Jenna wanted me—my touch. It wasn't even the sex. She needed me in a way that Cathy just doesn't.

C: I miss her too. I miss our connection, our kids' connections, miss the families being together. I wasn't really that mad at Roger for having an affair, because I can't give him what he wants. I can understand why he would look for that somewhere else. But I was mad at him because the affair meant we lost the relationship totally. She was a part of our lives, and then she wasn't.

(I have the sense that they are both in love with Jenna.)

J: There's a way in which Jenna drew you together.

C: I know it's upsetting, Roger, but she's right. It's like both of us felt better, both of us felt closer when Jenna was around. She stopped by, you know, after I knew about everything. I think I would have trouble if he talked to her separately all the time, but I can understand trying to help her when she's upset. I guess I miss her too.

J: We have to stop for today.

They cancel the next session. I call to reschedule, but they do not return my call. I call again. Roger calls back to say they will let me know if they decide they want more counselling. I am left wondering what hap-pened, as I did not see this coming.

   Eight months pass. Cathy calls again, asking if they can schedule an appointment right away. She comments that they would like to come in "a few more times". I attempt to schedule a session the next week, but Cathy calls and puts it off a month because Roger has work pressures and her mother is visiting. I decide to wait until I have them both together to discuss their prior exit from treatment and scheduling issues. Eventually they call again.

Session three

Cathy enters the office first, sitting at one end of the couch. Roger sits at the other end, leaving a space between them. Neither partner looks at the other. A few minutes pass. Cathy speaks.

c: We just don't seem to be making much progress on the closeness issues.

r: I told you that I'd simply given up on having that between us.

c: Maybe you're still in love with Jenna. I mean, I could understand it. I miss her too. [To me] He's had some contact with her, but he's told me about it.

J: [To Roger] Contact?

r: Yeah. She calls me now and then or she stops by my work. I mean, we haven't been sexual—that's over. She just needs the support.

c: Her husband's been really cruel about it.

r: I think he's just going to punish her forever. I don't know why they stay together. She's been unhappy for years, and he gives her no support emotionally [I think Roger is talking about himself as well] Maybe it's some kind of religious thing, like they need to stay together because that's what the church thinks they should do. A ridiculous reason, but people do it.

c: [To me] They're active Mormons, and she feels really guilty about her involvement with Roger. It was her bishop who told her not to spend time with us anymore. I don't know if Jenna really loves her husband. [To Roger] Do you think she does?

J: You're talking about Jenna's marriage, but maybe there's also a reference to your own. Cathy, you said earlier that you wonder if Roger is still in love with Jenna. That question sort of got dropped.

c: [She laughs nervously] Maybe I'm not sure I want to know the answer. I mean in some ways, it's okay if he is. I could certainly understand.

r: I told you I've decided to stay with you. [To me] That hasn't changed since the last time we were here. I made a commitment to our family, and I will keep that.

c: Yes, we're going to stay together.

J: I hear the decision, but maybe you two could tell me a little more about what's behind it, about what keeps you together, or how you feel about being together, about Jenna, about your family.

R: You want to know the reasons?

J: Not just the reasons. I feel like I don't have the whole picture, like there are pieces missing. You've announced this decision, but I don't know how you feel about staying together, giving up Jenna or even why Jenna happened in the first place. I'm just trying to understand.

R: What's to understand? I had an affair with Jenna. I felt close to her emotionally in a way I can't with Cathy. We've tried, and that's just not a possibility [With irritation to me] I've explained that to you before, so what's the point of going through it? [Cathy looks at me with a frightened expression]

J: I can see I upset you. I think that happened last time you two were here as well, and you two didn't come back for a while.

C: We were doing okay.

J: Maybe, but there's something about digging deeper into this that's intrusive and painful.

R: [Still irritated] It's just pointless.

J: I know this is frustrating, but can you two help me understand what is pointless about it?

R: I've made my decision, to stay with Cathy, so what does it matter how I feel about Jenna?

C: Well, it does matter to me. You don't have to stop loving her.

J: [To Cathy] I think you love her, too.

C: I do in a way, not sexually, but things were better when Jenna was around. We laughed more, our kids had fun, we had someone to talk to—I think we both talked to her, maybe instead of each other. We sort of took care of her I guess, but we were happier. Neither of us really liked her husband. We put up with him so we could be around her.

(I see that Jenna is a shared exciting object between them.)

R: Maybe I don't want to talk about her because I do love her. What's the point? She's not leaving Jim. I'm not leaving Cathy.

C: I'm afraid you will.

J: You can tolerate Roger loving Jenna, but not leaving you.

C: That's right.

R: See, so why talk about it? Therapy does no good. Talking about it will never change the reality. We cannot be close. That's an insolvable problem. I don't even know if I want to be close to Cathy anymore. I can live without it.

J: You've each decided you can live without closeness, and you see it as an insolvable impasse.

R: Right. We just live with it.

J: At a cost.

R: [Long pause] I don't know. You ask us things we just don't know the answer to.

J: I don't know if the two of you are going to stay together, are right for each other, can resolve this impasse. But you did come back here looking for something. I think there is a great deal that we don't understand. Some of it you want to know and some of it you are afraid to know.

C:
&   [Looking down] Yeah.
R:

C: [To Roger] So maybe we should come for a while? Do you agree?

R: Yeah. It's a good idea.

Roger and Cathy attended four more sessions, although they rescheduled one of the sessions for "work" reasons. The couple discussed Roger's drinking, particularly the distancing effect it had on Cathy and the ways he drinks to manage anxiety. Roger described wanting Cathy to initiate some physically affectionate exchange between them. They made some limited progress exploring their shared attraction to Jenna and what she represents. For Cathy, Jenna was the nurturing, attentive maternal figure she never had. Cathy hinted at a previous lesbian relationship with "a friend" before she met Roger, but the couple stopped treatment before it was explored further.

Jenna affirmed Roger's potency as a male, wanting him sexually and needing him emotionally. Jenna had idealised Roger during a time when he felt criticised by Cathy as he had by his parents. The couple did not stay in treatment long enough to explore the intergenerational patterns. Cathy was afraid Roger would abandon her and the children as her father did. In his drinking and infidelity, Roger repeats the acting out of his mother, whom he both longs for and hates. I always felt on the edge of losing them because I was easily perceived as harsh and critical, particularly by Roger, as my comments often felt like piercing intrusions. They distanced from me as from each other, living in separate quarters much of the time. I tried unsuccessfully to get them to talk about wanting to leave treatment rather than acting on those feelings, including exploring fears of vulnerability and close-ness. At this point, I decided they may need to come and go several times before they could engage fully. As I wrote this report, and after a five-month absence, they have just called again for an appointment.

Discussion of "Now you see us, now you don't: dealing with resistance in episodic couple treatment" by Janine Wanlass

Mary Morgan (London, England)

Janine has presented us with rich clinical material and her thinking about a couple that is hard to engage in regular sessions. Her ability to work with her countertransference and her interpretations were con-vincing. I will comment on the issue of creating a couple analytic setting, then on the nature of couple relationships, and then some unconscious meanings of "Jenna", in the presenting problem and in the transference to Janine.

Couples coming for therapy rarely have a "couple state of mind". Some partners feel the other is responsible for their unhappiness. Oth-ers might recognise the problem is shared, but don't usually under-stand what they create together. Their experience is often that anxieties, differences, and loving and hating feelings lead to conflict or with-drawal. We ask the couple to consider a way of thinking and being that they have not found in their relationship. As Janine recognises, despite Roger and Cathy's desperate need for help, change feels threatening to their relationship.

The couple state of mind, present in the therapist, is something we hope will become internalised into the couple's relationship as part of therapy. If one takes this position, then the essence of the first contact with the couple might be beginning to establish a different kind of space in which a couple state of mind becomes possible.

Session one

Janine tells us Cathy made the initial phone contact, and in the first session seemed anxious, speaking quickly and continuously. Although Roger stated he wanted to work on his marriage, she was not convinced, guessing he had complied with Cathy's insistence on seeking help. It is often significant which partner makes the initial contact and sets the therapy up in a particular way in the minds of either partner and sometimes in the mind of the therapist. In creating the couple therapy we bring all of this into the room—the way, as a *couple*, they approach difficulties.

This dynamic of Cathy instigating the therapy is underpinned by Janine's countertransference that Cathy is engaged and Roger is not. Half the couple wants to be here and half does not. Addressing the ambivalence the couple brings into the room as something that can be understood reduces the risk of acting out.

In this first session we learn there are communication difficulties, that they struggled following birth of their baby four years ago, that Roger drinks and withdraws, that Cathy worries too much about the children at the expense of the couple relationship, that Cathy was neglected and Roger had an affair. We begin to get a sense of a couple overwhelmed by anxiety. Probably the relationship never offered containment. They both seek other means of dealing with their anxieties: Cathy vicariously through the children, Roger turning to alcohol and then to an affair. Perhaps Janine wonders whether therapy can to provide the containment that is missing when their way of supporting each other has broken down. I was wondering, "What was their way of supporting each other and why did it break down?"

Following this first contact Janine reflects on object relations concepts, attachment theory, and link theory to understand this couple—which all provide meaningful ways of understanding the individuals and the couple. I was interested in her comment that she experiences the couple more like a pair of young siblings than lovers or parents, and that developmentally they are held back because of unmet childhood needs for nurturance and feeding.

Janine's countertransference reflections suggest that this couple experienced limited maternal containment. We do not know much yet about each partner's early development. I wonder if they got together like two children supporting and nurturing each other as best they could, with sex playing an important role. With the arrival of children,

Cathy could no longer support both Roger and the children, and met her own needs by caring exclusively for them. Roger turned to soothing himself with alcohol and his computer.

Jenna seems to have an important function for them both. They feel more like a couple and family in her presence. Can Janine (who has all the same letters in her name plus an "I" as Jenna) provide this function? I don't know if Jenna is her actual name but it is even more interesting if Janine chose the name as if, consciously or unconsciously, there is the recognition of the Jenna they seek in her—but what is the "I-Jenna" object?

Session two

Session two starts with Janine's observations of the couple. The way they sit on the couch seems to highlight their need for support—Roger grasping the hard edges of the couch, Cathy, left unsupported, seeming to flail with no edges, like a couple that cannot support each other. Janine finds herself thinking of them as prepubescent fifth graders. These observations offer insight into what it might feel like on the inside of their relationship. Is this a couple propped up by each other at the beginning of their relationship like siblings? How can two people coming together for support transition into a creative couple, without transitioning into a containing couple relationship that could facilitate their development? When they report that since the first meeting a week ago they are already doing better, Janine wonders in what way? Is it that they have refound (even temporarily) their previous sense of being propped up by each other? Are they in the same space rather than in separate emotional quarters?

I wondered if this was an unconscious belief they had about relationships as a place in which siblings or fifth-graders support each other. If this is right, it probably worked for them for a while, briefly offering sexual and emotional closeness. This gave reassurance—a "soft place", in Cathy's words—which she no longer feels there is. Now that they cannot find that, their relationship feels like "a hopeless defeat" in Roger's words, leaving them angry.

Hearing more history, we get a sense that neither had this soft place with their mothers. We already learned that Roger's mother drank. Cathy says poignantly, "I remember wanting to be close to my mother, but she would just push me away. You know, like when you are a little kid, and you just want to stand next to her, feel her body next to yours. But she couldn't tolerate any of that childish foolishness." Roger and Cathy probably sought a maternal object in each other, which neither could provide, but they clung together for a while even as the relationship failed to develop.

I had two thoughts about the moment of friction when Janine suggested to Roger that he married someone who had trouble with closeness. Of course he was unaware of it, feeling he had married someone whom he could cling to. In that sense he does feel caught out. Second, and more importantly, I thought it was evidence of the lack of an internal creative couple. When Janine put a new and different idea to him, he experienced it as an attack rather than a creative opportunity. They want the "I-Jenna" relationship with Janine—a clinging borderline relationship not a creative couple. So when she is not in total agreement with them, they feel dropped.

Following Janine's interesting countertransference that they are both in love with Jenna, Cathy reports, "It's like both of us felt better, both of us felt closer when Jenna was around." This couple without edges relates by clinging together. Jenna was the glue. Do they break off contact at this point because they feel this internal phantasy is threatened?

I think at this point the couple is in a difficult place in relation to the therapy. Things have started to open up—their complicated feelings for Jenna, her loss and their unresolved feelings for her. With newly complicated feelings about Janine too, perhaps they fear that Janine will not be the "I-Jenna" to cling to, but a threatening separate person with her own mind. But perhaps somewhere this also offers hope.

Session three

It turns out that Janine made emotional contact with a part of them. Her capacity to relate to and think about them with her own separate mind, unconsciously might be a lifeline for this couple. So they contact her eight months later.

They bring to the third session their continued difficulty in closeness, and difficult questions about whether Jenna can be relinquished as both real and symbolic object. Battling this threat, the only thing they can agree on is a firm decision to stay together, rather like binding themselves to the mast of a ship tossed in a tempest. Although wanting

Janine's help, they are anxious and defensive. In this state of mind they cannot respond to Janine's questions about what keeps them together, how they feel about being together, about Jenna and their family. I feel that were Roger, for example, to talk honestly about how he feels about Jenna, he would break down, and they would both feel everything is unraveling. Unable to manage, in desperation they have tied themselves to the mast, but still fear it will not hold. So Roger is defensive with Janine's line of enquiry. She realises that "digging deeper feels intrusive and painful", provoking anxiety. They want to cling to their "decision", not investigate it.

Interestingly, Cathy comes to the rescue by saying she can understand and possibly accept that Roger still loves Jenna. Now the atmosphere seems favourable for Janine to say that she thinks "Cathy loves Jenna too". From this point in the session there is a reflective attitude about what Jenna embodies for both of them—something missing that binds them together. Roger acknowledges he still loves Jenna, but it is a dangerous place, so "Why talk about it? Therapy does no good, talking about it will never change the reality." Perhaps this could be a point to acknowledge just how fearful they have been of the therapy transferentially, and how this has kept them away.

Janine now addresses their ambivalence: they have held onto her as potentially helpful, and they fear for their fragility and impasse. This interpretation moves their perception of Janine from experiencing her in the paranoid-schizoid position, in which she is either the idealised therapist/Jenna who will glue them together, or the dangerous witch who will unwrap threatening feelings and from whom they have to flee. For the first time they are, with Janine's help, feeling contained enough to return for more sessions.

I think Janine is right when she describes this couple as two fifth-graders who developmentally have not yet become an adult creative couple. Their model of a couple relationship is of clinging to each other and to the "I-Jenna". After the couple lost this way of being, perhaps when the children intervened, when clinging cannot easily be maintained, Jenna provided this temporarily.

Working with a couple like this is demanding because of the deficits in their early experience and their compensatory defensive patterns of relating. For change to occur, they would have to allow the therapist to have her own mind, to give them an experience not about agreement but about having creative intercourse towards understanding. We hope the therapist's understanding of them as a couple might eventually help them to internalise a couple state of mind, supporting both the management of difficulty and further development.

Reference

Morgan, M. (2005). On being able to be a couple: the importance of a "creative couple" in psychic life. In: F. Grier (Ed), *Oedipus and the Couple* (pp. 9–30). London: Karnac.

EPILOGUE

This book has begun the exploration of many vertices of psychoanalytical thought about relationships between intimate partners and family members. Some of these depend on the psychoanalytical background of each community of psychoanalysts and psychotherapists, and some depend on more individual variation among practitioners—even when they share common theoretical and geographical points of view. This variety of perspectives and concepts shows us both differences and similarities between psychoanalysts and psychotherapists around the world, all of them dedicated to the growth and well-being of their patients, but who have developed differing approaches as they encounter the nuances of interpersonal interaction. In studying the family, we can see how psychic life is largely a result of the way in which people form links in their primary bonds, so we approach these clinical situations with couples and families not only in order to maximise our clinical effectiveness but also to conduct clinical research into the origins of the human experience.

Couple and family psychoanalysis is still in search of definition and development, both as an area of knowledge and as a distinct clinical approach within the psychoanalytic therapies. Its procedures are as different from those commonly applied to individual analysis as they are from those of the systemic family therapies, and because of this, their implementation explores a wider domain of important clinical challenges and research. Beyond mere clinical application, working with families and couples gives us the possibility of formulating new hypotheses about how families and couples work as the special small groups in which each individual grows, about how psychic change takes place in health, and about handicapping conditions that bring families to our attention for psychoanalytical work. And then there is the way that the study of people in their real world relationships expands our ideas about development and pathology, which can also be applied to work with individuals.

Nowadays we begin to see that multiple ways of thinking have led to diverse theoretical concepts, each of which can help us more fully to realise the potential of family and couple psychoanalysis. In this volume, with this in mind, we have undertaken our project of inquiry in order to build a more substantial methodological and theoretical corpus of knowledge and practice drawn from around the world.

Two main theoretical perspectives form the background of most formulations and interventions in this book: object relations theory, and the theory of the link or "*el vínculo*". In distinguishing the South American concept of "the link" from the object relations concept of "links in thinking" that derives from Bion, we seek to preserve the unique potential of both perspectives. Bion began a tradition of using the idea of a link to explore factors that lead to or impede mature thought, while Pichon Rivière's *vínculo* concerns the bonds that unite, divide, and organise people in their intimate groups, and that then organise the totality of the psyche. These two distinct areas are both central to our clinical thinking.

In this book, contributions from many analysts and psychotherapists in the form of case presentations and the discussions of those cases have also given us close-up views of the thinking process within the clinical mind, shedding light on the way each analyst and therapist understands the families and couples they see through allowing us to sit with them as they struggle clinically. Our intention has been to allow a creative debate about the ways in which intrapsychic, interpersonal, and contextual processes interact with each other. In this way, the field of unconscious mental life first described by Freud can be gradually extended, as we see how the unconscious is forged through relationships, which in turn are affected by the context in which they exert their effect—in which internal and external reality intertwine.

As we said at the beginning, this is the first book of a series devoted to exploring how different analytic backgrounds and theoretical concepts from around the world are used in everyday clinical practice with families and couples. We hope this offering from a diverse (and collegial) group of analysts and therapists, each addressing interpersonal links from his or her own perspective, will encourage other psychoanalysts and psychotherapists—experienced and novice alike—who are interested in this field of clinical work, enabling them to learn even as we have been learning, as we all work to enlarge our understanding.

Elizabeth Palacios and David E. Scharff
Zaragoza, Spain and Washington, DC, USA

INDEX